SHATTER *the* NATIONS

SHATTER *the* NATIONS

ISIS and the War for the Caliphate

MIKE GIGLIO

PUBLICAFFAIRS
NEW YORK

PublicAffairs
Hachette Book Group
1290 Avenue of the Americas, New York, NY 10104
www.publicaffairsbooks.com
@Public_Affairs

Printed in the United States of America
First Edition: September 2019

Published by PublicAffairs, an imprint of Perseus Books, LLC, a subsidiary of Hachette Book Group, Inc. The PublicAffairs name and logo is a trademark of the Hachette Book Group.

The Hachette Speakers Bureau provides a wide range of authors for speaking events. To find out more, go to www.hachettespeakersbureau.com or call (866) 376-6591.

The publisher is not responsible for websites (or their content) that are not owned by the publisher.

Print book interior design by Linda Mark.

Library of Congress Cataloging-in-Publication Data
Names: Giglio, Mike, author.
Title: Shatter the nations: ISIS and the war for the Caliphate / Mike Giglio.
Description: First edition. | New York, NY: PublicAffairs, 2019. | Includes bibliographical references and index.
Identifiers: LCCN 2019016895 | ISBN 9781541742352 (hardcover: alk. paper) | ISBN 9781541742345 (ebook)
Subjects: LCSH: IS (Organization) | Middle East—History, Military—21st century. | Middle East—History—21st century. | Middle East—Description and travel. | Giglio, Mike—Travel—Middle East.
Classification: LCC DS63.123 .G54 2019 | DDC 956.7044/3—dc23
LC record available at https://lccn.loc.gov/2019016895
ISBNs: 978-1-5417-4235-2 (hardcover), 978-1-5417-4234-5 (ebook)

LSC-C

10 9 8 7 6 5 4 3 2 1

CONTENTS

Stories are for those late hours in the night when you can't remember how you got from where you were to where you are.

—Tim O'Brien, *The Things They Carried*

AUTHOR'S NOTE

I AM INDEBTED TO THE LOCAL JOURNALISTS WITH WHOM I'VE HAD THE honor of working and sharing bylines. They are among the best and bravest our profession has to offer and were a constant reminder of why I chose it. I especially want to thank Munzer al-Awad, the friend and colleague who worked with me for years covering ISIS in Turkey. Though he appears in these pages, they do not do justice to the passion, skill, and humanity that defined his work.

None of the sources in this book were offered or given anything in exchange for the interviews and access they provided, except the promise that I would try to relay their accounts accurately—and, when necessary for their safety, protect their identities. Those whose names have been changed in line with this obligation are mentioned in the endnotes. I remain in awe that so many people in such difficult situations were willing to talk with me, sometimes at great personal risk, and that they believed enough in the value of reporting to share their stories. Whether they spoke with me directly in their native languages, or in mine, or with the aid of translators such as Munzer, as was most often the case, most dialogue is rendered in English.

GLOSSARY OF TERMS

Alawites: A religious group that broadly identifies with the Shia branch of Islam. Alawites makes up a minority of the population in Syria but hold much of the power. Syrian president Bashar al-Assad is an Alawite.

Al-Qaeda in Iraq (AQI): The insurgent and terrorist group that fought U.S. troops during the Iraq War. The predecessor to ISIS. AQI was founded by the Jordanian Abu Musab al-Zarqawi and eventually pledged loyalty to Osama bin Laden and al-Qaeda's global leadership. Many ISIS members and especially its leaders are AQI veterans.

The Coalition: The collection of local and international forces fighting ISIS. The Coalition is led by the U.S. but includes countries such as France, Britain, Germany, Australia, Canada, and the Netherlands, along with Jordan, Saudi Arabia, and the United Arab Emirates. The Coalition also includes local partner forces that are essential to the battle in Iraq and Syria.

dishdasha: A traditional robe.

emir: A local ISIS leader; the word translates to "prince."

EOD: Explosive Ordnance Disposal. The technicians who work to defuse bombs.

The Free Syrian Army (FSA): The moderate rebel alliance featuring many defected military officers and soldiers that received U.S. backing in the Syrian civil war.

hookah: A large water pipe used for smoking tobacco. Also known in the region as *narghile* or *shisha*.

IED: Improvised-explosive device, often a hidden explosive or roadside bomb.

Iraqi Counter-Terrorism Force (ICTF): The most elite battalion of the *Iraqi special operations forces*, which was created to work with U.S. commandos during the Iraq War and leads the war against ISIS in Iraq.

Iraqi special forces: See entry below. This term is used in this book to refer to ISOF.

The Iraqi Special Operations Forces (ISOF): The overall division of Iraqi special forces, who are the most effective soldiers in the anti-ISIS fight. They are also commonly known as the Counter Terrorism Service (CTS) and the Golden Division. To avoid over-using acronyms, I often refer to ISOF simply as the Iraqi special forces or the special forces. Though there were other Iraqi military units that called themselves special forces, any reference to Iraqi special forces in this book refers to ISOF.

Iraq War: The war that began with the 2003 U.S. invasion of Baghdad and formally ended in December 2011.

ISIS: The Islamic State of Iraq and Syria.

Istanbullu: An Istanbul native or resident.

Kurds: An ethnic group that traces its roots to ancient kings in Iran and makes up a suppressed minority in Syria, Iraq, and Turkey. Many Kurds dream of carving out their own state.

MRAP: Mine-Resistant Ambush Protected. A heavy armored vehicle that can sometimes withstand the blasts of IEDs and other explosives.

mujahideen: A holy warrior. The term is often used to refer to foreign fighters.

mukhabarat: The secret police in many Arab countries.

The Muslim Brotherhood: The political and Islamist movement across the Middle East that is the most powerful opposition faction in Egypt during the dictatorship of Hosni Mubarak.

The Nusra Front: The Syrian rebel group that eventually became the official branch of al-Qaeda in the country. Nusra and ISIS worked together until 2014, when they formally split as part of a larger rift between al-Qaeda and AQI.

peshmerga: The soldiers who control and defend the semi-autonomous Kurdish region in northern Iraq. The name means "those who face death."

PKK (The Kurdistan Workers Party): The parent group of the YPG that has been fighting a decades-long insurgency in Turkey and is labeled a terrorist group by the U.S. State Department.

Rojava: The Kurdish-dominated land of eastern Syria.

Sahwa: The Awakening. The U.S. campaign during the George W. Bush administration's troop surge that empowered local Sunni fighters to take on AQI during the Iraq War.

Salafis: Hardline Islamists who seek to make the world more like they believe it was during the time of the Prophet Muhammad.

shabiha: The pro-regime civilian death squads in Syria, known by the locals as "ghosts."

shalwar kameez: Traditional outfit of baggy pants and shirt.

sheikh: An honorific in Arabic usually reserved for powerful men and religious leaders.

Shia: The second-largest branch of global Islam that follows the lineage of Husayn ibn Ali, the grandson of the Prophet Muhammad who was killed in the battle of Karbala. Shia Muslims make up the dominant population in Iraq as well as Iran.

Sunni: Islam's largest branch. Sunni Muslims make up the majority of the population in Syria and are a large minority in Iraq.

VBIED: A vehicle-borne improvised explosive device, or car bomb.

Yazidis: The religious minority based around the Sinjar mountains in northern Iraq.

YPG (The People's Protection Units): The Kurdish militia and local PKK affiliate that dominates Rojava.

MAP OF THE REGION

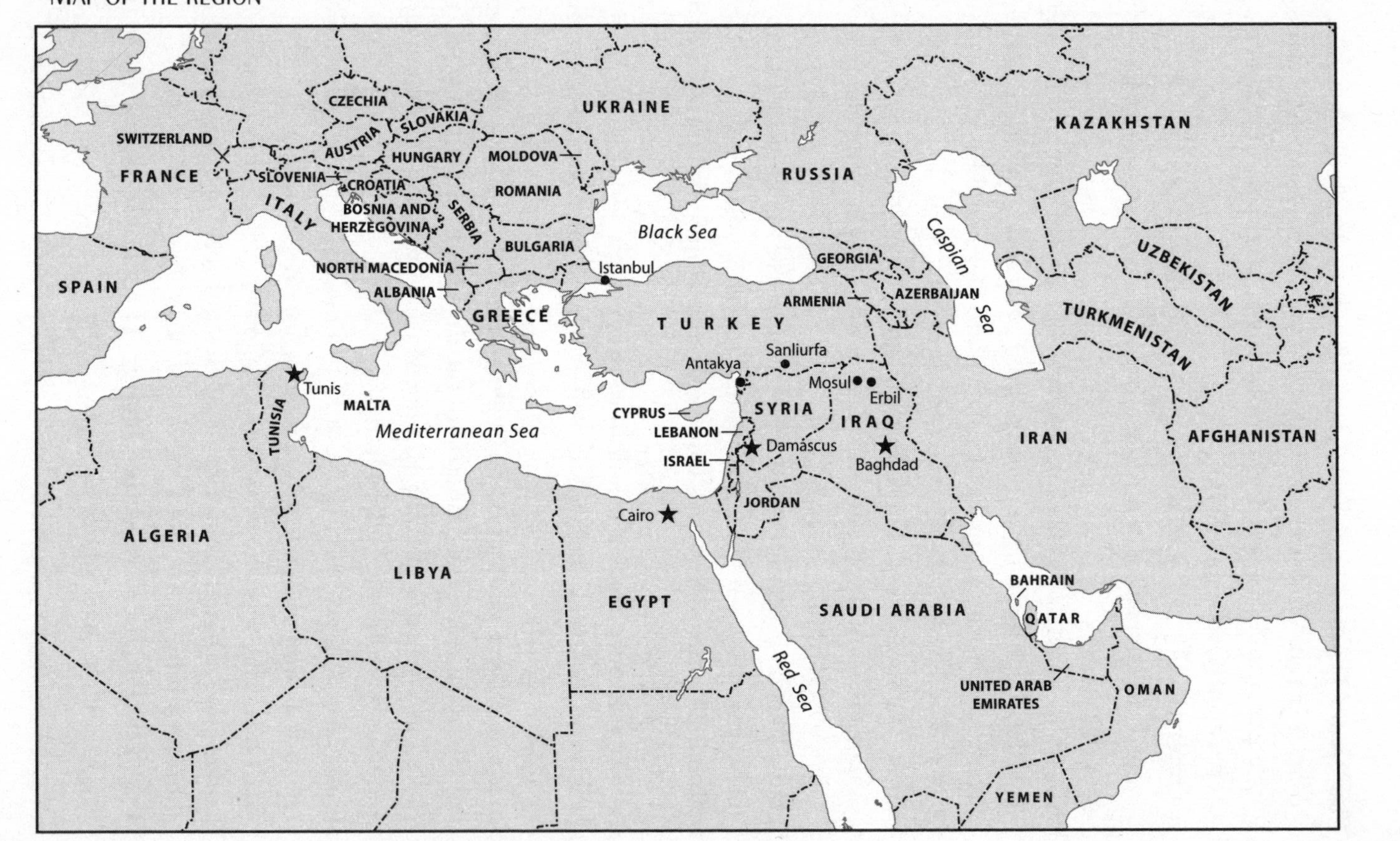

THE ISIS "CALIPHATE" AT ITS HEIGHT

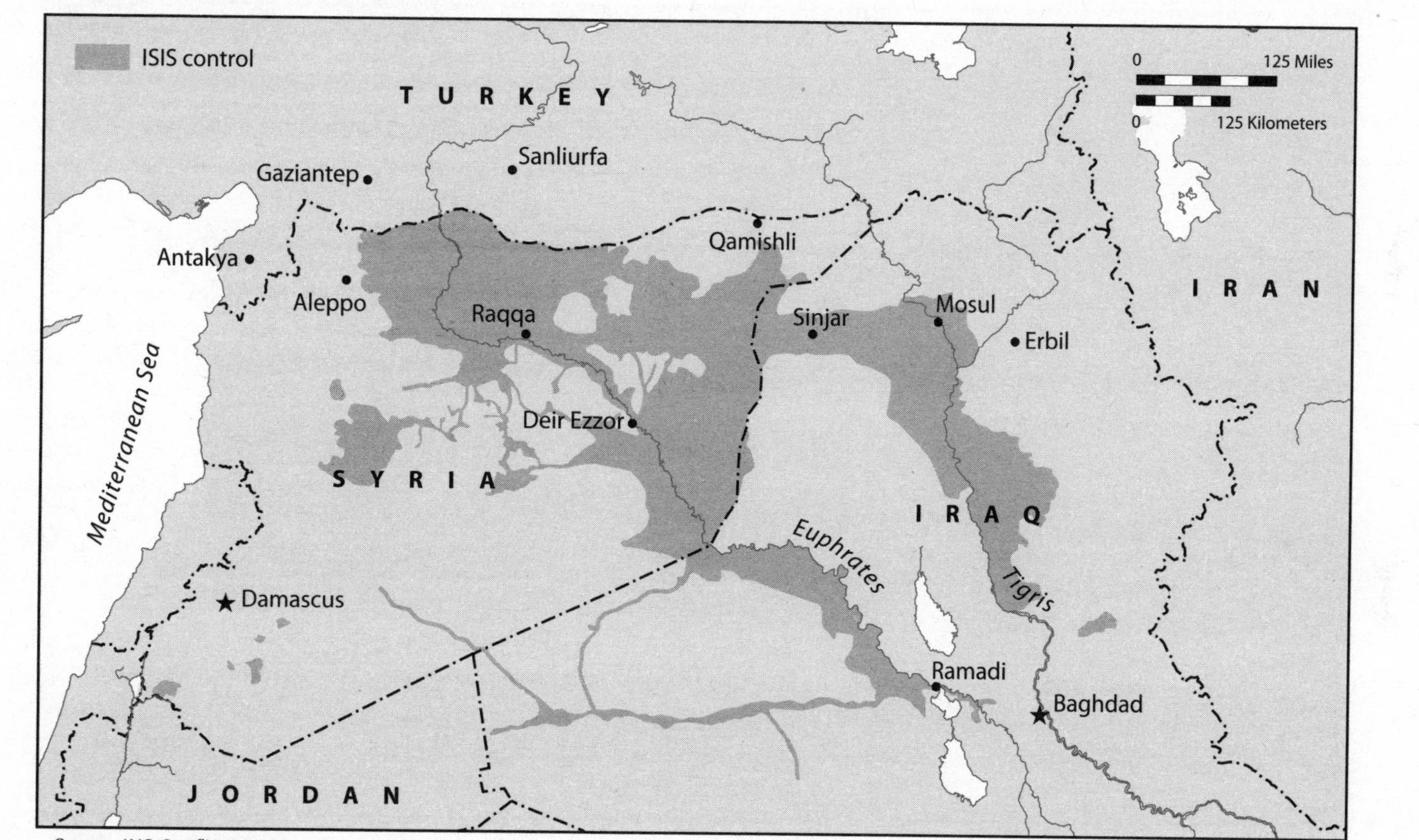

Source: IHS Conflict Monitor

Control of Iraq and Syria in July 2014

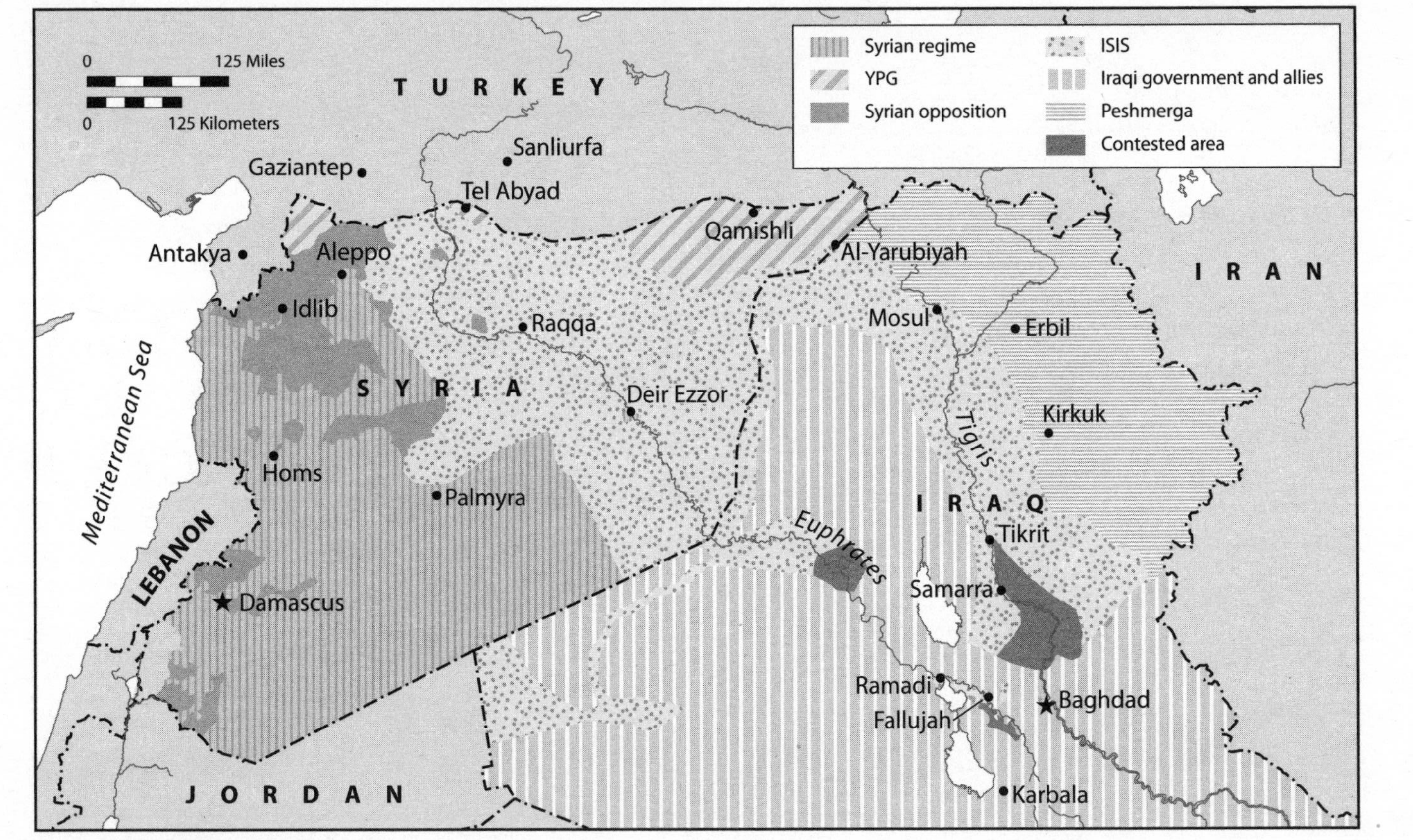

Source: People Demand Change

Key sites in the offensive for Mosul

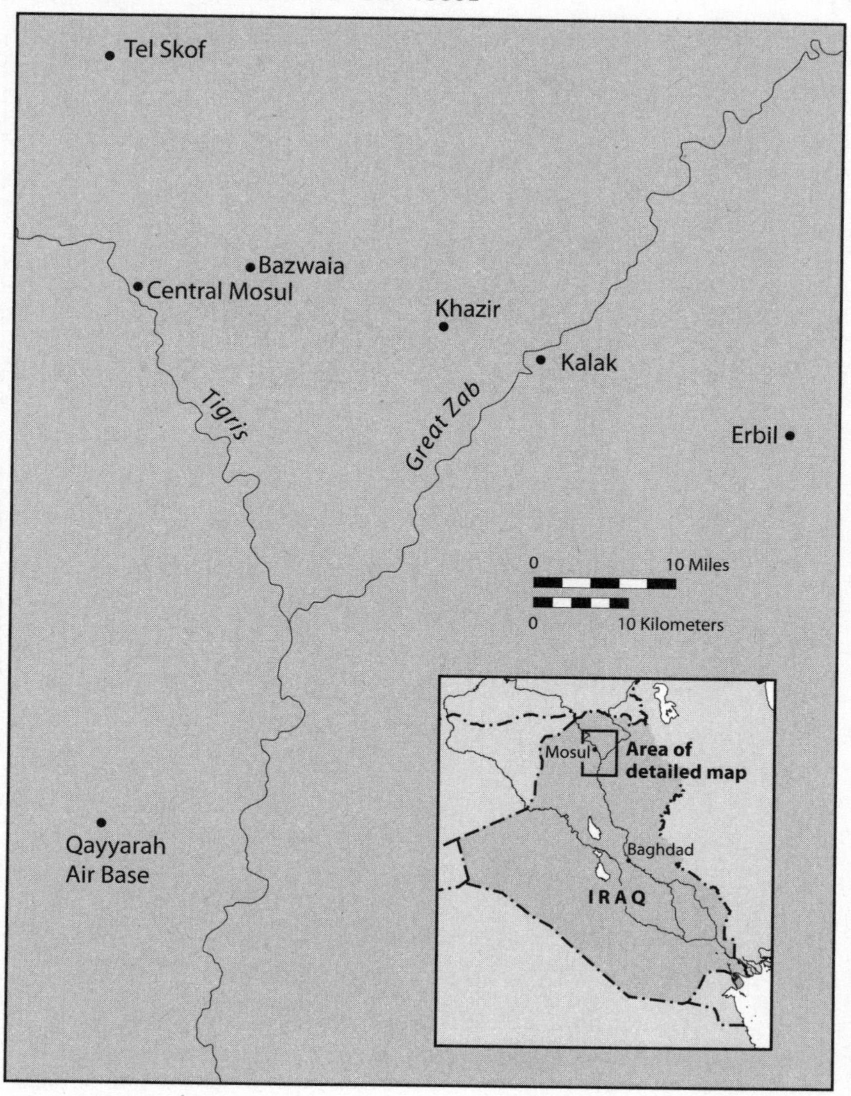

Control of Syria in July 2017

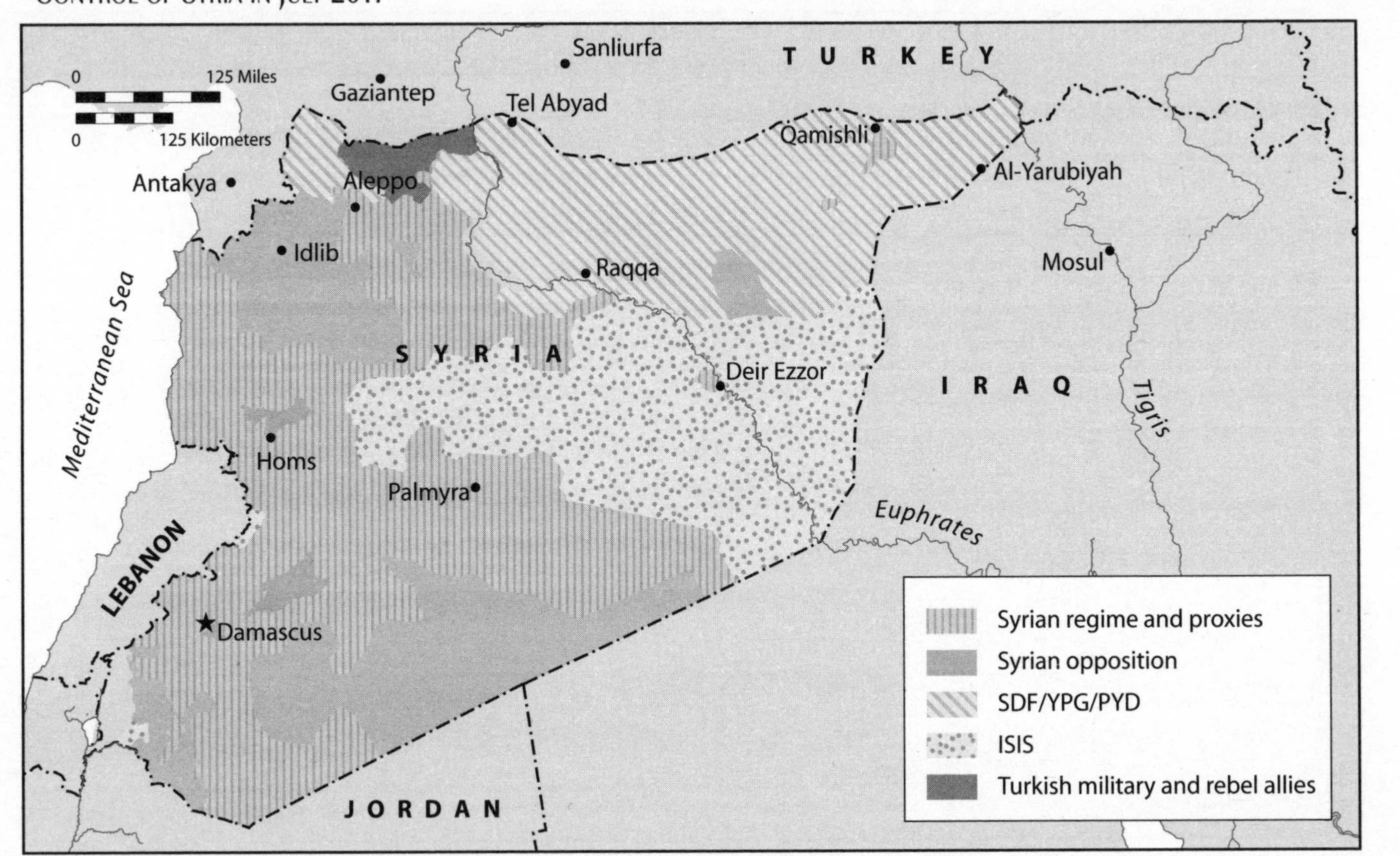

Source: People Demand Change

PROLOGUE

Mosul, Iraq. February 2017.

ABDUL-WAHAB SWORE IT WAS A TRUE STORY.

His eyes were reflected in the rearview mirror as he sped his pickup through battle-beaten country. To the left, the setting sun cast a polaroid haze across brown fields and squat stone farmhouses. To the right was a ridge of mountains. Ahead was flat road and a darkening sky.

"There was a big soldier named Will—" That's how Abdul-Wahab put it. He pronounced the name "Wull."

"Wull, Wull." He sounded it out a couple more times, like he hadn't said it in a while.

He slowed the truck to roll through the final checkpoint manned by the Kurdish militia, whose green-and-red flag snapped in a bitter wind. A soldier in a scarf manned a machine gun on the barricade that marked the boundary. From there the road led sixty miles through territory controlled by the Iraqi military, to the edge of Mosul and the last bastions of the ISIS caliphate.

Will was one of the American special forces sent to Iraq more than a decade earlier to kill insurgents. The nights of the Iraq War had been filled with U.S. commando raids, and the Americans had created

Abdul-Wahab's elite battalion to do the raids with them, an Iraqi version of the Delta Force or SEAL Team Six. The battalion had an English name—the Iraqi Counter-Terrorism Force—and was known by its initials, ICTF, which the men sewed onto their uniforms and painted on their Humvees. The Iraqis admired their American mentors. They picked up the special forces ethos, wore baseball caps and sunglasses, used words like "fuck" and "bro" and "dude." But Will was different, Abdul-Wahab said. "He would lose control."

Abdul-Wahab kept his foot on the gas pedal as he raced through a Christian town that seemed to be empty. ISIS had destroyed some of the houses, and the ones still standing were dark. Not a soul was visible except for a trio of Iraqi soldiers who sat on a leather couch on the roadside.

The photographer Warzer Jaff was in the passenger's seat; I was in back. Abdul-Wahab's M16 was by my feet.

An ICTF veteran in his forties who had given up fighting, Abdul-Wahab had been ferrying Jaff and me to and from Mosul for months. He was stocky and gruff and expert at passing through the myriad checkpoints that led to the front lines, always knowing what to say or whom to call or when to gift his sunglasses to an inquiring militiaman. He was an ideal wheelman for navigating the strange tapestry of the alliance, with all its varied forces flying their banners around the city like armies in a medieval siege. His commanders used him for special transport: of weapons and supplies and officers who wanted to escape for a night to the hotels of Erbil, the Kurdish capital and nearest outpost of modernity, a place where they could find a decent dinner and booze or visit a mall or swim in a pool, and grasp at a moment of normalcy on the edge of the world's most brutal war zone. As grumpy as Charon, he was forever making the forty-five-mile journey between the two valley cities, and when Jaff and I had no other way to get to the war, we went with him.

A folk song about an old battle was playing on the radio. "You made your tribe proud of you . . . I can hear them scream."

Abdul-Wahab was still talking about Will. First he began shooting animals on patrol. Then, on a raid one night, he shot an old man as he opened his front door. Abdul-Wahab said he'd seen it happen. The man's daughter was screaming, beating her chest in grief, and Will said something like, "I just gave him an injection, he's sleeping," and threw a mattress onto the old man. He killed a teenager in front of his mother, jamming his gun into the boy's mouth. Abdul-Wahab said he saw the boy's mangled head. He killed one man as Iraqi medics were treating him. He killed another while he lay in bed beside his wife.

I asked what had happened to Will. Abdul-Wahab said he didn't know. Will was transferred one day, and that was the last he'd seen of him. But he reckoned that a man like him must have met his judgment eventually.

What he was telling me, I knew, was a ghost story. It reminded me of old reports of torture and orange jumpsuits and dead civilians, and that what America asked of its soldiers could unhinge them. The war that defined my parents' generation, in Vietnam, had the draft and civil unrest with it. By the time the Iraq War started, when I was eighteen, America had a volunteer army, so people like me could carry on without worrying that our number would be called. The country still found itself with a guilty conscience, though, and in this war, with ISIS, the only U.S. soldiers on the front lines were the secret kind, small groups of commandos whose every mission was classified, while U.S. pilots and drone operators dropped bombs. It was left to local soldiers like the men of Abdul-Wahab's battalion to do the bulk of the fighting, and as far as most Americans and their politicians were concerned, the war was out of sight and out of mind. In a way it made sense: fewer Americans lost their lives or their minds or committed war crimes. There were fewer stories like Will's. Yet, in this new kind of U.S. war that culminated in Mosul—the deadliest urban battle in which America had engaged in at least a half a century—the toll was still being paid by the local soldiers who were U.S. allies and by the civilians who were dying by the thousands in the cross fire. And I worried about the psyche of a country that still considered itself at war but was more disengaged than ever from it, with no sense of shared sacrifice or even collective responsibility. On the one hand, Americans seemed obsessed with ISIS, roiling with every terror attack, while on the other they made little effort to understand the enemy or the local soldiers doing most of the killing and dying to stop it.

Swaying in the cab of Abdul-Wahab's truck during our halting journeys to the front lines—the checkpoints more frequent, the sentries more intense as we neared the fighting—I sometimes imagined the helicopters that had moved like a mass-transit system over the American battlefield in Vietnam and the correspondents who had used the choppers almost at will to traverse it. There were times when the war with ISIS felt looser and wilder. From Istanbul, where I lived, I could fly economy to cities such as Baghdad, Antakya, Berlin, and Erbil, all of them theaters in the same sprawling conflict. I could meet one day with the smugglers and fixers who worked for ISIS and on occasion with ISIS members themselves, and the next find myself on the other side of the mirror with the men who were confronting the jihadis: a Syrian rebel, an American artilleryman, a German border guard. Yet the closer I came to Mosul, the heart of the extremist statelet ISIS had carved into the map, the more the feeling was one of constriction.

Abdul-Wahab left us around midnight at a small country home on the approach to western Mosul. The ICTF was using the house as a rear base, and we unrolled our sleeping bags on a floor crowded with soldiers. A gunner called Bis Bis was on the phone with his mother in Baghdad, who put his son on, who said he wanted a new ball. Other soldiers were snoring. I took a couple of swigs from a pint of whiskey and pulled the bill of my hat over my face and fell asleep to the sound of U.S. airstrikes, which shook the walls through the night.

———

It was still dark the next morning when I awoke to the rumble of the battalion's idling Humvees.

They were American-made and weighed 7,000 pounds with thick tires that came up to my waist. They were encased in metal armor, scarred by bullets and shrapnel, and painted black, like the armored bulldozers that would accompany them. Each Humvee had a turret on its rooftop outfitted with a heavy weapon: a machine gun or an antitank rocket system or a grenade launcher. The letters "ICTF" were stenciled on the turrets. The men of the ICTF had probably killed more extremists than any soldiers in the world, because they were good but also because they had been fighting for more than a decade. In recent months they had also taken so many casualties that if they were a U.S. unit, a commander would have declared them combat ineffective and pulled them from the battlefield. The soldiers wore uniforms that were the same apocalyptic black as their Humvees. Some looked like American commandos in their ball caps and wraparound sunglasses. Others covered their faces in checkered keffiyehs or black ski masks emblazoned with skeleton faces.

The men stepped into their Humvees, and Jaff and I took our places in the one we'd been assigned. Sitting in the back seat, I could see my breath billowing in the cold, and my legs were shaking from it, twitching and bouncing, my knees rubbing against the driver's seat. Beside me were crates of .50-caliber bullets and the legs of the gunner, who was standing in his turret. Jaff sat in the front passenger's seat with his camera. A native of Iraqi Kurdistan, he had fought Saddam Hussein's forces with the Kurdish militia, then made his name during the Iraq War as a local reporter with the *New York Times*. Now married to an American journalist, with a seven-year-old daughter, he lived on Manhattan's Upper West Side.

The convoy crept north in a column through the sallow dirt of abandoned farm fields, curling along a path that sappers were clearing of improvised explosive devices, or IEDs. The Humvees rocked and groaned as they rolled forward. Their shells rattled intermittently, as if shaken by an unseen hand, from airstrikes.

All the while, we were under the gaze of mechanical eyes. Cameras under the wings of the U.S. warplanes overhead could zoom to any spot on the battlefield. Predator and Reaper drones that looked like windowless prop planes circled noiselessly, beaming full-motion video to coalition command centers in Baghdad, Kuwait, and Tampa. The feeds showed the path the battalion would take, first traveling through the booby-trapped fields, then moving past an island of half-built apartments, and finally entering a neighborhood called Tel al-Rayan that marked Mosul's southwestern edge. After four months of brutal street fighting, ISIS still had not been dislodged from the half of the city on the western bank of the Tigris, a swath of territory that extended from an outer ring of working-class suburbs to a densely packed downtown and the ancient, winding streets at its center. For more than two years the coalition's cameras and satellites had watched as ISIS militants built defenses, raising dirt ramparts and laying tank traps, moving back and forth in their pickups, their faces covered. They also dug tunnels and buried mines and laid explosive traps through the streets and houses.

As the column of Humvees kicked up dust, the ICTF soldiers looked out through thick, bullet-resistant windshields, some of them cracked from prior battles. Through the window in my door, a textbook-sized slab of murky glass, I saw the island of abandoned apartment buildings about a hundred yards ahead through the chalky dirt. A muzzle flashed from one of them, and bullets from a heavy machine gun streamed toward us. They made a sound like the chirping of birds as they whizzed around the turret. Some flew into the Humvee's armor with a clank. The feeling this gave me was always the same, both riled and afraid, like a trapped animal taunted by someone rattling its cage. Our gunner returned fire, each burst from his .50-caliber weapon sounding like a car crash inside the Humvee's metal shell.

The Humvees fanned out from the column and advanced toward the attackers, blankets and mattresses flapping from the backs of some of them.

An airstrike hit the apartments—it felt like standing in the middle of a thunderstorm. Smoke and dirt burst into the sky, and for a moment there was silence.

Then, amid the constant chatter on the radio, came the words that the soldiers always listened for: *sayarrah*, *mufakhakha*. They could sound almost beautiful, even in a gruff commander's Arabic, but they meant "car bomb."

A vehicle approached from the distance, a red pickup truck outfitted with makeshift armor, trailing a long cloud of dust. Our gunner swung his turret to track it, firing, his body contracting. Hot casings jangled down, and I swatted them from my legs. A bullet smacked our windshield and cracked it. Then the pickup disappeared into the hills.

ISIS made its car bombs in factories and outfitted them with metal armor and enough explosives to incinerate a building or a Humvee. For months they'd been coming, one after another, at the soldiers, the pilots speeding through the fields and streets like the War Boys of *Mad Max*, blazing forward in their clanking, up-armored death machines, chasing suicidal glory.

They had killed some of the battalion's best soldiers in this way. Of all the forces aligned against ISIS, the soldiers of the ICTF were its deadliest enemy. They were elite and attacked with the support of America's air force and intelligence, but at the same time they were soldiers of Iraq. They were men like Ibrahim Abu Hamra, aka Red, the Humvee's driver, a meaty sergeant with cream-colored skin and strawberry hair who looked Irish. He was a longtime ICTF soldier and new father who had managed to maintain the fiction to his wife that he worked a desk job. To my right, peering through the milky film of his reinforced window, was Mohamed al-Khabouri, who'd joined the battalion a decade earlier alongside his older brother. The brother had been killed years ago by ISIS's predecessor, al-Qaeda in Iraq (AQI), which, as far as Mohamed was concerned, locked him into war with every iteration of the jihadis until it was finally done. He was prematurely bald, with owl-like eyes that gave him a haunted expression. The gunner, newer to the battalion, was no more in the Humvee than a voice from above and a dangling pair of legs.

Gunfire erupted at the head of the convoy, and then the air around me seemed to expand like a balloon and burst as the car bomb exploded. The gunners in the lead had destroyed it before it reached the Humvees. A little black dog ran past my window, moving quickly through the empty fields. Mortar rounds fell around the Humvee, the bombs whistling down and shrapnel punching into the metal armor. Out my window, the apartment buildings were getting closer. I saw another pickup truck speeding away from them, toward ISIS territory.

The convoy continued its slow progress until the first buildings of Tel al-Rayan appeared on the horizon, marking Mosul's city limits. An armored buggy was driving up and down the column of Humvees, delivering Styrofoam boxes of fish and rice for lunch, when I heard a buzzing overhead. The soldiers who'd gathered around the buggy scattered. One grabbed his automatic rifle and fired into the air. There was a streak of white, an explosion, and then a soldier limping. Soon there were more—little consumer drones that ISIS had rigged to drop grenades. The men lashed out as if at a swarm of insects, running in circles and shooting wildly.

The same drones sold at Target or on Amazon were being used by ISIS to conduct surveillance and coordinate mortars and car bombs. I learned later that the coalition was trying desperately to stop the drones, to jam their communications, but ISIS had technicians too, and they kept changing the frequencies the drones were flying on, staying a step ahead. Both the soldier tasked with jamming the drones and the jihadi working to thwart him were American. The ISIS war was strange this way: two global armies clashing at a vanishing point where the distant past seemed to blend with modernity. We were rolling into places that ISIS had dragged back to medieval times, and yet it was hard not to feel that they were also pushing toward the future, spreading their radical vision on social media and broadcasting their beheadings on YouTube in HD. ISIS preached a savage extremism that advocated an eye-for-an-eye code of justice, institutionalized rape, and promoted the taking of slaves. It was also making a sophisticated play in Western politics, infiltrating terrorists among the refugees moving into Europe and betting that their attacks would fuel xenophobes and populists to help along the clash of civilizations ISIS preached. It was a war of GPS-guided missiles and advanced IEDs, and it was also a war of long-haired jihadis fighting men in skull masks as the two sides charged in their metal war machines.

———·———

> *You are my war club, my weapon for battle—with you I shatter nations . . .*

This biblical passage, from the book of Jeremiah, captures something, for me, of a war that could feel expansive in its stakes and in its age-old themes. There was the idea of a historic struggle promoted by both ISIS and its enemies, and the reality of suffering, and a swath of death and destruction from which people tried to draw meaning.

Jeremiah had prophesized that Jerusalem would be destroyed as punishment for idolatry. Then the Babylonian army had carried out God's wrath. More vengeance was coming—now Babylon would be punished. But in these lines it's unclear whom God is addressing. It could be Jeremiah, or the king of Babylon, or Cyrus of Persia, or the word of God itself, or something else. I had spent six years tracking the conflict as it built to its bloody climax in Mosul, from the first days of the Arab Spring, and I knew that all sides believed they walked on the side of God and that war was always justified this way.

> *. . . with you I destroy kingdoms, with you I shatter horse and rider, with you I shatter chariot and driver, with you I shatter man and woman, with you I shatter old man and youth.*

The people I met around the war often based their stories on ideas like retribution and atonement. And their struggles played out in places like Sanliurfa, in southern Turkey, where I could meet ISIS-linked sources in a shopping mall and then walk a mile to a reflecting pool said to have hosted Abraham. In Mosul, which had been home to some 2 million people, the war was waged around the tombs of the prophets Daniel and Jonah as airstrikes thundered across the Nineveh plains. Mosul was where ISIS had declared its caliphate and where defeat would signal the caliphate's demise, and when soldiers said they were on the front lines of some deeper, global struggle, it seemed to blend with the history of the place. From the moment ISIS's fighters had captured Mosul and declared themselves lords of a terrorist empire, the question was not if it would fall but when. Their so-called caliphate was too crazy to last, and ISIS seemed to like it that way. The suspense was not about whether ISIS would win but how it might change the world before its cities fell and how many of America's allies it could kill along the way.

The battalion pushed into the edge of the city the next morning. This time our Humvee was first in the line. The gunner had his .50-cal cracking like a jackhammer as he strafed a rooftop from which we were taking fire. He was yelling down through the manhole, but it was hard to hear him above the din. On the street before us, laundry hung from a balcony, and a water tanker leaked from bullet holes. To the right, a second convoy was attacking the ISIS flank. Something exploded next to our Humvee, rocking it on its frame. The gunner kept pounding. Then there was an eruption from the second convoy. I saw its lead Humvee engulfed in oily black smoke and flames. It had been hit by an antitank missile, and all four soldiers inside it were dead. The vehicles behind it retreated. Some soldiers ran out with a medical kit, but they were hit by a mortar round. When the dust cleared, I could see one of them lying on the ground, waving for help. We rolled forward.

From there, time passed in a haze. One minute I was screaming at Jaff over the racket of the gun, and the next we found ourselves silently feeding chains of golden bullets to the gunner, as the fighting intensified, knowing we had displaced two soldiers who would otherwise have done the job. And then, during a lull in the battle, I was eating rice and beans from a Styrofoam lunch box.

As I ate, a man in green stepped out from behind a building at the far end of the street. An antitank rocket launcher rested on his shoulder. The Humvee's gunner fired, and the man was gone. We waited for anxious minutes, scanning for any sight of him, until an airstrike hit, collapsing the building he'd been hiding behind. The Humvee crept deeper into the neighborhood. From a rooftop, someone waved a white flag. Drones buzzed, and a grenade hit with a deafening crash on the metal roof above my head. Then Mohamed screamed, "Car bomb!"

"Where?" Red asked.

"Here!" Mohamed said. He was looking out his window. "Right here!"

Red kicked the Humvee into gear. The big tires had been shredded by bullets and shrapnel and were flat. He jammed his boot on the accelerator, and the Humvee moved slowly forward.

The gunner wasn't firing. He ducked down from his turret and closed the hatch.

I could see the car bomb coming, less than twenty yards away and gaining on the Humvee. It was encased in a shell of armor that had been painted a gleaming white. The windshield was covered by a sheet of black steel, obscuring the driver.

It looks like a spaceship, I thought.

Just ahead was a dirt barricade, and with no other choice, Red gunned the Humvee into it. He pounded the gas, and the tires spun.

PART I

BEGINNINGS

CHAPTER 1

THE MARTYR

New York City. January 2011.

SIX YEARS EARLIER I WAS STARING AT MY COMPUTER IN THE DRAB *Newsweek* offices in downtown Manhattan. I clicked on a Gmail chat box, waiting for a man who called himself El Shaheed, Arabic for "the martyr," to appear online.

I was twenty-six and struggling to find my place at the storied magazine, which was cutting staff and bleeding money. I had a temp job on the foreign desk and wore dress shoes that squeaked. The online meeting had been arranged by a former Egyptian activist living in Washington, DC, who claimed that El Shaheed was preparing to lead a revolution on the streets of Egypt, from the internet.

I'd never been to Egypt and knew only the basics about its politics: that it was a brutal police state, that octogenarian dictator Hosni Mubarak was a major American ally, with a military that received $1.3 billion a year in U.S. aid, and that he had ruled for three decades. But huge street protests had recently brought down the dictatorship in Tunisia, the small country wedged between Algeria and Libya on the southern coast of the Mediterranean Sea. Activists there had used

Facebook and other social media platforms to subvert censorship and organize, and I'd written a story about them.

In the chat box, I saw that El Shaheed was typing.

elshaheeed: I'm here
need to leave in 30 minutes
so lets make the best use of the time

I asked who he was, but he'd only say he was the administrator of a Facebook page that was going viral in Egypt. He'd created the page the previous summer as a campaign against police brutality—the El Shaheed moniker paid tribute to a young computer engineer who'd been bludgeoned to death for no apparent reason by police. Since then, El Shaheed and some friends had been using the page to explore new kinds of dissent, like flash demonstrations that were recorded and posted online to commemorate the action. Egyptian singers living abroad had made music videos for the cause that racked up views on YouTube. In comments on the page's posts, people vented about the daily oppression they faced, and each time people liked a post or a video, it was flagged for all their friends to see. It was a vivid example of the still-new power of social media.

Four days earlier, on January 14, the same day Tunisian dictator Zine El Abidine Ben Ali fled his country, El Shaheed's Facebook page had posted a call for a countrywide protest, and this time the target was Mubarak. The protest was scheduled for January 25—and on its events page on Facebook, tens of thousands of people had clicked the box that said they'd be attending. The page had more than 375,000 followers and was growing quickly.

elshaheeed: thats how powerful a virus can be
me: a virus—why did you use that word?
elshaheeed: cause its infact a virus
no one can control it

once its out
it goes everywhere
its unstoppable

The secret police had begun to question well-known activists, trying to find out the identity of El Shaheed. He was receiving emails with suspicious links, and Facebook accounts with profile photos of pretty women were sending him messages, saying they wanted to meet.

elshaheeed: I'm taking as much measures as I can to remain anonymous
But of course I'm scared

It was past midnight in Egypt. We'd been talking for over an hour. He let slip that he had a wife, who was getting angry that he was still online. He also mentioned that he put in long hours at a demanding day job.

El Shaheed said he was working with veteran activists to help the protest move from the internet to the real world. Many had previously suffered through beatings, imprisonment, torture, and the deaths of comrades. They were spreading word among their contacts, planning routes, and readying lawyers, trauma doctors, and medical supplies. I called some well-known Egyptian activists, who confirmed what El Shaheed had told me, and published the story online.

On January 25, protests erupted across Egypt on a scale far greater than even El Shaheed had expected. In Cairo alone, some 200,000 people turned out. Police fought the crowds with clubs and tear gas. Some protesters were shot dead; hundreds were arrested. But as night fell in Cairo, protesters occupied Tahrir Square, an expanse of concrete in the city center ringed by faded colonial apartment buildings and old hotels. News channels around the world broadcasted live-streams of Tahrir from the rooftops, showing a sea of men and women crammed shoulder to shoulder, chanting and singing, the crowd shimmering with the flashes of the cameras on their mobile phones.

In the days that followed, the regime instituted a state of emergency as the protests spread across the country. The Facebook page put out a call for an even bigger protest, naming it "A Day of Rage."

"This time no one is organizing so far. A lot of organizers are arrested," El Shaheed told me in our chat box. "We are hoping it will virally spread, and people will assume responsibilities." He shared with me a Google doc that showed dozens of users working in real-time to edit the language of the manifestos that were appearing on the Facebook page and the chants protesters were shouting in the streets:

"Change, change, leave, leave."

"Bread, freedom, social justice."

"The people want to overthrow the regime."

I was surprised to see how connected many Americans felt to the drama, following the protesters not just on the news but through their Facebook and Twitter feeds, interacting with them, sharing and liking, and adding to their momentum. All of it fit with a certain mind-set at the time, halfway through Barack Obama's first term—the feeling that it was possible to sit at your laptop and like your way to a better world.

It was the beginning of what was optimistically being called the Arab Spring: first Tunisia, then Egypt, and then rumblings of like-minded protests planned in places such as Libya and Yemen. Dissenters were organizing even in Syria, where the Assad dynasty was one of the world's most oppressive autocracies. A special euphoria was building around the movement in the United States, where many felt that the protests showed that a spirit of American freedom was emerging in a traditionally autocratic region. The shadow of the Iraq War had defined America and its relationship with the rest of the world for almost a decade, and Obama had risen to the presidency based in part on his promise to move on from the conflict. He'd given a major foreign policy address, in 2009, in the reception hall at Cairo University, just across the Nile River from Tahrir. The speech was called "A New Beginning," and Obama used it to champion things like "the ability to speak your mind and have a say in how you are governed" and "the freedom to live as you choose. Those are not just American ideas, they are human rights, and that is why we will support them everywhere."

U.S. troops were still fighting al-Qaeda in Iraq, but Obama was planning to bring them home by the end of 2011. The Arab Spring seemed to offer a new way for America to influence the Middle East. The young Arabs were not just chanting for the same ideals Obama had outlined but organizing around them with the aid of Facebook and Twitter, Androids and iPhones. The euphoria of that moment, with Americans sitting at their phones and laptops and feeling connected with protesters across the Arab world, was central to the darkness that followed. I would meet rebels and activists in the ensuing years who never got over the sense of betrayal that came when, as they were still in the midst of their struggle, the rest of the world lost interest and severed the connection, leaving them on their own to be killed and jailed and co-opted and otherwise erased from history.

The Syrian activist who snapped one day, tied up a man, and prepared to behead him in the name not of jihad but of liberalism, as an act of defiance to say, *I'm still here*; and the oil smuggler and ISIS fixer who supported the caliphate even as he risked his life so many times to help me, whose anger at America and the West was all the more intense because he'd once been a revolutionary; and even those who carried out the darkest of ISIS's missions—at times they all seemed to be looking back to this moment, for justification, so they could see themselves not as killers or terrorists but as soldiers of retribution.

There was something else. To be living a drab life and then, through your phone or computer, to feel engaged with an exciting new world, only to look away from your screen and find yourself still trapped at home, could be life altering. Much later, sifting through a cache of thousands of personnel files of ISIS's foreign fighters, I would read their bios and realize that they had experienced a similar pull.

On the Day of Rage, protests across Egypt swelled to their greatest size yet. The regime seemed on the verge of collapse. Then El Shaheed went missing. His friends contacted me using his handle online, saying that they were running the page in his place. He'd been dragged into a car by men in plain clothes who were probably secret police. As the days passed, word of El Shaheed's disappearance began to spread among the crowd in Tahrir Square. Eventually, his friends told me who El Shaheed was: Wael Ghonim, a thirty-two-year-old Egyptian, who was a short and bespectacled executive at Google. He lived with his wife in Dubai but had flown to Cairo for the protests. He was released due to political pressure, and before his friends rushed him to Tahrir, we spoke on the phone for the first time. I asked how it felt to be unmasked. "I hate it, but it was out of my hands," he said, sounding weary. Then he added, almost in a whisper, "A lot of people died." Mubarak stepped down four days later.

I turned to the cyberactivist movement in Syria, where the dictatorship was even more brutal than Egypt's had been. "The regime will bring all its force and military, and this will frighten a large number of people," said a veteran organizer named Razan Zaitouneh—one of many Syrians I spoke to who would soon be exiled, murdered, or disappeared—as she was planning one of the first small protests in the capital, Damascus. "But that wasn't the only purpose of this call. It's about breaking the fear and breaking the silence in Syria. And it's the start."

CHAPTER 2

LEO

Damascus, Syria. March 2011.

LAWAND KIKI WAS BORN IN 1979, THE FOURTH AND FINAL CHILD OF a dissident couple in Damascus. His mother told him that, in her native Kurdish language, his name meant "he who is loved." When Lawand was fifteen, he fled to America with his family and applied for asylum, settling in Fairview, New Jersey. Lawand finished high school there and learned to speak English with the same thick Jersey accent as his mostly Irish and Italian American neighbors. He did a spot-on De Niro impression and memorized lines from *Analyze This*. He was the kind of guy who made friends easily, chatting up the regulars at the deli and pizzeria. People around the neighborhood knew him as Leo—Leo from Henry Street.

When Leo was in his early twenties, his dad died, and he helped to support himself and his mom. He drove a limo and sold knockoff designer jeans from the trunk of his Lincoln, letting customers know that the jeans were fakes because he didn't have the heart to rip them off. He preferred to feel like they were in on the scam together: *These look just like real Diesels, and they're only forty bucks*. The family's asylum application had dragged on and was denied after his father's death; Leo eventually overstayed his visa. He was arrested by immigration agents in the winter of 2006 and held in detention. After three months, he was deported to Damascus. When he arrived at the airport, it was his first time in Syria in more than ten years.

The *mukhabarat*, Syria's secret police, detained him from the plane. The officer who beat and questioned him in a dimly lit interrogation room at the airport was suspicious of Leo's time in America and accused him of being in the CIA. Eventually, he released him into the city.

In those first months back in Damascus, as Leo wandered the vaguely familiar streets, he was jarred by the poverty and repression he saw. Like any Western tourist, he walked in awe around the Great Mosque and the sprawling bazaar that surrounded it. In another part of the capital, he could visit the Four Seasons Hotel and a high-end shopping mall that sold real versions of the fake designer clothes he'd once hawked from his Lincoln. But as he settled into a working-class suburb called Rukneddine, in a bedroom of the colonial-era home in which his paternal grandfather had been born, he realized that many Syrians couldn't afford to own a car or sometimes even to buy meat. He also noticed that no one would talk politics out of fear of the secret police who'd given him such a violent welcome home. "The walls have ears," people warned in hushed tones. Thousands of political prisoners filled the country's many jails.

Leo wanted to return to New Jersey, and he called his mom on Skype every day, but his deportation order barred him from America for a decade. So he started ringing up relatives and old friends from grade school, trying to find a new community. Over time, he began to fall in love with the ancient city. He sometimes thought he could feel Damascus breathing. Already settled in the earliest recorded history—Damascus is mentioned in the oldest surviving records of the pharaohs and in the book of Genesis—the city had served for centuries as a crossroads, drawing in religious and ethnic groups from across Eurasia, North Africa, and the Middle East. It was home to deeply rooted communities of Sunni and Shia Muslims, Alawites, Christians, Circassians, Druze, and Kurds. The diversity was, on the one hand, part of what made Syria vulnerable to the kind of sectarian tensions that had led to civil wars in Iraq and Lebanon. On the other hand, it was part of the city's unique charm, and if Leo squinted, standing amid the different peoples and accents in Rukneddine, he could catch glimpses of his adopted American home.

In time he found that he'd built a tight-knit circle of friends, like in New Jersey. He was part of a crew of twenty- and thirty-something Syrians who convened to play PlayStation and *tarneeb*, a Syrian version of Spades. Or they'd sip *mate* tea from small glasses stuffed with herbs as they passed hours in the city's cafés, puffing tobacco from hookah pipes made of colored glass as the water lightly bubbled in their oblong bases, their voices blending with the sounds of the city.

In March 2011, the month after Mubarak stepped down in Egypt, protests began in Daraa, a former Roman garrison city forty miles south of Damascus. The protests were a response to police brutality, as in Egypt. Local cops had arrested and tortured children for spray-painting antiregime graffiti. They castrated one of them, a thirteen-year-old boy, before they returned his body to his family. The protests in Daraa began to grow when security forces fired on the crowds, then spread to the rest of the country. The protests were peaceful, led by the same kind of liberal, tech-savvy activists as in Egypt, but the response from the Syrian security forces was far deadlier. Hundreds of people had been detained and dozens more shot dead in the streets by the time Syria's young president, Bashar al-Assad, prepared to address the crisis in a nationally televised speech.

Assad, a forty-five-year-old ophthalmologist, had been living in London when, eleven years earlier, he became the leader of Syria, following the deaths of his father and older brother. Some, like Leo, saw hope in the young and modern image he projected. Assad was defined for them not by the abuses of the *mukhabarat* but by his promises of reform, by his willingness to dine in public with U.S. Senator John Kerry, and by his glamorous wife, who'd just received a profile in *Vogue*. Leo bought into Assad's talk of incremental change and believed he was working to fix the brutal and corrupt regime he'd inherited. It was just after 8 p.m. in Damascus, and Leo stared at the TV in his fading apartment in

Rukneddine, waiting for Assad to appear on the screen. He thought the speech would be historic: Assad would prove himself the reformer he'd long claimed to be, apologize for the bloodshed, and push for peace. *This is a crisis, and he's gonna fix it*, Leo thought. *Don't worry. Everything's gonna be fine*.

As Assad approached the podium, the regime-sanctioned parliament broke into thunderous applause. "I am sure you all know," Assad said, "that Syria is facing a great conspiracy."

Assad rambled on, leveling accusations that the protests were part of some international treachery and warning of "plots being hatched against our country." He threatened the protesters and any Syrian who supported them. The applause continued on Leo's TV. "Burying sedition is a national, moral, and religious duty; and all those who can contribute to burying it and do not are part of it," Assad continued. "There is no compromise or middle way in this."

The speech went on like this for more than an hour. Assad stopped often to accept standing ovations, smiling. He made jokes. *He's not saying anything that means anything*, Leo thought, suddenly afraid. *Instead he came out laughing*.

In the summer of 2012, Leo arrived with the first surge of Syrian refugees into Turkey, uprooted again, with $100 in his pocket. Civil war had erupted at home, and the mountainous region of southern Turkey that shares a 565-mile border with Syria had become the main staging ground for the rebellion, where fighters could rest and resupply under the watch of a friendly Turkish government. The ancient cities that dot the region were overtaken by the strange ecosystem that comes to life on the edge of a war: rebels, activists, aid workers, and gunrunners, spies, hustlers, and operators of all kinds, and journalists. Newly arrived in Turkey myself, I was amazed when I met Leo amid this blur of faces. It was almost like a dream: a refugee who hailed, like me, from the sprawling towns that ring New York City and greeted me with an accent thicker than my own.

"What's up, bro?" he said.

He was wearing a T-shirt and jeans, his jet-black hair pulled back behind his ears, his brown eyes glowing with a warmth that softened the fact that he otherwise looked like a typical Jersey tough guy. He was still disoriented from his journey.

After Assad's March 2011 speech, the crackdowns had become deadlier, and the protests had spread. Assad tried to rally his supporters by inflaming sectarian tensions that dated to the division of Islam between Sunni and Shia in 680 CE. Assad and the core of his regime were Alawite, a religious minority in Syria combining some Christian and ancient Zoroastrian beliefs with the tenets of Shia Islam and broadly identifying as Shia. Leo was from another group on the periphery—the Kurds, an ethnic minority that, while predominantly Muslim, was politically suppressed in Syria as in other Arab countries. If someone had asked him before the war how he identified, though, like many of his friends he would have said simply that he was Syrian. Most people were more interested in unity than in division, but the danger of sectarianism was that it existed as a reservoir for the cynical to tap. Assad peddled conspiracy theories that Sunnis were planning to massacre minorities, and his security forces fired live rounds and sometimes artillery into the protests, hoping to overshadow their message of peace. At the same time, he released hard-line Sunni Islamists en masse from the extremist breeding grounds of the regime's prisons to aid his claims about Sunni radicalism. Among the first refugees fleeing into southern Turkey were many Syrians like Leo who once had bridged sectarian divides. As one young activist there told me later, "I met the most beautiful people I ever knew in jail."

At first central Damascus had been mostly isolated from the unrest, but Leo could feel it creeping toward him. Neighbors and friends were sucked into the conflict. A salesman who worked in a shop that sold designer shoes was arrested at a protest, and when he emerged weeks later, he was marked by torture and filled with rage. A seller of hairstyling products who'd been giving food and blankets to the protesters simply disappeared from his shop one day. There were whispers that he'd been betrayed by another of Leo's friends, a chef who backed the regime.

A screenwriter was arrested—he had been speaking against Assad in the cafés—and he, too, was never heard from again. Three brothers who worked as wedding planners became members of the *shabiha*, the pro-regime death squads that the locals called "ghosts." All across Syria, military personnel were defecting rather than obey orders to fire on the crowds, while bands of civilians, like the former shoe salesman, armed themselves.

Around this time, from a safe house not far from Rukneddine, the Syrian dissident and intellectual Yassin al-Haj Saleh, a supporter of the protests, issued a warning. "The Syrian revolution is starting to regress into a primordial condition; a 'state of nature.' . . . The state of nature is characterized by social dispersion, direct reactive responses, violence—all characteristics of a society losing its self-control and its ability to act uniformly," he wrote in an essay published online. "A state of nature is the equivalent of a civil war—a sectarian war, in which murder leads to murder . . . and hatred animates hatred."

One night in Damascus, Leo stood on a friend's rooftop, watching as a military chopper hovered just above him until he saw it spit a rocket into the streets, shattering another piece of his city. He decided to flee. He called an Alawite friend working as a security officer for the regime, who advised him to drive to a border crossing with Lebanon. There, Leo met another Alawite from his old crew. He took Leo's passport into the customs office, stamped it himself, and brought it back to the car—a final favor inspired by the kind of kinship that was deteriorating so quickly.

"Take it easy," the friend said.

"You want anything from Lebanon?" Leo asked.

The friend paused. "Bring me some tobacco," he said, "if you ever come back."

Leo spent three days in Beirut, sleeping on the floor of a half-constructed home. Then he took a flight to Istanbul, boarded a bus headed south, and rode for sixteen hours to the border with Syria, hoping to find work as a translator in the new wartime economy.

CHAPTER 3

BORDER

Antakya, Turkey. July 2012.

I ARRIVED IN SOUTHERN TURKEY NOT LONG AFTERWARD. I WAS SENT BY *Newsweek* overnight, taking flights from London, where I'd been based as a foreign correspondent, to Istanbul and then to a city called Antakya, twenty-five miles from Syria. By then, in Egypt, the Islamist Muslim Brotherhood had outmuscled liberal activists and put one of its enforcers into the presidency, as the generals plotted a return to power, while in Yemen and Libya all order was collapsing. Only Tunisia was on a path to democracy. Syria was the Arab Spring's last great struggle, with the potential for transformational change and, at the same time, profound suffering and violence—two sides of a spinning coin. A few days earlier, rebels had assassinated four members of Assad's inner circle in a Damascus bombing and then launched a surprise incursion into the northern city of Aleppo, Syria's commercial capital and most populous city, which sat thirty-five miles from Turkey. Suddenly, it seemed that they could beat Assad, and journalists from around the world were arriving in the Turkish border region around Antakya. A taxi took me from the airport to a small hotel called the Narin, where I'd heard some of the correspondents were staying. I put my bag on the floor of a thin-walled room and fell asleep.

The next morning I woke to the sound of children playing at a school beneath my window and began to make my way around a city that had found itself transformed into the international hub of the rebellion. Situated in a valley on the Orontes River, which stretches north from Lebanon through Syria and into Turkey, where it flows into the Mediterranean Sea, Antakya had often been on the frontier of history. Called Antioch in the Bible, it drew the first Christian evangelicals, including St. Paul, who began his missionary journeys from the city. Cut into the surrounding mountains is an ancient church in which St. Peter is said to have preached, where an escape tunnel in the walls testifies to the dangers early Christians faced. Even after the emperor Constantine made Christianity the religion of the Roman Empire, Antioch kept its edge as home to spiritual radicals like St. Simeon the Stylite, who spent a life of prayer confined to a small platform on a pillar.

Antioch also sat amid the shifting front lines in the struggle between the Persian and Byzantine empires that preceded the birth of Islam in the seventh century. In his book *In the Shadow of the Sword*, the historian Tom Holland recounts the most notorious attack Antioch suffered over the centuries, at the hands of the Persian shah Khusrow I in 530 CE:

> But Khusrow, even as he swaggered and plundered his way across Syria, had more in mind than mere extortion: he wanted to stage a spectacular. Accordingly, he aimed directly for the richest prize of all, "the fair crown of the East." . . . The people of Antioch did all they could to prepare for the looming onslaught: by sending to Palmyra and Damascus for reinforcements, and to Simeon on his pillar for a miracle. The news brought back from the stylite, however, could hardly have been any bleaker. God Himself, speaking to Simeon in a vision, had revealed His plans for Antioch—and they were terrible.

> "I will fill her with her enemies," so the Almighty had declared, "and I will abandon the greater part of her population to the sword, and those who survive to captivity." And so it came to pass.

Time and again Antioch was razed by enemies and rocked by earthquakes and afflicted with plague, but it always survived. The Antakya I found that summer, renamed when it became part of the Republic of Turkey in 1939, still moved to a rhythm of its own. Women in halter tops walked past bars and ice-cream stands down modern streets that faded seamlessly into an old town that belonged to another time, where mazes of cobblestone pathways wound along the dusty walls of homes built in the old Arabic style, their rooms facing onto courtyards, and uniformed schoolchildren dashed past women in headscarves. Antakya had been part of Syria under the Ottoman Empire, and many residents spoke both Turkish and Arabic, making it a natural destination for the rebels and refugees moving across the border and the foreign interlopers who followed them there. The newcomers appeared suddenly and conspicuously, as if a storm surge had crashed through the city and receded, leaving human debris.

The Narin Hotel had an open-air café on its second-floor balcony that overlooked one of Antakya's main streets. It attracted the outsiders, who sat at their tables over little hourglass-shaped glasses of clay-brown Turkish tea, eying one another, conversing in muted tones, conspiring. Journalists met with Syrian fixers who offered passage on the old smuggling routes that cut through the dusty hills into Syria and access to the expanding constellation of rebel groups: the Brigade of Oneness, the Brigade of the Redeemer, the Syrian Falcons, the Free Syrian Army, the Syrian Martyrs' Brigade. Representatives of these groups wore collared shirts and slacks to meet with the moneymen who'd flown in from Gulf countries with cash that could buy weapons and pay salaries. Foreign governments were also intervening. America, Britain, and France already had been providing the opposition with things like communications equipment and medical supplies, while Turkey, Saudi Arabia, and Qatar were giving them small amounts of weapons. Diplomats and spies fanned out through the city.

It was hard to know who was who or what to make of their stories. One night I met a man who'd flown in from Saudi Arabia to channel support to rebel groups, and as we sat on the Narin balcony, smoking cigarettes and drinking beer, he showed me clips of himself on talk shows at home, dressed in the white robe and headdress of a sheikh, as he called in the name of God for aid to the rebels. On another night on the same balcony, I met a Tunisian veteran of the religious wars in Chechnya and Afghanistan. A drunken American told me he worked for Campbell's Soup and was going to scout business opportunities in Syria.

All the while more people were coming across the border from Syria. Often the journey into Turkey was as simple as a dash through the hills, and if the border guards fired their rifles, it was usually into the air, as a halfhearted warning. Those who could afford the modest fees could hire a smuggler to walk them right through the border gates. One day I paid $50 to an old man who'd been in that business for decades. He took my arm with one hand, and as he walked me past the customs booth and into Syria, with the other hand he gave the guard a little wave. "Everyone here eats from my soup," he told me. Sometimes so many people crowded together on the Syrian side of the border gate that the guards just gave in and opened it. The less fortunate of the new arrivals filled white tents in the refugee camps that were being built near the border; the first time I visited one, outside a mountain town thirty miles south of Antakya, the war lurked just over a ridge, flashing and rumbling. Other refugees packed into apartments in the border towns and in Antakya, driving up real estate prices. Syrian activists took over cafés with their laptops. You could find rebel leaders inside the right hookah bars and restaurants, taking leave from the fighting. Many would eventually make their way to the Narin balcony.

It was like a wild game of speed dating all through the summer on that balcony and across Antakya and the surrounding towns and cities. I'd wake in the Narin to the morning announcements at the school below and then meet four, five, six people in a day, one face blending in with the next—the commander with the eye patch, the defector-general in the tracksuit, the American diplomat in the floral shirt, the aid worker in the cargo pants. For years afterward I would run into one or another of them, and there would be a flash of guilty recognition between us, as if we shared some secret sin.

One hot afternoon, I stepped into an apartment building, walked up a few flights of stairs, and entered a sparsely furnished flat. Inside, a man lay on a mattress, scratching at a leg that had been amputated just above the knee. Another sat on a couch, staring at a television tuned to the channel guide. His shirt was rolled up to reveal a hole in his stomach, covered by a plastic bag that showed his intestines and sagged with yellow fluid. The men had been rebels, caught up in the moment, and then the wave had passed right over them. They'd been taken in by a doctor, a refugee himself, who turned his apartment into a makeshift convalescent home. These homes were popping up all around southern Turkey as the war worsened and the wounded were pushed away from overcrowded hospitals. Some were more professional, with trained nurses on staff, like the one where I found another fighter, just back from surgery and still in the grips of anesthesia. "Oh, God. Everything is destroyed," he said as he rolled his head from side to side, chanting in a singsong voice like an oracle. "But it's okay. We will kill you. We will kill you."

For all its repression under Assad, Syria was a relatively well-educated country, and citizens of prosperous cities like Aleppo had a hard time making sense of the demise of their former lives. I met a man named Mustafa, newly arrived from Aleppo, as he sat with his wife and children on the floor of a house near the border, which was crowded with refugees. He mimicked the motion of turning meat on a grill, explaining that people had gone about their lives, barbecuing through the summer, until the war reached them. "I used to tell my friends, Hama is completely destroyed, so is Homs, so is Daraa, and you are having a barbeque," he said. "They used to say, 'No way. Nothing will happen here.'"

He couldn't believe that the regime was bombing neighborhoods after rebels took them. Assad had turned his fighter jets on his own cities. "We didn't expect it to be like this at all," Mustafa said. "But the situation has gone mad."

He was interrupted by a relative who owned a copy shop near Aleppo University. "Just imagine that you were at home in New York and Obama started shelling you!"

Mustafa, a barber, had kept canaries in his shop. When the regime began to bomb a neighborhood across town, the birds screeched and fluttered in their cages. Then the shelling grew more frequent, and finally the bombs hit his neighborhood too, destroying a store, exploding in a park. Mustafa passed the days alone in his shop, the canaries screeching nonstop. Eventually he gathered his family and fled, but not before giving the keys to his shop to a rebel he knew and asking the man to keep an eye on the birds. He hoped the refugee experience would be something like a prolonged trip abroad, and he called the rebel every day to check on the canaries. Several Aleppo residents had left the same man with their own keys and requests to look after their homes and plants and pets.

I first met Leo on the Narin balcony not long after my conversation with Mustafa. We realized that we'd grown up not far from one another, in similar places, and were about the same age. We agreed to work together as journalist and translator.

Leo had been filtering back and forth across the border since his arrival in Antakya, finding work with an Associated Press crew and an amateur documentary team. On one of his assignments in Syria, he woke in the middle of the night to a mortar attack. "It was crazy," he recalled. "Everyone was running around in their fucking underwear." After that he swore off returning to the war zone. *Newsweek*, on its way to going bankrupt, could no longer support war trips, and my editor had threatened to fire me if I ventured into the fighting. So Leo and I focused instead on exploring the border region and its role as the world's gateway to Syria and its suffering.

It was oddly comforting to see the conflict through the eyes of a Syrian refugee who was also just a guy from home. Leo had lost his naiveté about Assad, but he wasn't an activist. He just wanted an end to the war. "It's all so fucked up," he often said, shaking his head. The accounts of men and women speaking from the depths of confusion and pain came to me in his thick New Jersey accent, and it was easy to imagine that the people we met could be anyone from anywhere. As we traveled hundreds of miles around the border between houses and camps and cafés, I often wondered who from my own hometown could take their places—who might run the checkpoints, who would fight, who would help the wounded, who would leave. We sometimes spoke by Skype to friends of his who'd stayed behind in Damascus, like the muscle-bound nightclub manager who sat before his computer's camera in a graphic tee and explained how he spent his nights as an assassin, killing people around the city whom he suspected of working for the regime. Soon after, he was killed himself.

It was hard to remember that Leo, too, was suffering, with no family around him and almost no possessions. The first time I handed him his weekly salary, he walked straight into an electronics store beside the Narin and bought an iPad with a mobile data plan. He plugged in the factory headphones, signed into Facebook and Skype, and began chatting with his mom in New Jersey and his family and friends from Damascus who had scattered everywhere. After that I almost never saw him without the iPad—he usually had at least an earbud in—as we traveled up and down the border.

The rebels we met were a mix of soldiers who had defected, first-time fighters, and Islamists. Those who'd left the Syrian military had mostly joined the Free Syrian Army, or FSA, an alliance of rebel groups that were more professional and moderate than their counterparts. They portrayed themselves as modern versions of America's revolutionary patriots and had the support of many of the activists who'd started the protests. They wanted U.S. backing. In August 2011, Obama had stated that Assad should step down, leaving many Syrians to wonder what America might do to make it happen. Rebels could take encouragement from the fact that so many representatives of the U.S. government were in southern Turkey. In a city 115 miles northwest of Antakya, Leo and

I were welcomed at a seminar run by State Department diplomats to train opposition activists, and we knew such gatherings were occurring regularly. The United States was providing rebels with equipment like computers, night-vision goggles, and ambulances while also sending aid to the opposition councils that had been set up to govern rebel-held territory. We also learned that CIA officers were holding meetings with rebel leaders, asking what kind of weapons they needed.

Yet, as summer turned to fall, the factions gaining strength in the rebellion were not the moderates who sought to be U.S. allies but the hard-line Islamists, many of whom had established steady sources of support via backers like the Gulf financiers I'd seen on the Narin balcony. The most extreme groups were being joined by veteran mujahideen like the Tunisian I'd encountered, who were heading by the hundreds to southern Turkey to enter Syria. One night at a café near the border, Leo and I met three Syrians in their early twenties who'd joined the most ominous of these Islamist groups, the Nusra Front, which had taken in the greatest number of mujahideen. It would later come to light that the Nusra Front was founded by veterans of al-Qaeda's war against America in Iraq, but at the time U.S. diplomats were still wondering what to make of it. The three young men arrived for our meeting dressed in prayer caps and *shalwar kameez*. They reminded me of children playing behind their beards as we shared pastries and tea. They told us about the services, such as food and water and medical care, they were providing to civilians in Syria. "The Nusra Front is carrying out the work of God," one of them said. They affected the strident, formal speech of TV imams, and Leo did a riotous impression of them as we made the drive back to Antakya, laughing all the way.

The regime in Damascus, in fact, was not collapsing. It was carrying out more airstrikes. Each day brought more destruction, more civilian casualties, and more momentum for those among the opposition who wanted a response that was more extreme and more sectarian. As the war grew darker, so did the mood in southern Turkey. I moved from the Narin to an apartment with a balcony that overlooked the Orontes River, where Leo and I sat and smoked hookah. One day that winter, we walked across the hall to greet some new Syrian neighbors and learned that one of them was making bombs. He asked if I'd let him have a solar-powered battery charger I'd received as a Christmas gift. When Leo and I walked into Antakya's bazaar on another day, to buy a propane furnace to light the coals for our hookah, the shopkeeper assumed that he was a rebel and I was a foreign fighter. "I know you're just going to use this to make a bomb," he said, sounding dejected, as he handed Leo the furnace.

We had befriended the owner of a cell phone shop that was always crowded with Syrians. He was a Turk who supported Assad but also sold SIM cards and phone credit to rebels, who could pick up Turkish mobile service in northern Syria and sometimes strode into his shop to hand him thick wads of cash. The owner loved to talk politics—he'd lecture me at length about how America would destroy Syria, just like Iraq—and whenever I visited, he'd pour me coffee and beckon for me to sit. On a chilly night in January, with the shop busy as usual, I met a man who told me he was headed to a weapons drop at the border and invited me to come.

I'd been tracking the flow of weapons to the rebels. Many Islamist factions were having no problem getting arms, and I wondered what America was doing for its allies. I'd spoken with Syrians who recounted meetings with CIA officers at luxury hotels around the border region, during which the Americans had asked for wish lists of weapons and promised that the United States would help to defeat Assad. This was the start of a years-long CIA program that saw some rebel factions receive weapons and ammunition channeled via Saudi Arabia, Qatar, and Turkey.

My new acquaintance and I walked to his apartment and waited for the lead smuggler. At around 10 p.m., a man with long gray hair and a matching beard entered the apartment in a crisp gray suit. His name was Abdulrahman al-Halaq, but the rebels knew him as ZaZa, one of the most powerful smugglers in northern Syria. ZaZa changed into a black tracksuit, and I asked him if he approved of my plans to come along. "Even if you were my own brother, I would kill you if I saw you there," he said.

He agreed to have a beer and talk for a while instead. His shipments seemed to have the approval of the Turkish government, and he intimated that they were part of the covert program run by America and its allies. He said he mostly sent automatic rifles and that the heavy weapons and surface-to-air missiles that the rebels had been promised had never materialized. He also said that even the lighter weapons he did receive were in short supply—just enough, in his estimation, to keep the balance from tipping to either side. "They give us ten bullets so that when we run out we have to come back for more," he said. It was a line I would hear again and again from the CIA's rebel allies over the years as America kept them alive but made sure they never got too strong, wary of what might happen if Assad were defeated. "If they gave us twenty, we could advance, but they don't want that," ZaZa continued. "They just want to balance the power of the regime."

Leo was a natural hustler, well equipped to survive in the wartime ecosystem around the border region, but the hopelessness was wearing on him. He saw what was happening to the Syrians around him, as even prominent rebels and activists were reduced to relying on the piecemeal support of their foreign benefactors for survival. Someone from a European embassy requested to meet Leo in Antakya one night. Whoever this person was or whatever he wanted, I wasn't surprised that he'd be interested in meeting a well-connected English-speaking Syrian. Leo couldn't have known where the meeting would lead, but for him it was like a door in a locked room opening. He bought a suit from one of the stalls in the bazaar, put it on, and slicked back his hair. "How do I look, bro?" he asked, and then he walked out into the city.

On one of our last late-night drives along the border, as we sped through a sideways rain down a highway that looked onto Syria, Leo began to tap on his iPad, writing a Facebook post that expressed the bewildering sense of upheaval he was feeling.

"I discovered that I'm one of the world wonders," he wrote. "One day I'm in Syria, and the next day I'm not. The next day I'm in America, the day after I'm not. One day in Germany, one day in China. One day in Dubai, the next day in Canada."

The words seemed to blend his personal story with that of every Syrian refugee.

"Sometimes I'm in Lebanon, and the next time I'm not. Sometimes I'm in Jordan, and then the next time I'm not. One day in Saudi Arabia, and the next day in Turkey. No family or a mother. And my father is gone. One day I'm hungry, and one day I'm not. One day I'm in a house, and the next day I'm not. One day with a country, and the next day without."

The road curved, and Syria passed in a blur beyond the hills on the driver's side.

"I left my friends, and then the next day I saw them again," Leo wrote. "And then they stayed where they are, and then I left them again. One day I'm safe, and the next day I'm not. Right now I'm nothing, but at the same time I'm everything. Did you understand anything? And if you didn't, that's how my life exactly is right now."

He published the post. A few minutes later, he said quietly, still staring into the glow of his iPad, "It already has eight likes."

CHAPTER 4

REVENGE

Cairo, Egypt. August 2013.

As the war worsened in Syria, Egypt erupted in bloodshed that marked the official death of the Arab Spring for anyone who still hoped it could be revived. I felt the pendulum swing, toward something much darker, as a crowd pulled up paving stones to pile atop their meager, sandbagged barricades on a street in eastern Cairo. Some ripped branches from the city's sickly trees. A man with a white beard stooped to grab a stone, then raised his eyes. A convoy of armored personnel carriers rumbled forward, painted in the midnight blue of Egypt's internal police.

They stopped fifty yards from the protesters. I ran up to take a picture, but the vehicles began rolling again, past me and up to the barricades. Soldiers stood tall in their turrets, looking down at the panicked crowd. They wore masks. The air cracked as they fired a volley of tear gas grenades, and for a moment there was silence, the vapor hanging. Then they raised their automatic rifles and fired into the fog.

There were thousands of people in the encampment, all supporters of Mohamed Morsi, the Muslim Brotherhood enforcer who'd been Egypt's president for about a year until he was jailed during a military coup six weeks earlier. The protesters had been camped since around the Rabaa al-Adawiya mosque in the Nasr City district of Cairo, turning the neighborhood's middle-class streets into a carnival of Islamists from around the country. The bloodshed was meant to let Egyptians know that the generals would tolerate no further dissent.

As I paced behind the armored vehicles, the police continued firing into the crowd. Behind me, loudspeakers blared, urging the protesters to surrender, while inside the camp, Muslim Brotherhood leaders screamed through loudspeakers mounted on the minarets of the mosque: "No! Don't leave! It's a trap!"

Some protesters threw Molotov cocktails. The firing from the police intensified.

"For God we lose our lives," a voice on the mosque's speakers cried.

Eventually I was joined by Louis Jammes, a willowy French artist in his fifties, and his twenty-five-year-old friend, Mahmoud Abou Zeid, who introduced himself by the name his friends called him, Shawkan. He had deep-set eyes, a chiseled jaw, and an easy, confident manner. Fluent in English and wearing a T-shirt and jeans, with his hair pulled into a hipster bun, he would have been at home on the streets of New York or Los Angeles, just like many of the Egyptians who'd defined the revolution in its early days. Now those of his comrades who hadn't sold their souls to back the military coup were either in jail or toiling in obscurity. Shawkan had found a different path, as a journalist, documenting the revolution's destruction as a photographer with a London-based freelance agency.

The three of us stood together for a while, watching as the police continued to shoot and kill the demonstrators. Then Shawkan walked off with his camera to take some pictures.

I heard a commotion behind me. Police in plain clothes and flak jackets were roughly arresting a man, who was screaming. When I approached to get a better look, the men in the flak jackets surrounded me. They pulled my backpack from my shoulders and my phone from my jeans. Someone hit me in the face. My head snapped sideways, he hit me again, and then I was being punched from all directions. My wrists were pinned behind my back with zip ties. My wallet left my pocket, my belt left my waist, and my watch left my wrist. Someone had me by the collar. He announced to the gathering crowd of police that I was an American journalist, and they cheered as he jabbed me in the chin. Then he dragged me to the metal box of a prison bus and threw me into it.

Inside, protesters were crammed shoulder to shoulder along the thin benches that lined the walls, and more were on the floor. One man was crumbled in a corner and moaning. Many had been beaten before being put in the bus, and the guards were beating them some more. Soon Shawkan and Jammes were beside me. We fell to our knees as the bus began moving.

The Islamists muttered prayers around us. The air was thick and hot, and with my arms pinned behind me, I labored to breathe. Sweat soaked my jeans and shirt as my chest pressed against the knees of two men who sat on the bench in front of me. Each had one hand bound to his neighbor's. With his free hand the man on my right pulled out a small phone and surreptitiously placed a call, pleading for help, as his fellow prisoners whispered sharply for him to hide it. The driver saw him in the rearview mirror and yelled to a guard, who marched back into the hold, pushing bodies aside until he was wedged behind me. He grabbed the phone and punched the man, but with my body as a buffer he couldn't strike at full strength. So he pushed me forward with one hand and beat the man with the other, using me for leverage. I laid limp in his victim's lap, feeling the shudder of the blows.

The guard beat the prisoner with a rage that seemed inspired not just by the offense but also by the fact that it had forced him to assert his authority, trapping him in it. The bloodied men around us were bearded, some in slacks or jeans and others in *dishdashas*. They were the same kind of men I'd seen crying when word of the coup came down, wandering the streets in shock, so sure of their hold on the world until that moment. After Mubarak's ouster, the liberal opposition had been riven by infighting. The well-organized Muslim Brotherhood had outmaneuvered them, dominating parliament and winning the presidency, then stocked the security forces and government ministries with loyalists, and then jailed and tortured liberal activists who were once their allies. Sensing an opportunity, Egypt's generals had secretly funded a protest movement that called for the military to reclaim power; the counterrevolution was centered on a Facebook page and led by young, tech-savvy activists. Tens of thousands of Egyptians, many of them oblivious of the conspiracy and others simply not caring, joined the protests, and soon the army's tanks were rolling through Cairo's streets.

Sweat was running down my face, and one of the men on the bench produced a little rag and used it to pat my forehead and cheeks. For years afterward I could feel the sweetness of that act, as I considered that the man, like most of the thousands of Egyptians who were arrested in the crackdowns, had either been killed or was buried irretrievably inside one of the country's prisons. The bus stopped, and the back doors swung open. A sports arena towered above us as we were marched through a jeering crowd of cops. Inside the arena, on a basketball court, more police surrounded a cluster of prisoners who were kneeling in rows between the three-point lines. Our group knelt to join them. I knew Egyptian police often tortured political prisoners soon after they were processed, but as I fretted over this, an officer grabbed me by the arm and pulled me off to the side. Soon Jammes was beside me, and we realized we would be released. We watched in silence as the court filled with more protesters. In the stands, a man who'd been shot in the shoulder laid on his side, moaning for what seemed like an hour, until some paramedics arrived. As they carried him away, he turned back and shouted, "May God let Muslims win!" The kneeling men responded with a halfhearted murmur.

The zip ties were cut from my wrists, and Jammes and I were led to the exits. Shawkan remained kneeling amid the rows of prisoners.

We stepped from the arena and learned of a death toll that would climb past 1,000. Among the dead were three Egyptian journalists and a veteran British cameraman who'd been shot, by a police sniper, in the forehead. Smoke rose on the skyline as I walked past a few riot cops sitting on a curb outside the arena. "Please don't be angry," one of them said.

A week later, in Syria, the Assad regime would launch its first large-scale chemical weapons attack against rebels and civilians, killing hundreds with poison gas in a Damascus neighborhood a few miles east of Leo's old apartment in Rukneddine. And Obama would decide not to keep his pledge to enforce a red line over the use of chemical weapons in the conflict, signaling that America was prepared to leave Syria and the rest of the region to its suffering and to the coming surge of extremist violence. In Egypt, Islamists slaughtered police in retaliation for the massacre at Rabaa, driving the security forces to respond with greater brutality. I visited Kirdasah, a Cairo suburb near the pyramids, where the police station was charred from an attack that had killed eleven officers. The blackened walls were pocked with bullet holes and scrawled with fresh graffiti: "This is the price for injustice. God will have victory." I'd spoken earlier by phone with the wife of the station's commander, a police general who'd died alongside his men, and as she described her heartbreak, the couple's daughter, a college student, repeated something in the background. "God will take revenge on my dad's killer," the girl said three times. When I visited one of the elders in Kirdasah, he spoke of vengeance too. "Of course the police are also looking for revenge. They will take revenge," he told me. "But don't worry, we are alert. Do you think we will wait for them to come and kill us? Believe me, people in Kirdasah are kind people. They weren't born carrying guns. But beware of kind people when they are angry. If the police came here tomorrow and killed all the men, the next day there would be triple the number."

The bloodshed he predicted came not long afterward to Kirdasah and to all of Egypt. Disenchanted Islamists carried out bombings and assassinations across the country and turned the northern Sinai desert into the site of an insurgency. At the same time, many were turning their attention beyond Egypt's borders, falling in with the fighters from around the world who were traveling to southern Turkey to join the next great struggle that was beginning in Syria.

Through it all—through everything that happened over the next five years as the ISIS caliphate rose and crashed—Shawkan would remain in prison, brutalized by the guards and wracked by hunger strikes and depression, a testament to the dashed hopes of the Arab Spring. He would appear in court from time to time, and the cameras would catch him pale and haggard, fading like a memory.

PART II

TERROR

CHAPTER 5

SIGNS

Eastern Syria. November 2013.

I STEPPED UP INTO A SCHOOL BUS WITH MY RUCKSACK AND BODY armor and was surprised to see the faces of schoolchildren looking up at me.

I'd thought the bus was just cover for the smuggler, but he also appeared to be its regular driver, and it must have been the end of the school day. The students lowered their eyes as I squeezed down the aisle and sank into an empty seat.

Three months after the Rabaa massacre in Egypt, I was headed to Syria, working for a new publication, *BuzzFeed*. With me was the photographer Yusuf Sayman, who stuffed himself into the row in front of me with his own armor and camera bag. We stayed quiet on the ride as the bus made its usual stops along a dirt road that led from the edge of a Turkish town to the Syrian border, dropping off the uniformed children at their homes. When the last was gone, the bus kept driving until we reached a clearing where two smugglers sat beneath a tree.

We waited with them as dusk settled with a chill that hinted of winter. As the sun sank below the horizon, more travelers emerged, walking toward us from the surrounding fields. One man said he lived nearby, in the relative safety of southern Turkey, but worked in Syria at an oil refinery. His commute was a sprint along the smuggling paths just ahead, which cut through a minefield stretching beyond the razor wire that marked the border.

He was the first to tell me the story of the strange jihadis who had appeared in the forgotten patch of Syria beyond the mines. "They have got big beards, and they have keys hanging around their necks, and they say, 'Allahu akbar,'" he said. He lifted his arms into the air. "And they explode."

Over the next week I would hear the tales several times—of men with long beards and wild, flowing hair and a love of bombs and death. It was said that they believed the keys on their necks would open the gates of paradise. In some tellings, they even carried spoons in their pockets, to dine with the Prophet Muhammad when they got there.

Night fell with a heavy blackness. The man was talking about bombs, in the suicide vests the jihadis wore and in the cars they drove into markets and hospitals. One of the smugglers grabbed my body armor so we could move fast, and we joined the stream of men, women, and children rushing toward the border, the bags rustling and bouncing as we ran. Somewhere in the darkness the Turkish gendarmes guarding the border were shooting and shouting. We slipped through a hole in the razor wire.

A few weeks earlier, from Turkey, I had called a friend in Syria on a shaky Skype line. His name was Barzan Iso, and he was a partisan with the little-known guerilla faction that controlled the swath of northeastern Syria that I was entering. We used to drink together in Istanbul, my newly adopted home. Barzan had been living there as a political exile even before the war, but over the summer he'd returned to Syria. The civil war, more hopeless than ever after Assad's chemical attack, was fading from the international news. The Arab Spring was dead. But Barzan told me that something dangerous was rising in its place and arranged my trip with the smugglers so I could see it.

Yusuf and I hurried along a path the smugglers had cleared through the mines, which stretched for miles across the no-man's-land that separated the two countries. The sounds of shouts and gunshots faded. We slowed to a walk, and the travelers around us dispersed into the night, leaving us with our smugglers. I saw a light glowing from a little shack that sat atop a hill. We walked toward it.

Inside, a man in army fatigues sat at a desk with a great ledger opened before him. He asked for our passports with the routine formality of a customs officer and began to copy the details into his well-worn book. Dogs barked outside. We were standing in what seemed to be a farm shed.

The war had divided Syria into little fiefdoms where each armed group strove to install its own bureaucracy. Sometimes it felt like one big, violent game of house. You had to be careful not to offend anyone, but you also had to make sure not to let them ruin your passport. On a trip Yusuf and I had taken into rebel territory early in the war, a fighter had met us at the border in a ratty sedan and driven us to the first checkpoint, where a billboard ad for an FM radio station read, "Welcome to Free Syria." A man with a beard approached my window waving an entry stamp. I brushed him off, and we rolled past the billboard and into a wasteland of bombed-out buildings and mud flats crowded with refugee tents. The battalion that controlled that crossing was ousted by a rival soon after, and it continued on and on like that. Yusuf, a burly chain-smoker from Istanbul, had run a bar in Manhattan's East Village before becoming a journalist. He had a phrase he'd use in the war's early days in his scratchy jazz-man baritone: "mickey mouse." There were mickey-mouse checkpoints and mickey-mouse courts and mickey-mouse bombs that exploded on their makers and a mickey-mouse missile that turned in the air and came back at the people who fired it. One time he hitchhiked into Syria with the mickey-mouse brigade.

The man at the desk wanted to keep our passports until we returned to sneak back into Turkey, but we protested, and he relented. Our guide arrived—a twenty-five-year-old who wore a pistol holstered at his waist—and led us to the back of a pickup truck. We bumped along to the nearest town, where a family sympathetic to the local guerillas welcomed us at their home with a late dinner. We sat on the floor over plates of meat and cheese and again heard the story of the men with the beards and keys.

The next morning we headed toward the regional capital of Qamishli in an old Astro van. The road wound past farm fields and oil refineries and through checkpoints run by nervous soldiers. We were far from the places like Damascus and Aleppo that had been the focus of the civil war. There, U.S.-backed rebels and their Islamist counterparts were still watching as the territory they'd captured was carpet-bombed. Here it was different. This land was controlled by the Kurds, the ethnic minority with roots in ancient Iran to which Leo belonged. The Kurds accounted for about 10 percent of Syria's population and were concentrated mainly in the northeastern corner of the country, an arid and lightly developed region between Iraq and Turkey. The Kurds called it Rojava.

Syrian Kurds were oppressed under the Assad dynasty, which viewed them as potential separatists. For decades, the regime had carried out campaigns of forced assimilation and ethnic cleansing against its Kurdish citizens. At times it forbade giving children Kurdish names. When the Kurds had protested over their treatment a decade earlier, they were killed in Rojava's streets. Many had been wary of participating in Syria's Arab Spring uprising, understanding the kind of suffering the regime was capable of inflicting. Instead, when the civil war erupted, Kurdish leaders made a deal with their longtime enemy in hopes of keeping Rojava out of it. The regime ceded control of Rojava to the Kurds and allowed them to raise a militia, called the People's Protection Units and known by its Kurdish acronym as the YPG, to defend it. In return, the Kurds promised not to join the rebellion. Since then, amid this uneasy detente, Rojava had been spared.

But in recent months the violence had come to Rojava in an unexpected way. The Kurds were under attack along their boundaries from the most extreme of the Islamist rebel fighters, including the bands of wild-haired jihadis I'd been hearing about. It could seem strange for these radicals to have set their sights on such an out-of-the-way slice of territory if you only saw Rojava through the lens of the war between the rebels and Assad. But to a jihadi planning to start a new war—and to draw the outlines of a new country—Rojava was valuable real estate. It stretched for some two hundred miles along the Turkish border, which was still the gateway not only to the war economy of southern Turkey but also to transit routes to Europe and beyond. Rojava also abutted two Syrian cities that extremists were quietly working to control. Raqqa and Deir Ezzor were little known outside Syria, but they and their environs were home to Syria's main oil wells and a combined population of more than 2 million people. They also sat along the desert highways that led to two key cities in Iraq: Ramadi, the capital of Anbar province, and Mosul.

As we sped along in the Astro van, the road was mostly empty. When it passed through small towns, though, it was lined with banners, flying like flags. On the banners were photos of YPG soldiers—young men and women who looked down with stony faces at the passersby. They were locals who'd been dying by the dozens in their battle with the jihadis. "No one talks about us. We didn't see anything on TV," our guide said.

On the outskirts of Qamishli, we waited at the roadside for an escort, a pair of pickup trucks with armed militiamen in their beds. One went in front of the van and the other behind it as we entered the city. As part of the deal that had been struck, the regime still controlled a few key facilities, plus the airport and the city's main road. The soldiers in the first pickup tensed when they passed regime police standing in black uniforms on the roadside. Eventually, we arrived at a Kurdish security headquarters ringed by roadblocks and guards. The regime flag flew from its own security building just across the street.

In the headquarters, we were greeted by a framed photo so large it was almost life-sized. It showed a haughty man with a thick moustache and an odd, recoiled look on his face, as if he'd just smelled something surprising. This was the Kurdish nationalist leader Abdullah Ocalan, who'd spent the last fifteen years in solitary confinement in an island prison off the coast of Turkey, where the government had also spent decades suppressing its Kurdish population. He was the founder of the Kurdistan Workers Party, or PKK, which had been carrying out an insurgency in southeastern Turkey since the 1980s and was designated a terrorist group by the U.S. State Department. The YPG militia that controlled Rojava was a PKK franchise, founded at the start of the civil war by a handful of senior PKK members. The YPG seemed to be of another place and time, a throwback to leftist radical groups that flourished across Europe during the presidencies of Jimmy Carter and Ronald Reagan. They preached a neo-Marxist doctrine with a communal politics and deployed cadres of women fighters. The troops wore identical brown athletic sneakers that looked like Nike Air Force Ones and called each other *heval*, or comrade. Some were PKK veterans, and others were farmers and tradesmen recruited to help hold the lines. Their ardent secularism made them anti-Islamist and a natural enemy for the jihadis.

I sat for tea with a Kurdish security officer in his forties, Jewan Ibrahim, who wore a green flight suit with a green sash around his waist and a green jacket. There were plenty of Kurds who had opposed the YPG's expansion in Syria and its deal with Assad, but they had been forced out, and the YPG now controlled all aspects of Rojava's security and politics. Ibrahim said he didn't regret anything. "That is how we kept our city," he said of the deal. "Otherwise, it would be destroyed, like Aleppo. We learned from our revolution. We learned not to destroy our cities."

Another reason to avoid a fight with the regime was the new enemy. Ibrahim said the same extremists who'd been attacking Rojava were gaining influence over the rebellion. While the deal with Assad was holding, cease-fires that the Kurds had struck with rebel groups were fraying as the rebellion changed. All across opposition territory, fighters linked to al-Qaeda were seizing pockets of turf in silent coups, like a snake gobbling up small prey as it lay in wait for something bigger. The jihadis were installing bureaucracies that were far more efficient than anything the rebels had tried before, establishing tax systems and demanding tribute on everything from weapons to cotton and grain. And they were targeting areas with resources such as oil that could be sold on the black market. Most of the other rebel groups relied on outside benefactors to survive—from the private donors in the Gulf to the intelligence services of countries like Saudi Arabia, Turkey, and the United States. The jihadis had a different plan. They wanted to become self-sufficient. The most brutal and effective was a group whose name telegraphed its ambition, the Islamic State of Iraq and Syria, which locals referred to by its acronym: Daesh in Arabic, or ISIS.

ISIS had grown out of the Nusra Front, the extremist rebel faction whose young, idealistic members Leo and I had met near Antakya, and the two groups were in the process of splitting. Ibrahim said that the foreign mujahideen who'd been arriving in Syria were now concentrated in the ISIS ranks. In one recent battle, he said, "I saw people from Europe with my own eyes." The fighters were still coming to Turkey by plane and could reach Syria easily across the border. Remnants of AQI, the al-Qaeda faction that had fought U.S. troops during the Iraq War, were meanwhile crossing into Syria from Iraq. "The al-Qaeda in Syria is now even stronger than the one in Iraq," Ibrahim said.

The Kurds had been the only group so far to stop the jihadis—driving them from a city called Ras al-Ain, seventy miles to the west, and from several towns—perhaps because many Kurdish fighters were veteran insurgents too. But they were being attacked regularly: there were car bombs, suicide blasts, and IEDs planted on the roadside overnight. A recent bombing in one small city had left fourteen civilians dead. Ibrahim said the jihadis were employing the same tactics they'd honed against the Americans in Afghanistan and Iraq. "The people who are planning this are very intelligent," he said.

Graffiti was scrawled around Qamishli, still visible beneath fresh layers of paint. "Our leader is the Prophet Muhammad," read one. "I will sacrifice my father or mother for the Prophet," read another. At the checkpoints that lined the roadways, soldiers tried not to stand in groups, believing it would make them more of a target. They paid extra attention to cars with male drivers and no passengers and to men with beards. They dug through pickup beds and opened hoods and trunks. They crawled on the ground to peer under flatbed trucks. "We're afraid for our lives," said one, who was seventeen.

One night, at an outpost near the front lines outside Ras al-Ain, the city where the Kurds had recently driven out extremist rebels, soldiers stayed warm in a tent beside a stretch of road. The sea of black around them was disturbed only by the occasional onward creep of headlights. A forty-six-year-old farmer and father of four from a nearby village said that, as the jihadis advanced on Ras al-Ain, he'd decided to pick up a weapon for the first time in his life. He had a short training session, learning to handle an assault rifle and operate its safety, and then joined the battle. "Whoever says he's not afraid when he goes to fight is the biggest liar," he said. "I was forced. There was only one thing in my mind: not to let any foreigners take my land."

He recounted the enemy's fighting style with awe. They fired rocket-propelled grenades, or RPGs, from the middle of the street, unconcerned with taking cover, and sprayed bullets as if they had an unlimited supply. More seasoned soldiers at the outpost said the jihadis also had well-trained snipers and fighters who could operate heavy weapons and tanks. "Their snipers are so good," said one, holding up a bandaged hand to make his point.

The next morning we drove east to a town called al-Yarubiyah on the border with Iraq. It was unremarkable except for the convergence of two major roads: Iraq's Highway 1, which extended to Mosul, and Syria's M4, which went to Raqqa. The jihadis had seized it months earlier and held it until the Kurds freed it the previous week.

On the road into town, carloads of residents were returning. Flatbed trucks were piled high with furniture; one was packed with a flock of sheep. "I feel that I am born again," said a man who passed with his wife and six kids through a checkpoint the YPG had erected to screen the new arrivals.

In al-Yarubiyah, people ambled past buildings reduced to rubble and reopened boarded-up homes. Some had been looted. Pilfered belongings were strewn across a warehouse—an overturned armoire, spilling out girls' clothes; a scattered deck of UNO cards; a medical dummy, opened up to reveal its insides. Soldiers picked through the mess, examining the clothing, tapping at a dusty tambourine. Sunlight filtered through bullet holes in the building's metal siding.

Graffiti covered the town, the black spray paint extending across wall after wall, spelling out religious exultations and verses from the Quran, written out in exacting calligraphy. It ran along the gates of shuttered storefronts; it was stenciled onto telephone poles. It covered the former state security building, burned out and bullet-riddled, which had been converted into an Islamic court.

Most residents had fled when the rebels arrived. Those who remained recalled a foggy transition among the town's new overlords. Fighters who seemed moderate at first were replaced with—or superseded by, or became themselves—fighters who were ardently Islamist. They began to impose a draconian code, forbidding residents from listening to music or smoking cigarettes and forcing them to fast and pray. One man, who owned a grocery shop on the main road, spent two nights in jail for owning a hookah. Bread prices skyrocketed, and fuel became scarce. Residents tried to avoid confrontation. "It's a black-and-white world for them. You can become their enemy very fast," the grocer said.

One day, at the intersection outside the grocer's shop, the jihadis trotted out two dazed-looking men—one younger, the other maybe in his fifties—and presented them as agents of the Syrian army. The accused might have been sedated. They put up little resistance as the jihadis cut off their heads. The grocer said he stood and gawked. Another man recounted vomiting on the street. Another, who was twenty-five, said he recorded the scene on his phone. I asked to see the video, and he replied, "I deleted it, sheikh." He had addressed me by the honorific for Islamic scholars, by mistake. Embarrassed, he explained that this had become a habit. "They ordered us to call them sheikh," he said. "And if you didn't say sheikh, then you had a problem."

On the edge of town, at the border gate, what in peacetime had been a small administrative building stood unmarked by the ubiquitous graffiti. Inside, Kurdish soldiers had found cartons of TNT and the makings of a car-bomb factory. They'd hauled most of it away, but some items remained—thick metal cylinders to hold the explosives, sacks of aluminum powder to enhance the blasts, and metal ball bearings, taken from a local cement factory, to serve as shrapnel.

The bomb factory sat beside a large building where cargo trucks from Iraq and Syria once met to exchange their loads. Its vast floor was empty except for a collection of metal plates, which had been arranged neatly into rows. Each had been stenciled with the same careful script, the text tightly packed. "There is no god but God, and Muhammad is the messenger of God," the plates read along the bottom, and above that, written like an official seal: "The Islamic State of Iraq and Syria."

I stepped out into the sunlight and saw a policeman wandering the lot around the building. I asked if he knew the purpose of the metal plates. They were signs, he said. He pointed up at the yellow poles that marked the border, overlooking Syria and Iraq. "They wanted to take part from here and part from there," he said, motioning from side to side, "and become the Islamic State."

CHAPTER 6

ABU AYMAN

Antakya, Turkey. February 2014.

A REBEL COMMANDER NAMED MOHAMED ZATAAR SAT ON A LIVING room couch in Antakya on a cold February night, taking a break from the war across the border in Syria. He was eager to return. "There is a new battle starting," he said, staring at the door. He decided to call his enemy.

He dialed the number for a shadowy jihadi known as Abu Ayman al-Iraqi, one of the most notorious men on the chaotic battlefields of northern Syria. Zataar led a battalion of moderate rebels called Wolves of the Valley and had made his name fighting the Assad regime. Abu Ayman was a leader with ISIS. Like the Kurds, Zataar and a handful of other rebel commanders had decided to turn their guns on the group shortly after the New Year, setting off an internal war. A former dealer of fake antiques, Zataar considered himself one the original rebels, and he despised the extremists. He told me he'd come to see ISIS as a greater threat than Assad. "We are fighting a war against terror," he said.

The phone rang, and someone answered on the other line. Zataar asked to speak with Abu Ayman, whom he referred to as "the sheikh." Then he hung up. He said Abu Ayman would call him back.

Unlike the other groups in the rebellion, ISIS kept itself hidden. Even the Nusra Front, the official franchise of al-Qaeda in Syria, made statements and gave occasional interviews to the press, but ISIS had remained silent. Yet it had a reputation for brutality that was growing as it pushed ever more aggressively to overtake the rebellion. Its biggest feat to date had come in January, when it officially took over Raqqa, the city on the Euphrates River in eastern Syria, after driving out rival rebels. All across opposition-held Syria, its ruthlessness gave it the advantage as it assassinated rivals and kept the population under control by imposing hard-line Islamic law and, much like the Syrian *mukhabarat*, torturing and killing civilians.

Abu Ayman had become a symbol of this ISIS ethos. He was said to have killed one well-liked moderate commander in cold blood and tortured and executed the soldiers of another rival, leaving their bodies by the roadside. When a local cleric was sent over to mediate, the story went, Abu Ayman killed him too. He was one of ISIS's top commanders in Syria, but like the group's other leaders, he released no audio or video statements and revealed nothing about his identity. His nom de guerre simply meant "Ayman's father, from Iraq." He was a so-called emir, or prince, who was responsible for a swath of territory that bordered Turkey—one of a handful of regional leaders who answered to ISIS's top commander, another Iraqi called Abu Bakr al-Baghdadi. It was said that most of the group's most senior figures were Iraq War veterans of the al-Qaeda insurgency, and it later emerged that Abu Ayman was an early AQI member and a native of Mosul, with a degree in English from the city's university.

Zataar said the two men often spoke, usually to negotiate things like prisoner exchanges. His iPhone rang, and he placed it on the coffee table and put the call on speaker.

"My dear Abu Ayman, listen to me," Zataar said in his lispy Arabic. "Let's talk man to man."

By his own admission, Zataar, who was forty-six, spent four years in prison for his business dealings, during which he continued his work and bought three new homes. He'd been free for a year when the uprising began and quickly formed his own fighting force—because, he'd told me, "nobody can take the decision not to be involved in this revolution." He had a brash and wind-blown air, wrapped in a black cardigan, his greying hair swept back into a thick, frizzy mane. He rested a big fist on the coffee table as he spoke, flipping a paring knife through his fingers. He seemed to take pleasure in the strange intimacy of a battle in which he could pick up his phone and jaw with his rival.

"Abu Ayman, just for you to relax, I will let you know something: you are fighting people who don't lie down before oppression," Zataar said.

"Yeah?" Abu Ayman replied.

"And who will never allow anyone to subjugate one person from among the Syrian people," Zataar said.

"To me, Islam is higher than the Syrian people," Abu Ayman said.

"To me it's the Syrian people, brother," said Zataar.

It was clear that each commander took the fight personally. They bickered like hardened rivals, each with his own complaints, from stolen weapons to broken cease-fires. As Zataar spoke, two of his men leaned forward in their seats around the coffee table, silently nodding and pumping their fists—or when it was Abu Ayman's turn, throwing up their arms in exasperation. The background noise suggested a similar scene on Abu Ayman's side. Zataar often seemed to be toying with Abu Ayman, mocking him with his tone, trying to rile him. He skinned and ate oranges as the conversation dragged on.

Lamenting a broken truce in a village called al-Zanbaq, Zataar said, "You went into al-Zanbaq and took our horses, Abu Ayman, and went into our homes and took our clothes."

"You listen to me—what horses?" Abu Ayman said.

"Brother, I have genuine Arabic horses, and they took them," Zataar said.

"Who took them?"

"You took them!"

"Do you see a hair of your horses here? We didn't take them."

"I got them back. No problem."

"We didn't take the horses!"

"Abu Ayman, just listen to me, you got into our houses, and checked them out, and took our women's clothes."

"This is not true!"

The two men then argued about the treatment of prisoners. Zataar accused Abu Ayman of executing one of his men and of beating another, whom he referred to as Sheikh Ibrahim, and shaving his beard.

Abu Ayman discussed the matter with someone nearby. "The guy with me now knows Sheikh Ibrahim," he said, and put the man on the line.

"May God be with you," the man said.

"May God give you life," Zataar replied.

"In the name of the one who raised the skies without foundations, I will say what I have seen with my own eyes," the man said. While Sheikh Ibrahim had been beaten briefly by an ISIS fighter, he explained, "I immediately stopped him."

"Are you Abu Mansour?" Zataar asked.

"I am Abu Mansour or another man, it is no difference."

"Just listen to me, Abu Mansour. Our guys asked you to bring a Quran for them, but you brought a divergent version of the Quran."

"God forbid."

"Man, do not say God forbid," Zataar said impishly. "I beg you just to be honest."

"Oh Lord, this is a huge lie."

"You brought them a Quran, and the guys discovered that there were mistakes in it."

"Oh Lord, this is a huge lie. Oh Lord, this is a huge lie."

"Didn't Sheikh Ibrahim tell you that there were mistakes in the Quran?"

"We have foreign fighters—they may have brought Warsh's version, which is different from Hafs's version. Our brothers from Morocco and Tunisia read Warsh's version, if you know about versions."

"I don't know about versions," Zataar said.

Later Zataar offered Abu Ayman a promise: "God willing, if we catch you, we won't kill you."

"Why?"

"I promise you."

"Why won't you kill me?"

"I will make you live among us for at least a year, so you will know who we really are."

"A whole year—good."

"And then I will release you to go wherever you want."

"Good."

"That's a man's promise, God willing."

"Your generosity overwhelms me and makes me want more," Abu Ayman sneered.

As the call wore on, for well over an hour, Abu Ayman switched between goading and persuasion. Like a seasoned evangelist, he took the insults but never stopped with an unlikely effort to win Zataar to his cause.

"Just listen to me: let me see the truth about you. I might be mistaken, or you might have the wrong impression about me. Come and let's meet," Abu Ayman told Zataar. "We are people like you, and if you see us as mistaken, come and advise us and teach us."

"All the people are crazy, but only you are wise!" Zataar said, mocking him.

He chided Abu Ayman for the use of suicide bombers, for the violence against local rebels, and for his hard-line religious views. He also brought up the allegation, made by many rebels, that ISIS collaborated with the Assad regime. "You came with a concrete plan to kill Muslims in the name of Islam," Zataar said. "I am not telling you that you are *mukhabarat*, but no one treated Muslims as badly as you did."

Time and again, on the other hand, Abu Ayman accused Zataar and his allies of being manipulated by foreign intelligence. "I am not saying that you have no relation to the revolution, but I am saying that you people have [foreign] friends, and you go to Turkey and sit there and listen to things that make God angry," he said. "You sit with godless and faithless people, and strange things occur."

This, of course, was partly true. Rebels in northern Syria still received much of their supplies from their foreign backers via Turkey. And

Zataar and his allies were angling for U.S. backing, which Zataar would receive eventually.

"Just listen to me: Is [Recep Tayyip] Erdogan, the prime minister of Turkey, godless and atheist?" Zataar asked.

"Yes, he is godless and an apostate," Abu Ayman replied. "He does not rule in God's name, but in the name of a fake constitution."

"If Erdogan is an apostate, who in the world is not godless and is a Muslim?"

"From the presidents, no one. All of them are godless."

"What about the people?"

"All the lands that were once ruled by Islam are Islamic countries, and the people in these countries are Muslims. But the men ruling them are godless."

"You have no evidence that you have succeeded once in your life," Zataar finally said. "In all of the countries where you tried [to take control], you failed, and the people hated you."

"That was because of traitors and conspiracy," Abu Ayman replied.

Both men were referring to Iraq. At its height during the Iraq War al-Qaeda had controlled large swaths of Sunni-dominated territory near the border with Syria, and U.S. troops had finally defeated it by turning local tribes against it, once the population had begun to revolt against the group's extremism and brutality. It was called the *Sahwa*, or Awakening, and involved the U.S. military arming and supporting Sunni fighters who hailed from the same branch of Islam as the extremists. ISIS, run by AQI veterans like Abu Ayman, had not forgotten this, and in fact he'd been gathering intelligence on Syria's rebels for months, anticipating that they and ISIS would become enemies. For the next ten minutes, Abu Ayman fretted and ranted that a version of *Sahwa* would return in Syria, led by rebels like Zataar.

"The West has understood the game. They won't send anyone whose name is William or Benjamin. They'll send people named Ahmed and Mohamed and Abdullah," Abu Ayman told Zataar in his Iraqi accent. "The American soldier is expensive, so they will use people from among us—and this is the truth of the battle, they will use you—in the fight against us."

America was not yet involved in the fight against ISIS. But Abu Ayman seemed certain that it would be drawn in eventually and felt he knew what its strategy would be: to enlist local forces rather than send ground troops of its own. And while he knew America wanted to move on from the Iraq War, in a way he and ISIS's other leaders were still fighting it.

"I might get hit by a mortar and be killed, and you might live longer than me, but remember my words," Abu Ayman said. "They [America] will use you, and they will unite you with Bashar's army, and with an interim government, and they will promise you seats in parliament, and such things—the same as they did with the Sunnis in Iraq."

He continued: "The West will sell you cheap. They sold your grandfathers and our grandfathers. And for hundreds of years the West has been controlling us, and they keep these tyrants over our heads."

Since Zataar and his colleagues took their orders from the United States and its allies, Abu Ayman reasoned, "You will kill us and we will kill you. We have no other options—either you cleanse us or we cleanse you, because the decision is not yours."

"Good for you, Abu Ayman," Zataar said. "This is the right decision. Listen to me, sheikh: these are the only honest words that you have said."

"This is the only solution," Abu Ayman repeated. "Either you cleanse us or we cleanse you."

CHAPTER 7

FEAR

Baghdad, Iraq. June 2014.

PANIC SWEPT THROUGH THE MILITARY BASE AS THE SOLDIERS' CELL phones chimed. "ISIS is coming," the messages said.

The base was on the outskirts of Mosul. It was late June of 2014. An Iraqi sergeant called his commander for reinforcements. "Dabber halak," the commander said. *Figure things out on your own.*

The Ghazlani base, next to Mosul airport, was ringed by tall concrete walls. For three days the Iraqi soldiers there had waited in their shadows, listening for word of the ISIS advance through Iraq's second-largest city. The rumors came piecemeal. ISIS militants were said to have seized the banks downtown. They were said to have opened the cells of the city's prisons, adding hundreds of inmates to their ranks. They were said to have crucified Iraqi soldiers in the streets. It was inconceivable. On the official rolls, more than 30,000 troops were stationed in Mosul, which was home to some 2 million people. The troops at Ghazlani were part of a quarter-million-strong army that had been trained and equipped by U.S. troops, intended to be a legacy of stability. But if ISIS was coming to the Ghazlani base, the sergeant knew, the rumors must be true. Much of Mosul had fallen already. Now the militants planned to raise their flag above the airport to emphasize the fact that they controlled the city.

The sergeant was an experienced soldier who'd received U.S. training like many of the men stationed there. They had American weapons—M16 rifles, artillery, armored Humvees—and he felt they could resist. But the troops around him were already pulling off their uniforms. Grudgingly, he did the same. *How could so many soldiers, with so many weapons, collapse so swiftly*, he thought as he joined the crowd running toward the base's main gate. Then he heard gunfire. ISIS was already waiting outside the entrance, shooting the fleeing soldiers. Men began to push and trample one another. The sergeant kept calm, ducking unnoticed through a side entrance. He blended into the crowds of civilians fleeing on foot along the road outside.

Mosul was a diverse city but served as an epicenter for Iraqi Sunnis, who'd seen their power fade after the U.S. overthrow of Saddam Hussein, a Sunni who had repressed the Shia majority. The Great Mosque of al-Nuri, whose improbably tilting minaret had defined the city's skyline since the twelfth century, was as conspicuous as the Leaning Tower of Pisa. During the Iraq War, al-Qaeda capitalized on the sectarian tensions the U.S. invasion had unleashed, turning Mosul, like other Sunni strongholds, into a seat of its insurgency. Securing the city had been a signature victory for U.S. troops and their Iraqi allies. Since the end of the war, Mosul had grown, sprawling outward on either side of the Tigris into expanding suburbs on the Nineveh plains. Residents had been going about their lives, strolling through the busy parks and shopping centers and posting updates on Facebook. Then ISIS invaded, a few days before the attack on the Ghazlani base, launching a blitzkrieg into the city from across the Syrian border in convoys of SUVs and pickup trucks.

As residents hid in their homes or fled, there were only small windows into what was happening in Mosul, like shouts in a dark forest. In one video posted online, bodies of Iraqi soldiers lay in the street. In another, a pickup rolled through the streets with black flags flying from its roof and masked men standing in the bed, their fists raised.

Iraqi leaders had become fearful of losing control over their Sunni cities, especially because they were guarded partly by "ghost soldiers"—imaginary troops invented to claim salaries that lined the pockets of politicians and high-ranking officers. ISIS charged into Mosul with around only 1,500 fighters, but with the Iraqis caught off guard, the battle became a rout. Scenes like the one that the sergeant witnessed were repeated at outposts around the city as soldiers fled, leaving their weapons and armored Humvees behind. ISIS decided to press its advantage, calling in reinforcements along the supply routes they had been busy securing in forgotten corners of eastern Syria. They also gathered new recruits from among the locals. From Ghazlani, they continued their assault south. The names of the cities along their path would have been familiar to American soldiers who'd seen so much blood spilled to secure them. With each new city that fell, ghosts of the past were raised. ISIS took Tikrit, the birthplace of Saddam Hussein, and then it advanced on Samarra, the holy city whose historic Shia shrine had been bombed by al-Qaeda in 2006, plunging Iraq into sectarian bloodshed. There were clashes in the town of Abu Ghraib, home to the notorious prison where leaked photos had shown U.S. soldiers subjecting Iraqi prisoners to humiliation and torture, making the orange jumpsuits worn by the prisoners into a lasting symbol of American hypocrisy in the eyes of many in the Middle East. And with that, ISIS had reached the outskirts of Baghdad.

In Istanbul, I stepped onto a Turkish Airlines flight to Baghdad. I was the only passenger. I picked a row in the middle of the 220-seat plane. As it rolled down the runway, the flight attendant began the safety demonstration. She pointed to the emergency exits, produced a detached seatbelt, and secured the buckle. Then she stopped, mid-presentation, looked down at me with a nervous laugh, and walked away, finding the whole performance ridiculous.

Mosul's fall was like a coming-out party for the extremist group that Obama had recently labeled al-Qaeda's "jayvee team." Just like that, ISIS owned a major city. The U.S. equivalent would be if it had taken Phoenix. Videos posted online showed ISIS fighters parading through

Mosul's streets with captured U.S. weapons, tanks, and Humvees. Other videos showed militants gleefully bulldozing the border line between Iraq and Syria, not far from the crossing at al-Yarubiyah that I'd visited with the Kurdish militia in late 2013. Governments were realizing that ISIS was serious about its intent to create an extremist state and that they had no idea how far it might extend. The previous day, on a phone call with a former Iraqi ambassador to the United States, when I said that I would be in Baghdad in the morning, he replied, "If it's still there."

There was no better showcase for the ISIS brand than what was happening in Iraq and the global panic surrounding it. Not even al-Qaeda, at the peak of its power, had ever controlled such a swath of territory. ISIS was the first terrorist group to promise its followers the chance to live its vision in the here and now, not just in the afterlife—and to call them to change the world by creating a new reality, not just destroying the old one. As ISIS seized oil fields, banks, and other resources, along with the Iraqi military's arsenal, it had more money and better weapons at its disposal than perhaps any terror group in history. Before my flight to Baghdad, I had called Syrian rebels like Zataar who'd been fighting ISIS and found them deflated. "ISIS will look like Christ the Redeemer," one Islamist but anti-ISIS commander told me, saying that many rebels were considering quitting less extreme groups like his in favor of joining the enemy. He predicted that ISIS would attract even more recruits as it stirred the demons of Iraq's sectarian war.

In Baghdad, military police in blue uniforms stood guard on street corners amid the choking traffic. Lines stretched out the doors of travel agencies. Anyone who had the means to get away was trying to. The holy month of Ramadan was approaching, and like the Syrian refugees who'd hoped their time away from home was only temporary, some people wanted to think they were going on an extended vacation. "It's a way to run away—a practical way to run away," said a businessman in his fifties who was booking a one-way trip to Europe for himself and his family. "I'll decide from there when to come back."

"I'll come back when it feels safe. But I have a bad feeling that there won't be an end to this," said a mother who'd bought tickets for herself and her son to Tbilisi, Georgia. She was worried about a new cycle of sectarian violence. On the day that ISIS publicized a massacre of some 1,500 Shia soldiers, four young Sunni men had turned up dead on the street of a Shia neighborhood in Baghdad. Then a car bomb tore through another Shia area. As Shia volunteers rushed to arm themselves and defend Baghdad from ISIS, Sunnis looked at their neighbors with alarm. "I think people have been brainwashed," the mother said.

With the army reeling, Iraq's top Shia cleric had issued a call to arms, urging young men to join militias to defend the country against ISIS. Shia militia had run rampant during the Iraq War, and some of the units now rising up were the same sectarian forces that had fought the Americans. I was reminded of this history as I walked one morning through Sadr City, the gritty neighborhood that had been the heart of Shia resistance against the U.S. occupation in Baghdad. The militia chief and political leader who lorded over the area, Muqtada Sadr, had called on his followers to show their strength. Bystanders thronged the wide avenues. I was pulled aside for selfies by young men with automatic rifles, by a sheikh with an RPG launcher. Before us stretched a military parade. Cadres of men in green fatigues trotted past in loose formation, holding their rifles at their chests, their silhouettes moving in miniature on the pavement as the sun burned overhead. They were chanting, "We are going to the fight." The people around me held up their arms, recording on smartphones. Young men in black ski masks marched past. Another squadron followed them, trotting in rows, their hands at their hips. They looked clean-cut and well fed in their jeans and button-down shirts and were wearing suicide vests stuffed with imitation bombs.

The Shia militia had been a boon to AQI, pushing more Sunnis into its ranks, and I thought ISIS would be happy to see the return of its old enemy. It was another way that the new war echoed the last one. It was important to remember how the sectarian tensions the U.S. invasion had unleashed a decade prior fueled the current conflict, not just in Iraq but in Syria—the siege mentality taking hold on both sides, the sense of ancient wounds being again reopened. At the same time, seeing things only through the Sunni-Shia divide ignored the fact that most Iraqis and Syrians did not think that way and that there had been long periods when the two branches of the faith got along peacefully.

I drove south, to Karbala, one of Shia Islam's holiest cities. With me was Saad Taha, who had come out of retirement to be my guide. Saad had been a legendary fixer during the Iraq War, but he'd grown tired of the work, and had been happily editing a children's magazine. The highway crossed over the Euphrates River and punched through the edge of the Arabian Desert, bringing us into Iraq's Shia heartland. Checkpoints lined the way, and at one of them, a soldier in black approached me. He was wearing a ski mask decorated with a skeleton's face, and a patch on his shoulder said "Special Operations" in English. He spoke English to me from behind the mask, asking where I was from and what I was doing there. I had never seen such a soldier before. He was a member of the Iraqi special forces—this was the first time I learned of the elite, U.S.-trained commandos I would later accompany into Mosul. I didn't know it then, but with the regular Iraqi army collapsed, the special forces were dying by the dozens in a desperate effort as the country's last line of defense. The masked man told us to be careful because more Iraqi soldiers had fled their posts to west. "They should be shot," he said.

In Karbala sits the shrine of Hussein ibn Ali, the grandson of the Prophet and the third imam of Shia Islam, whose massacre, remembered each year on the commemoration of Ashura, had precipitated the great schism in the world's second-largest religion. Beneath the elegant, glass-lined dome of the mosque, worshippers prostrated themselves in prayer, and beside the tomb of Imam Hussein, as its green glass glowed, the two women who'd welcomed us to the mosque, a member of its staff and a local journalist, conversed about ISIS.

"Have you found yourself a gun yet?" the journalist asked.

"Why?" the other replied.

"One has at least to protect herself, because when they get here, you know what they're going to do."

US intelligence officials were estimating ISIS's fighting strength at between 7,000 and 10,000 men. Though far smaller than the Iraqi army whose soldiers it had sent fleeing, ISIS could operate at times like a secret police force and was capable of inflicting terror. Before Mosul, after ISIS had captured parts of the two main cities of Iraq's Anbar province, Ramadi and Fallujah, it carried out an intimidation campaign there and across the country. This received little attention in America, but for months Sunni members of the Iraqi security forces and their families were subject to threats and violence. Government officials and bureaucrats in Sunni-majority areas like Mosul were targeted too, and so were members of the Sunni tribes who one day might threaten ISIS with another Awakening. There were ransom kidnappings, extortions, and assassinations.

A captain from Fallujah, who was in hiding in Baghdad, described how, after taking his home city, ISIS sent messengers through the streets to announce that members of the security forces should publicly renounce their positions and declare *tawbah*—repentance—or be killed.

ISIS had done its research. It had spies inside the government, military, and police. It knew who all the cops and soldiers from Fallujah were and where their families lived. The captain had been posted to a base elsewhere but sent his wife and children to Baghdad. As soon as they left, ISIS fighters moved into their home. He believed that ISIS could reach anywhere in Iraq and that its spies were tracking his movements. He said ISIS had access to government databases with the names, ranks, home addresses, and salaries of members of the police and military. "It is difficult to hide yourself," he said. "They have agents and spies everywhere."

CHAPTER 8

EAGLE

Sinjar, Iraq. August 2014.

> *Yazidis. I had never heard the word. How cruelly ironic that I should learn of a people's existence at the very moment it risked vanishing.*
>
> —Father Patrick Desbois, *The Terrorist Factory*.

The Sinjar Mountains stretch for sixty-two miles across the northwestern corner of Iraq, rising skyward after the suburbs of western Mosul disappear into the Nineveh plains and running east into the border with Syria. By August 2014, almost all the land between Mosul and the mountains belonged to ISIS.

The previous month, inside Mosul's Great Mosque of al-Nuri, the leader of ISIS had ascended the minbar to announce himself as caliph, resurrecting the title once used for the leader of global Islam. It was afternoon prayer on Friday, and the mosque appeared full as Abu Bakr al-Baghdadi gave his sermon, which was recorded by ISIS cameramen. Dressed in a black robe with a black turban and a long black beard, Baghdadi, then forty-three, was a minor religious scholar who had once worn the orange jumpsuit of a prisoner of U.S. forces at the detention centers of Camp Bucca and Abu Ghraib. After his 2009 release he'd gradually been promoted to the top role in al-Qaeda in Iraq as those above him were arrested or killed, and after AQI's defeat in the Awakening, he'd overseen its rebirth as ISIS. The caliphs had ruled grand and shifting empires across the Middle East, Asia, and parts of Europe from the time of the Prophet to the fall of the Ottomans in 1924. To the vast majority of Islam's 1.6 billion adherents, who considered ISIS a corruption of their religion, it was sacrilege for this extremist to call himself a caliph and describe the territory that ISIS now controlled as a caliphate. But Baghdadi had calculated that he could still draw recruits to ISIS with the call he delivered at the mosque, which was posted online.

"Do jihad in the cause of God, incite the believers, and be patient in the face of this hardship," Baghdadi said.

ISIS had conquered one-third of Syria and one-third of Iraq, and its territory across those two countries spanned a land mass the size of Great Britain. Shown on a map, the caliphate looked something like an impressionist painting of an expansive tree. A thick root traced northwest from the Iraqi cities of Fallujah and Ramadi before meeting the trunk, which shot up half the Syrian border, encompassing parts of the province of Deir Ezzor. From there the tree's crown stretched for two hundred miles in either direction. To the east, it curled over Raqqa and into the Aleppo countryside. To the west, it wrapped around Mosul, then drooped downward through Tikrit and Samarra to the edge of Baghdad. All told, the caliphate was home to some 8 million people, approaching the population of Israel, many of whom weren't ISIS supporters but were afraid to attempt an escape.

ISIS was surrounded by hostile forces. In Syria, it guarded front lines against the Syrian regime, against rebels like Zataar, and against the Kurdish fighters who'd been battling ISIS since Yusuf and I had traveled with them the previous winter. In Iraq, the southern borders of the caliphate pressed against the Iraqi military, which was still scrambling to regroup from its defeat in Mosul, and the Shia militia I'd seen rising in Baghdad. And on front lines to the north and west of Mosul was a collection of soldiers that ISIS had yet to confront.

These veteran fighters, called *peshmerga*, were cousins of the Kurds in Syria but more professional and better equipped, with a long history of defending their mountainous pocket of northern Iraq from invaders. The *peshmerga* had battled the forces of Saddam Hussein for decades and then worked with the United States to overthrow him. They still hosted an important CIA outpost in their capital, Erbil. They'd been partners in America's war on terror for more than a decade, but they were careful not to get involved when ISIS began its war against the Iraqis, choosing instead to build defensive lines outside the self-styled caliphate and wait.

Then, on the night of August 2, ISIS attacked the *peshmerga*. The decision brought it into direct conflict with America and led to a series of sudden, sweeping atrocities that shocked governments around the world into action. If ISIS had left the Kurds alone, the caliphate might have lasted. America and its allies might not have started their punishing campaign of airstrikes. I never found a good answer to why ISIS had done this. When I later met the Kurdish spy chief who led the war on ISIS from its north, sitting in his fortified mountain compound, he still couldn't make sense of it. A veteran Syrian journalist, Hassan Hassan, told me once that he thought the decision marked a split between the two main factions of ISIS leadership: the statists, many of them veterans of the Saddam Hussein regime, whose main objective was to carve out a Sunni territory and who used extremism to advance this goal, and the true fanatics, who saw their extremism as the end in itself and were driven by the blind hatred that came with it. The latter group saw the *peshmerga*, and the religious minority that lived under their protection in the Sinjar Mountains, as infidels. A French priest, Father Patrick Desbois, who would have his conscience stirred by the atrocities in Sinjar and dedicate himself to studying ISIS and its victims, had his own theory. He'd spent much of his life investigating the reach of the Holocaust, traveling around Eastern Europe to uncover mass graves. "They made the same mistake as Hitler. They attacked everybody," he would tell me in Washington, DC, as the caliphate neared its end. "Don't forget that Hitler also thought that *God is with us*. Officially God was with the SS. Officially God was with ISIS. The problem with that, when you are in a military analysis, is that sooner or later people will forget their limits."

Or maybe ISIS had taken a more calculated risk. It wasn't until the last moment, with ISIS at the edge of Erbil, that Obama grudgingly approved U.S. airstrikes.

On the night of August 2, at an outpost in Mosul, a young ISIS captain received word from his commander that the detente with the *peshmerga* was over. A Syrian from Raqqa whose friends called him Okab, or Eagle, he was known among his fellow jihadis for his daring. He was told to marshal his platoon of some twenty fighters for a surprise attack. Then he and his men rumbled out from Mosul in a battle convoy, headed toward the Sinjar Mountains and *peshmerga* lines.

The convoy rolled for eighty miles until it reached the outskirts of the town that marked *peshmerga* territory, also called Sinjar, which sat at the foot of the mountains from which it took its name. This was sacred terrain. The mountains had been home for centuries to an ancient religious group called the Yazidis, who combined beliefs from the great faiths that had swept through the region: Zoroastrianism, Christianity, Judaism, Islam. The religion stood out for its belief in angels and their presence in the ups and downs of daily life and was centered on a temple in a valley beyond that dated back more than four millennia, on land that had been settled since at least the twenty-fifth century BCE.

More than 100,000 Yazidis lived in Sinjar and in the mountains and valleys dotted with terraced farms around it. Their preservation through the years had depended on the isolation of their forgotten corner of Iraq. It was the kind of overlooked locale that ISIS had been targeting as it pieced together its caliphate; the town of Sinjar sat on a potential supply route between the twin ISIS capitals of Mosul and Raqqa.

A black scarf wrapped around his head, Okab jumped from the ISIS convoy with his assault rifle and led his men into the sleeping town. He expected fierce resistance from the *peshmerga* stationed there. As he rushed forward, he felt the familiar sensation of drawing closer to God and the thrill of knowing he was just a bullet from paradise.

Instead he saw the *peshmerga* retreating. Like the Iraqi army in Mosul, they'd been caught by surprise and panicked. The streets were unguarded. Okab pursued *peshmerga* fighters into the mountains, stalking them for more than an hour before returning to the town.

He found chaos in the streets. His fellow fighters were dragging Yazidis from their homes, shouting *kafir*, or infidel. They beheaded men in front of their screaming families. They tied up women and children and threw them into cars. Okab watched as more than fifty Yazidi men laid facedown in a roadside ditch, crying and praying, their hands bound. Then his comrades drew their automatic weapons and executed them.

Suddenly, the spell of extremism that he'd fallen under snapped. "Who gave this command?" he asked the fighters around him. "Why are you doing this?"

Each time he received the same reply: "These people are infidels."

Okab did nothing to stop the massacre. He stood and watched. He knew that ISIS treated dissenters harshly, and he began to fear the men around him, even those under his command, wondering if they'd detect his newfound doubt. He saw a friend, a more senior ISIS member, and asked him to stop the carnage. "I'm going to pretend you never said this," the friend said.

As ISIS fighters pressed deeper into the town, residents scattered. Many made it up the road that wound to the top of Sinjar Mountain, throwing off the clothes, toys, and kitchen supplies they'd brought with them as they climbed, items that would remain, baking in the sun, for months. Those who reached the top found safety behind a defensive line the *peshmerga* had established.

With thousands of Yazidis from Sinjar gathered on the mountaintop, the humanitarian effort to save them became an international sensation. News crews dropped down by helicopter to speak with survivors, who told of the thousands of civilians killed and the thousands more taken as slaves, many of them women and children.

People were drawn to ISIS for myriad reasons, and one of them was that it offered a religious justification for extreme violence that was otherwise outside any moral code. I heard stories of men in Sinjar who'd turned on their neighbors when presented with the opportunity to kill a man, or rape a woman, or take a slave—but I thought I saw it most clearly in the foreigners who flocked to the caliphate in the wake of Sinjar as ISIS's notoriety reached new heights. They were colonizers: Tunisians and Egyptians, and also Brits, Americans, Australians, French. They joined ISIS by the thousands in an international enlistment the likes of which no terrorist group had ever seen. There was something alarming in the fact that ISIS could draw so many people from the lands of its enemies, but there was also something wretched about these foreigners. They imagined they would be bigger people than was possible at home; they pursued base designs; they dreamed of the glamor of violence, having no real sense of it.

Then there were locals like Okab who had made their way to ISIS by degrees. As he stood amid the massacre in Sinjar, his mind reeling, he decided to leave. Saying he needed to check on a casualty, he caught a ride back to his base in Mosul. From there he returned to his native Raqqa, wondering how to detach from the group to which he'd pledged his life.

CHAPTER 9

ARRIVALS

Istanbul, Turkey. September 2014.

U.S. WARPLANES WERE IN THEIR SECOND WEEK OF AIRSTRIKES IN Iraq when ISIS posted a video online. In it, a masked man speaking fluent British English beheaded an American captive, a freelance journalist named James Foley, who'd been kidnapped more than two years earlier in Syria. The video was shot from multiple angles and expertly edited. Foley was on his knees in a desert somewhere in the caliphate. He wore an orange jumpsuit reminiscent of those worn by prisoners at Abu Ghraib. Afterward, the British executioner waved a bloody knife at the camera and said he would next kill another missing American journalist, Steven Sotloff, if the airstrikes continued, as ISIS knew they would.

The Obama administration issued a statement condemning the murder, and soon after the United States was also bombing ISIS in Syria. But the power of the video could really be felt in the response of regular Americans. ISIS went overnight from a faraway menace to public enemy number one. Polls showed support for military intervention rising. ISIS had made the same calculation that Assad had at the start of the civil war—that Americans would stomach all kinds of atrocities overseas except the killing of one of their own. In the summer of 2012, Austin Tice, a journalist from Texas, had gone missing while embedded with rebels in Damascus, and the U.S. government, along with Tice's family, held the Assad regime responsible. The regime denied the charge and even went as far, in the view of many experts, as to stage a video in an attempt to absolve itself. In the video, Tice was paraded down a mountain path by bearded men who spoke in a caricature of how jihadis might, like actors fumbling through their lines. The video ended with Tice blindfolded and on his knees, muttering, "Oh Jesus."

The Assad regime wanted to be left alone to crush the rebellion in Syria, but ISIS seemed to be inviting a clash with America and the West. If ISIS leaders believed their own end-of-days propaganda, then perhaps a land battle against the armies of the West in Syria would bring about the apocalypse they claimed to be awaiting. From a more Machiavellian perspective, there was nothing better for boosting ISIS's stature and bringing it recruits. It was an open secret that ISIS had been hoarding a number of the Western journalists and aid workers who had disappeared into the conflict. Europeans whose governments would pay had been freed for millions of dollars in ransom. American and British hostages—whose governments refused to pay ransoms—would be used for propaganda. Sotloff was beheaded in another video on September 2.

I heard the news that night as I climbed the steep stone staircases that cut through my hilltop neighborhood in Istanbul, when someone told me that a group of Sotloff's friends were gathering to mourn. Dozens of Western journalists were living in the city, scattered around the center, finding their place along the meandering, narrow streets jammed with small bars and cafés.

With the Middle East in chaos, Istanbul had become the last sanctuary, a place where you could be at the center of the storm and also sprawl out on a boat in the blue waters of the Bosporus or sit with friends for hours at the white tablecloths of the fish restaurants, smoking cigarettes and getting drunk on arrack. The city felt like a listening post from another era, as journalists and activists argued and conspired amid its faded Greek and Ottoman glory.

From the start of the war in Syria, alarmists had warned that it could spark the next world war, but to me it had shades of a different conflict, the Spanish Civil War, which instead of starting the next global struggle laid out the stakes and the battle lines. The revolutionaries in Syria had wanted not to overthrow the U.S.-led world order but to hold it to its own ideals. They'd been slaughtered as their imagined allies looked on, and ISIS had risen in the debris.

Not long after Sotloff's death, I was in a Turkish border town, Kilis, ninety miles northwest of Antakya, having lunch with a Syrian in his twenties who had a view of the immense pull of the conflict.

Abdulrahman had smuggled hundreds of foreign fighters into Syria, starting in the winter of 2012. By then it was clear that Syria's rebellion would get little international support, and even some moderate rebels welcomed the help of the extremist-minded foreigners. Abdulrahman was bombarded with requests from would-be mujahideen, which he received through a special Facebook account that his smuggling group used. "They came from all over the world," he said.

At first the men hailed mainly from Arab countries. But the reach of the conflict seemed to expand as it worsened. Soon there were Chechens, Albanians, Britons, and French. Some brought their wives. It was the start of a migration that would intensify after ISIS took Sinjar and Mosul. Abdulrahman eventually fielded mujahideen from as far away as China, as well as a handful of Americans.

He did the work because he wanted to make money and because he supported the fight against Assad and thought the jihadis were aiding it. He ticked off airports where he received the foreigners in Turkey: Istanbul, Hatay, Gaziantep, Antalya. He'd stand in the arrivals hall like any chauffeur, holding a sign with the jihadi's name. Often they greeted him gleefully. "They hug me, and I hug them back and really welcome them," he said.

When his charges didn't speak Arabic, Abdulrahman communicated with them using Google Translate on his phone. Some seemed lost; one man fled from him at the airport, convinced he was trying to kidnap him. Abdulrahman lost track of another jihadi, an American who only spoke English, after they had crossed into Syria and later found him wandering around a border village in a panic.

Abdulrahman was afraid to reveal much about the man in charge of the operation, whom he called his emir, or prince. The emir worked with ISIS, Abdulrahman said, and reached out to potential recruits through accounts on social media platforms including Facebook and Twitter, which the man operated in several languages. He sent the ones he trusted to Abdulrahman and his friends. After the foreigners arrived in southern Turkey, they were driven to the border. Then they were smuggled across the rocky trails into Syria. "They would have their dinner in Istanbul, their breakfast here, and their lunch in Syria," he said.

It was a booming industry for Abdulrahman—and for other smugglers—in towns and cities across the porous, 565-mile border between Turkey and Syria. And it was usually easy. Turkish authorities did little to stop them; sometimes the border guards simply let them cross legally, stamping their passports at official border posts. At first, Turkey seemed to be making the same gamble as the Syrian opposition—hoping that these mujahideen would help the rebels bring a quick exit for Assad. Turkey was now trying haltingly to crack down on the smuggling, but more than 10,000 foreigners had already joined ISIS, according to one U.S. estimate. Turkey also worried about blowback—if it pushed too hard against ISIS, it risked inciting terror attacks on Turkish soil. And so ISIS was adding daily to its ranks, almost effortlessly, and in the process redefining what a modern extremist group could be. At its peak, al-Qaeda had dozens of members with Western passports. They were tracked closely by Western intelligence services, which considered them to be a security emergency. ISIS had thousands.

In another Turkish border town, Karkamis, a veteran smuggler had told me that he was regularly coming across foreigners. "They are so easy to recognize, but the police don't care," he said.

Many Syrian refugees had lost their passports when they were uprooted. So the authorities opened the border at least once a week to let Syrians without documents return home—and when they did, the smuggler said, the foreigners walked in with the crowd. "You can see them sitting right at the café near the gate," he said.

As we finished our meal in Kilis, Abdulrahman said he'd wound down his business, wary of the kind of police attention that working with foreigners was bringing. But he still helped out his former colleagues from time to time. In an apartment nearby, he was hosting an Arab man who was preparing to enter Syria the next day. I drove to the apartment with him and waited in the car as he went upstairs to see if the man would meet me. He declined even to speak by phone. Whatever had brought him all this way, he was happy to keep it to himself.

CHAPTER 10

FRONTIER

Southern Turkey. October 2014.

THE MAN IN THE PHOTO WAS SMILING, POSING LIKE A TOURIST NEXT to three severed heads. He had a thick mane of black hair, a full black beard, and eyes that were brown and piercing. The heads were stuck on metal fence points, eyes cast down. They were arrayed on the gates of municipal building in Raqqa, looking out toward the public. I looked up from the phone that displayed the photo, and the same black-haired man was smiling at me. We were sitting on his living room floor in a Turkish border town near Antakya. "That's very nice," I said.

Mohamed was one of those people who lived in a permanent state of in-between where ISIS blurred into the rest of humanity—not an ISIS member but connected to the group in myriad ways and a part of the black market machine that kept the caliphate running. He smuggled oil, which was making ISIS millions of dollars a week. By the fall of 2014, ISIS controlled 60 percent of the oil-producing resources in eastern Syria and a handful of minor oil fields in Iraq. A few weeks earlier, I'd met a young petroleum engineer who'd worked in Syria's largest oil field, al-Omar in Deir Ezzor, when it was controlled by the Nusra

Front. He explained that after ISIS won the oil field from Nusra, it approached the staff at al-Omar as if the takeover had been something like a Wall Street acquisition, asking them to stay on and offering a pay raise. When the engineer refused, the offer increased. When he refused again, ISIS tried to kill him. It had also advertised positions for petroleum professionals as part of its online recruitment drive.

The oil pumped at al-Omar and elsewhere served many purposes for ISIS. It was refined into fuel for cars, trucks, Humvees, and generators. It also gave ISIS something to trade, in semisecret deals with the Assad regime and with rival rebel groups. Often obscured behind the group's sensational propaganda was the fact that, in addition to its cadres of foot soldiers and suicide bombers, ISIS employed a skilled professional class, including businessmen and bureaucrats, doctors and specialists. Some were true believers who had come from abroad. Others were locals who for various reasons had cast their lot with the caliphate. If you wanted to do business in ISIS areas, as people often explained it, then you had to be with them. Much of the oil was refined and sold on the black markets that surrounded the conflict—in Iraq, in Syria, and in the border region of Turkey, where the official fuel prices, which were sky-high, made it ISIS's most lucrative market. The refined fuel was driven from ISIS territory to the border, where it was pumped into Turkey via underground pipes and brought by men like Mohamed to Turkish businessmen who mixed it with the petrol at normal gas stations or set up their own illegal filling stops.

The United States had started bombing oil refineries and supply routes, and Turkey had vowed to stop oil smuggling on its border, but the trade continued. Mohamed had agreed to take me to see his piece of it.

He was a Syrian in his thirties who'd been living for two years in the border town, where he supported his wife and young children in their modest but comfortable home, along with some of his relatives. Another relative was a senior ISIS member in Raqqa, and Mohamed traveled there on occasion, selling civilian supplies. In Turkey his business was fuel. The small border village that received the oil pipes was controlled by one of the mafias that ran smuggling operations all along the border, and a Turkish smuggler from a rival clan had warned that if we were discovered, we would likely be beaten with stones. Beyond that, I worried that if Mohamed was found to have taken a journalist there, they might come for him and his family. But he was unconcerned. He had the easy air of a man who believed that God was in control of his fate.

With me was Yusuf Sayman, the photographer and former barman, and my friend Zaher Said, a Syrian activist who'd come along to translate. I was also working with a driver who went by the nickname Abu Salah, a husky Syrian about my age with an ever-present stubble, his eyes always shaded by a baseball cap. A cigarette smuggler by trade, he was good at talking his way through police checkpoints and never seemed rattled. He'd been waiting outside, figuring that the less he knew of what I was doing and whom I was meeting the better. When we called him in and presented him with the plan, he agreed to it with a shrug. So we piled into his minivan, which could have passed for a soccer dad's car if it weren't so filthy. Mohamed sat in the passenger's seat. One of his brothers, wearing a tracksuit, sat in the middle row alongside Zaher, who wore his hair in a frizzy ponytail. I sat in the back row with Yusuf. "Put your sunglasses on," Mohamed suggested, and I flipped on my tinted Ray-Bans. He took a disappointed look at me. "Never mind," he said. "You look even more American with them on."

We drove to the village where the operation was based, turning from the main road onto a narrow dirt one, which was lined with great piles of trash. No representative of the government was permitted to enter here, Mohamed explained, including garbage collectors. Thin teenagers stood sentry, peering into the van's windows as we rolled slowly past. Some of the trash sat in shallow pools of oil. The road was lined with cheaply built concrete homes, but as we traveled further, some were encased in newly built walls. I saw a Mercedes parked behind a gate that had been left partially open. A motorcycle rolled alongside us, and the passenger on the back took a long look at us. The road bent around a curve, and I noticed that the houses were getting nicer and larger. Finally we arrived at a dusty lot. This place that helped to pay the salaries of ISIS fighters and fund the group's slick propaganda was dismal and grimy. Men smeared with mud and grease sat in folding chairs as refined fuel eked from hoses that emerged like hydra heads from the ground. A hundred or so seventeen-gallon drums were stacked beside the men in the chairs. Abu Salah pulled the nose of his van right up to them, and he and Mohamed jumped out, asking loudly about the prices. I watched them pretend to haggle as a wiry man used a long hose to fill a minibus, placing the hose into a tank hidden underneath it. There were probably more in the roof and inside the frame, to hide additional fuel as the driver brought it deeper into Turkey.

Mohamed returned to the van and asked if we wanted to see one of the black market filling stops where he sold the fuel he normally purchased here. He directed Abu Salah to a hamlet a few miles away, a couple hundred yards from Syria. We stopped beside an old farm building, where fuel drums were stacked against the walls of a cow pen. Abu Salah decided to fill up and bought about $50 worth, enough to fill his tank. He stuck a piece of hose into a massive drum and began to suck hard on the other end, huffing on the hose for more than ten minutes to get the fuel moving. He swallowed some accidentally from time to time and then stumbled around the cow pens, gasping as fuel dripped from his beard. Cows lowed nearby. When the fuel was finally flowing, he poured it into a rusty can. He tipped the can into the van's gas tank, then rocked the van furiously to help it go down. "I have fuel right now from here to here," he finally said, exhausted, pointing from his neck down to his chest.

Every last thing was being pillaged from Syria—oil, antiquities, metal, grain. It wasn't just ISIS, but they were the most efficient, systematizing and formalizing the looting. Mohamed stood upright beneath a post-summer sun, his arms folded behind his back. He gave a grand smile, nodding at me with an air that said he was not helpless in the face of the country's destruction. "All things are coming from Syria right now—it's the mother of the world," he said, his deep voice booming. He repeated this several times: "Syria is the mother of the world."

Many Syrians I met had an origin story centered on an act of violence that marked the divide between the person they had been before the war and who they had come to be.

Mohamed told me his on one of those elastic nights I would pass in the years that followed on the floor of his small courtyard, over dinners of slow-cooked meat and rice and pots of sweetened tea, all prepared by his never-seen wife and brought to us by his skinny son, who would arrange the plates on a sheet before us and fold himself into his father's shadow.

It was the story of a woman, beautiful and young, a gift, to him, who showed the virtue of what God permitted a man. She rode horses bareback—he spoke with awe. *She could really ride.*

She was a Sunni like him, but she had a relative who supported Assad. Mohamed said he'd learned that the relative had been killing revolutionaries. Sitting cross-legged, his posture, as always, preternaturally straight, he betrayed no emotion in the telling. He went to the relative's house and, in a brutal, ugly struggle, killed him.

He became a rebel. By then the country was tilting irrevocably. He fought with a battalion that considered America an ally, and he believed that the Western world was on his side. Syria was a closed-in place—made that way by the Assad family over its decades in power. Suspicion of America, Israel, and Europe was taught in the curriculum from the early days at school. But Mohamed was from a historic city that received a regular stream of tourists, and he felt a bond with them, though he didn't speak their languages, as he watched them walk with wonder amid the ancient streets. "They are open people," he would say—open to Syria, open to foreign worlds—and he admired them for it.

Even then, though, before the war, he had been a blurry man, someone who walked between different worlds. He was a tradesman. He was also a black-market operator, selling illicit goods to make money on the side.

Being a rebel didn't pay the bills, especially after Mohamed moved his family to Turkey, where the lira was strong and rising against his paltry monthly salary paid in Syrian pounds. He got his start as an oil smuggler by tying a heavy barrel to his waist and dragging it across the border himself. In those days a different militant group was drilling the oil, and the rebels who controlled the border were not ideological, just mercenary. The Turkey-Syria border had been rife with oil smuggling long before the war. As a Turkish smuggler once told me, it took only the "permission" of the gendarmerie, the Turkish paramilitary force that controlled the border, in the form of small bribes. A third-generation smuggler from a family with decades in the trade, he'd started filling cars rigged with hidden tanks at the cheaper gas stations in Syria and driving back to Turkey when he was a teen.

But the trade was transformed by the war. Rebel groups targeted oil resources from the regime in eastern Syria. Strapped for cash, they smuggled some of the fuel to buyers in Turkey. It was a booming business by the time Mohamed joined in early 2013.

In the evenings, he would receive a call from a commander in the Free Syrian Army, the U.S.-backed rebel coalition, telling him to head to the Syrian side of the border. Over in Turkey, the gendarmerie would clear a path in the hills, lighting it with the floodlights on their armored trucks. Back in Syria, vehicles bearing oil drums would arrive: buses, pickup trucks, taxis. He would take a drum, tie it to a rope, and drag it one hundred yards across the border to vehicles waiting on the other side. He might repeat the trip twenty times before daybreak along with hundreds of fellow smugglers. Other men hauled everything from cows to sugar and tea. If he made $1,500 in a night, he would give $500 to the FSA commander and another $500 to the Turkish border guards. "You can't really say that we are smuggling oil, because we take permission from the Turkish side and the Syrian side," he said. "But since it's under the table, we call it smuggling."

When ISIS began to turn its attention from fighting the regime to taking territory from fellow rebel groups, it focused on areas rich in oil. As it gained new oil fields, Mohamed kept smuggling. The trade created a windfall on the Turkish side of the border.

"You couldn't step anywhere without stepping in oil," another Turkish smuggler recalled to Yusuf and me one day. He had received us in a downbeat auto body garage, pulling down the metal gate behind us so we wouldn't be seen. As my eyes adjusted to the darkness, I saw a generator and a stack of rusty drums. For him the oil was a once-in-a-lifetime opportunity, and he was using the money to put himself through trade school. For ISIS, the profits were start-up funds as it built its caliphate, buying weapons and paying salaries. It turned profits from the oil it sold, the fees it charged to middlemen, and the taxes it collected at any checkpoints through which the oil passed.

Mohamed enjoyed being a part of the ISIS machine, and over time I would watch him do other work connected to the group, from selling artifacts to providing safe haven for its fighters in Turkey. Wherever in the black market ISIS set its sights, he found a way to play a role. Among his large family were several ISIS members, including the relative in Raqqa. And Mohamed knew even more ISIS members from his large circle of business associates and friends. His connection to the radicals that were taking on the Western world along with the Assad regime, both of whom he blamed for the Syrian people's suffering, seemed to give him a sense of pride. Each brutal and outrageous act—like the beheadings, which flew in the face of everything the U.S.-led order stood for, and showed the lie of its belief that the world had moved past the ugliness of history and into modernity—Mohamed saw as something like defiance.

In some ways he reminded me of a lapsed Catholic—he sometimes drank, he had a girlfriend in another town, he smoked constantly, and I never once saw him pray, but he still identified as an Islamist and often expressed support for the idea embodied in the ISIS name, of building a hard-line Islamic state. ISIS offered him a kind of agency. I had seen other Syrians act this way, like the young driver Abu Salah sent in his place one day, who decided that he couldn't waste this moment with an American in his back seat and spent a three-hour drive playing ISIS chants. Music was forbidden, so the sound of men chanting was overlaid incongruously with machine-gun fire and the sound of clomping horse hooves.

Sometimes Mohamed opined on how the ISIS cause was noble, and its realized vision would be beautiful if only the West would allow it the space. At other times he mocked the extreme religiosity that the group, especially its foreign fighters, practiced and preached. One day he said that foreign jihadis were destroying the group. Another, he told me his younger brother was getting ready to join ISIS in Syria, saying it was the only way he could find a job and afford to get married.

Sometimes Mohamed and his kin aligned with ISIS, and sometimes they didn't, but no matter what, through their business connections and family ties, they were always close to it. It was part of the genius of the ISIS survival strategy, tapping people like this and allowing them the freedom to come and go, their shifting positions in relation to ISIS giving it flexibility. It was a shadow network that was always there but also gone the second you turned on the light.

With me for most of the fall as I traveled up and down the border region in Abu Salah's minivan was Munzer al-Awad, a thirty-three-year-old journalist from Daraa, the city where the protest movement had started. Munzer had been an activist then, and he was exasperated to see what had become of his country and his failed revolution as we met with smugglers like Mohamed. We'd only recently begun working together and had first met Mohamed while searching for the kind of contacts who could bring us into this underworld, which seemed important now that criminals and jihadis had taken over the war. He hadn't joined me on the trip to see the oil-smuggling operation with

Mohamed because he was away for a few days, chasing a tip for a different story along the Turkish coast.

He was tall and rangy, with a prominent chin and a widow's peak, and I sometimes joked that he looked like a hitman. In fact, whether by disposition or by what he'd endured, he could never hurt anyone. He would meet anyone and face any danger, yet at his core was as soft as the center of a sunflower.

It was an eerie time, full of eerie movement, as people struggled to settle into the new reality. One day Munzer and I were in Akcakale, which sits just north of the Syrian border and was the gateway to Raqqa, thirty miles to the south. ISIS had established control over the Syrian side of the border. In an open-air café, a jittery man explained how he'd been part of a smuggling operation until ISIS took over and ordered the men to stop their work, because it had its own smugglers. When his crew kept working in secret, four of them turned up dead one night.

At Akcakale the Turkish guards kept the border gate unofficially in operation, from time to time swinging open the hatch to another world. If you asked the Syrians waiting on the dust-packed street, they would say they were going to visit family, and many of them probably were. Some also traveled back and forth across the border for work. One day we met a man who had a business running supplies into Syria from Akcakale, packing them into a big handcart and walking them across the border; he lifted up the metal gate of one of his shops to reveal stacks of used tires. It was big business in ISIS territory: fuel was cheap, and residents relied on their cars to get around. He also sold car parts, carpets, clothes, and electronics. "I send everything, as if to a regular state," he said.

The trader listed other top-selling items around the border: from children's toys and lightbulbs to conservative religious clothing, lingerie, and jewelry made from Indian gold. MP3 players were sent with the promise that they wouldn't be used for music. He refused to deal with alcohol and cigarettes at all. There was a booming business in new iPhones but also a pressing need for staples such as grain, sugar, and cooking oil. "They are living on imports," he said. "These are the basic nutrients of life."

As Munzer and I covered hundreds of miles with Abu Salah in his dirt-smeared minivan, I noticed that he was filling up exclusively on illegal fuel. He seemed to know every illicit filling stop along the long stretches of well-lit highway. He would get out to rap the door at shacks that sat in the shadows of the normal gas stations, with their bright Exxon or BP signs, or pull in back of the small Syrian restaurants that had begun to line the roadside, where sleepy attendants sat waiting with their hoses and rusty drums. He lived in a tent in a refugee camp with his two young sons and his wife, and when they checked in on his cell phone, he would often become upset, worried about his kids, who were struggling in the camp's overcrowded school. He was taking all the money that he charged me and socking it away.

Munzer and I were back in Istanbul by the time we published a story about the underground oil economy. Not long after, the Turkish government sent more than 1,000 security personnel on a raid into the smuggling town I'd visited with Mohamed. They destroyed eight miles of underground pipeline and detained thirty-seven people, Turks and Syrians alike. They also seized twenty vehicles, with license plates belonging to provinces all over Turkey, and weapons. For a time after that, the oil trade dried up on that stretch of the border, and a lot of people lost their jobs, including Mohamed. It was just before Christmas the next time Munzer and I saw him, and I wondered if he'd be upset. But he was proud instead. The season had moved into the start of a cold winter, and Mohamed said he hoped the price of oil would come down for the people in Syria if it was harder to sell in Turkey.

CHAPTER 11

BEHEADING

Gaziantep, Turkey. December 2014.

Over beers one night in a hotel near Turkey's border with Syria, a prominent human rights activist outlined a plan to commit a grisly homicide.

Malik was one of Syria's best-known activists. He'd made his name in 2011's peaceful protests and was one of the revolution's most ardent liberal voices. He hadn't committed an act of violence in his life, even as the revolution turned to civil war. But he was desperate.

As 2014 drew to a close, secular, pro-democracy Syrians like Malik, who had once led the uprising, were depleted and increasingly irrelevant. ISIS was dominating the rebellion and its narrative. Savagery like the beheadings of Western journalists and aid workers got more attention than the activists ever could. ISIS had released a new video showing one of these beheadings days earlier—this time, it was an American aid worker, Peter Kassig, whom Malik had considered a friend.

In response, he told me as we drank, he and some colleagues had come up with a plan—part revenge and part attempt to be relevant again. They would go to Syria and buy an ISIS prisoner from another rebel group. Then Malik would behead the man on video and release it.

Or maybe he wouldn't have the stomach for a beheading, he conceded as the night wore on. In that case, he'd shoot the man in the back of the head.

The prisoner had already been selected: a foreign jihadi said to embody the worst of ISIS's blind extremism. The fee that Malik would pay to buy him, thousands of dollars, had been procured. Malik and a few friends would cross the border the next day. "We're at a stage in Syria where our principles aren't going to help us," he said.

He hoped the video would send a message to both ISIS and the West—that Syria's moderates were still there—even if it meant adopting the same brutal tactics ISIS employed. "When it comes down to it, who's more effective at getting a voice?" he asked. "I've seen that ISIS is very effective at getting a voice."

Yet he also knew the video could suggest that his moderate movement had lost its soul. "It's saying: Look at us. Look at what we're doing. We know it's fucked up," he said. "But we're in a conflict where no one is paying attention to us."

"We're sort of lost," he finally said. "As an activist, I have no idea what the fuck to do."

One of his colleagues—another young and respected activist, who was with us—was having similar thoughts.

"Oh, man. This shit is driving us crazy," he said. "It makes it hard for you to determine right from wrong. I mean—you still want to be a very cool person, a moderate, someone who is passionate about his cause. But at the same time, you feel like there is nothing you can do to change this moment, to change the revolution. This is a desperation move."

Not long after, Malik, this second activist, and a handful of others traveled into Syria as planned. They bought the ISIS prisoner and sat him on a metal chair in a concrete room. They had a handgun and a shotgun, but that didn't seem to frighten the man. As they set up their lights and video camera, he asked, "Will you put me on TV?"

Malik interrogated the ISIS fighter and began to see him as tragically deluded. Then he remembered his rage at the suffering ISIS had wrought. He named the Western journalists and aid workers the group had beheaded on camera and asked the man how he'd like to suffer the same fate. "I don't know," the man said, looking up at him with a shrug.

Malik found himself boasting that he could do it. Yet he couldn't help but see the man's humanity. He took him from the chair and was soon driving him toward the Turkish border. He gave him some money and said he was releasing him on the condition that he leave Syria and never return. The man left the car without agreeing.

"I couldn't hurt him," Malik said later, when I called from Istanbul to check on him.

He felt that he'd kept his principles. He knew this wouldn't be enough. "I feel that the world will forget us and forget what we stood for," he said.

CHAPTER 12

GATEWAY

Istanbul, Turkey. December 2014.

IF YOU ASK AN *ISTANBULLU* WHERE TO FIND PLANT FOOD OR PESTICIDE, you will be directed to a shopping arcade in an underpass beside the Galata Bridge, in the neighborhood of Karakoy, where these items are sold in rows of identical shops. Fishing equipment is sold a few blocks over, where nets and harpoons hang from awnings and mannequins in wetsuits clutter the sidewalks. A little further along are the shops that sell construction supplies, crowded together along the narrow streets of the Persembe Pazari, one after another, hard to tell apart. Neighborhoods like these are vestiges of another age in the timeworn city, before the internet and the phone book, when buying a certain thing meant going to a certain place—engagement rings in Nisantai, wood products in Tahtakale. Modern Istanbul has its chain stores and shopping malls but also plenty of areas where the old style remains, if for no other reason than the classic Turkish mind-set that says *because things have always been this way*. Down the hill from Taksim Square is Cukurcuma, home to the antique sellers. Further west, in Galata, are shops stacked with musical instruments. On the nearby hilltop in Sishane, store windows are filled with light fixtures, glittering above the sea. Eminonu has the spice bazaar, and Sultanahmet is home to the carpet traders. Aksaray, a working-class neighborhood in the heart of the conservative Fatih district, is home to the human traffickers.

The neighborhood was founded in the fifteenth century by migrants from a region in central Turkey of the same name, which translates to "the white palace." They were brought to Istanbul by its conqueror, Mehmet II, to help populate the city with ethnic Turks after his victory over the Greeks. The transitory feel of the place has continued into the present day. Aksaray is home to the city's main bus depot, a seething compound that sees long-haul arrivals from places as far as the Balkans and Iran. Traces remain of the immigrant communities that have sprouted in the neighborhood over the years, from the riotous Georgian restaurant hidden in a corner of the bus depot to the Iraqi cafe and Iranian restaurant on the streets around it. In the fall of 2012, when Munzer, the Syrian journalist with whom I'd one day travel along the Turkish border, stepped out from a taxi and into the disorienting crush of Aksaray for the first time, he was surprised to find new Syrian restaurants along its streets. Syrian refugees like him crowded by the hundreds into its parks and squares as agents of the human traffickers canvassed among them, working to fill their smuggling boats.

He had arrived at the Istanbul airport two hours earlier, still caught in the mental fog that trailed him after his confinement and torture in one of the Assad regime's prisons. The only thing he could communicate to the taxi driver was that he was Syrian, and so the man drove him to Aksaray. Unsure what to do with himself, Munzer found a cheap hotel, sat at the bar, and ordered a drink.

Refugees like Munzer had been receiving this sort of welcome to Aksaray for decades, the neighborhood serving as a gateway from one world to the next. Before Syrians, it was Iraqis fleeing the carnage of the U.S. war. In the 1980s, it was Iranians, fleeing the newly established Islamic Republic. All of them were directed to smugglers who worked from hotels and offices and seemed to be part of Aksaray, as enduring as the medieval fountains along the busy streets. The particular smugglers changed with whatever national or ethnic group was passing through at a given time, taking over from the traffickers who'd come before them, always with the Turkish mafia providing protection from police. The traffickers sent their charges onward to Europe and beyond: by plane, via the land borders with Greece and Bulgaria, both a three-hour drive away, and on dangerous voyages in overcrowded migrant ships.

By the time Munzer and I began working together, in the fall of 2014, the Syrian refugee crisis had become the worst in modern history. People were fleeing ISIS as well as Assad, and more than half of the 4 million people who'd left the country were spread around Turkey, joined by a rising number of Iraqis. When Munzer arrived in Aksaray in the fall of 2012, there were 80,000 Syrian refugees in Turkey, but as Assad's warplanes strafed the country's cities, it was clear that the deluge was coming. Munzer had been one of the early revolutionaries, flying home from an accounting job in Doha to help organize the protests when they began in Daraa, his home city. Eventually the *mukhabarat* arrested him at his home, and he was thrown into the unlit basement of a prison. In all the time we spent together over the years that followed, Munzer would reveal only fragmentary details of what had happened to him. It wasn't until our last night together in Istanbul, in fact, that he opened up about what he experienced. Until then I knew only outlines—that he had been tortured repeatedly, that he had tripped over dead bodies in the pitch black of his crowded cell. I knew that he'd been released only by what he considered a freak chance and that the rest of the dozens of people he was imprisoned with were almost certainly dead. In a database run by a monitoring group in an effort to keep track of the tens of thousands of men and women who'd disappeared into the regime's prisons, Munzer himself was listed as deceased.

When he first arrived in Aksaray, he tried and failed to find a job—as a waiter, as a cashier. He spent a lot of the money he had on alcohol. Then he used the last of it to book passage on one of the smuggling journeys to Greece, hoping to get to London, in the belief that the limited English he spoke then might help him find work there. Instead he was detained by the Greek authorities, who sent him back across the land border into Turkey. Out of money and options, he took a bus from Istanbul to Antakya, looking for work as a translator for journalists.

We met for the first time, briefly, a few months after that. A mutual friend, a Syrian who worked for the *New York Times*, told me that he knew a former activist with a wild story. The three of us met at a hookah bar in Antakya. I noticed the hard, brooding demeanor that gave Munzer his assassin's aspect, along with the incongruously easy, almost mantis-like way that he carried himself, a former karate champion who now smoked three packs a day. When he told me the story that he wanted me to publish, I decided he was crazy. Since arriving in Antakya, he'd had no luck finding work with Western journalists—his English was poor, and he could barely understand me. Yet he was enraged with the corruption he saw among the rebels operating around southern Turkey, and he'd decided he would expose them on his own. He embedded himself with one battalion that controlled a lucrative stretch of the border and spent weeks collecting evidence like a DEA agent: voice recordings of the commander discussing drug running and other illicit business and even text messages of the man trying to purchase red mercury, thinking it could be used to develop a chemical weapon. He wanted me to publish it all.

The battalion was working with the Turkish government, and I knew that if I ran a story, there was a good chance it would get Munzer arrested or killed. When I told him this, he said something I would hear from him many times later on, when something we were doing risked his safety: "I just want to show the truth." Lying, I told him I'd think about it, believing that though he was a natural investigator, he also had a death wish. After we left, I told my friend to let Munzer find a way to get himself killed that didn't involve me.

Two years later, in the summer of 2014, I was drinking one night at a restaurant near the border when Munzer walked in with a couple of German journalists. He seemed more balanced than when I had last seen him, and he greeted me in much better English. We had a beer, and he explained that although he'd never seen his wild story published, he had managed to establish himself as a fixer and translator, working with European news teams. He'd even moved to a neighborhood not far from my own in Istanbul. Since I was looking for a partner who wanted to work not as a fixer but as a fellow reporter, and Munzer was eager for the chance to start sharing bylines, we agreed to start by trying our longshot story about oil smugglers. Munzer also had a unique set of contacts of his own in the human traffickers he'd first encountered on his ill-fated journey to Greece, who trusted him in part because they'd known him at his lowest.

It was from these contacts that he first heard an alarming rumor—that ISIS was slipping fighters in among the thousands of refugees and migrants leaving Turkey on boats bound for Italy and Greece.

This nightmare scenario was not yet a focus of Western governments, which had been incensed by the establishment of ISIS's physical caliphate and were still scrambling to put together a plan to destroy it. By now other countries, including the United Kingdom, Germany, and France, had joined America in its air campaign. ISIS had vowed retaliation. At the same time, it was pushing, as its propaganda made clear, to make Muslims everywhere see that they were in conflict with the West, whether they wanted to be or not. Prime targets for ISIS were those Muslims already living in the West—it wanted to show that despite what they might think, they could not peacefully exist there. It wanted to put liberal democracies, which said they welcomed all kinds of people, to the test. An ISIS attack, especially by someone who had slipped into Europe posing as a refugee, might create a backlash against Muslims in the West. ISIS knew that there were populists and nativists who would seize on this.

On a cold afternoon in December 2014, Munzer and I took a taxi to Aksaray. We walked down a set of stairs and into a bar lit dimly by halogen lights. Men in leather jackets sat at tables with women in tight jeans and miniskirts, smoking hookah pipes. The trafficker we'd come to meet was alone at a table in the center of the room. As we joined him, he said the café was run by smugglers and that he'd picked it for our meeting because it was "safe" from police.

A former white-collar professional in his thirties, he used his smuggling business to support his young family in Europe. He'd been doing the work even before the Syrian war, smuggling Iraqis and other desperate migrants to the continent, but he said business had picked up considerably. According to Frontex, the EU's border agency, more than 20,000 refugees, many of them Syrians, had already been smuggled from Turkey into Greece and Bulgaria alone that year. He charged $2,500 for each refugee he sent by speedboat from Turkey to Greece. He said he viewed it as "humanitarian work," on top of the profit he made. But he'd grown uncomfortable with the turn this work had taken.

He had a connection to an ISIS official, who, in the fall, had sent a man his way. He recalled him as a clean-shaven client who looked "like a simple refugee." The two struck up a friendship, and he learned that the man was an ISIS member. The man was blunt about his reason for heading to Europe—he wanted to be ready to stage attacks there. "The Western world thinks there is no ISIS in their countries—that all the jihadis have gone to fight and die in Syria," the trafficker said. "But this man said, 'No. We are sending our fighters to take their places.'"

After the ISIS man landed in Greece, he sent more people the trafficker's way—over the months that followed, about a dozen, the trafficker said. Each paid more than the other passengers on his boats. "They are waiting for their orders," he said. "Just wait. You will see."

He described himself as an ISIS supporter, sympathetic to the militants' campaign against the West and admiring of their professed piety. That was why he initially agreed to put the ISIS members on his boats, he said. "In the Quran it is written that if they come to fight you, then you must fight them," he said. "And [Western nations] are bombing in their country."

While he had no problem with the idea of ISIS fighters attacking government targets in Europe, though, he'd eventually found himself with a guilty conscience and had stopped taking on ISIS clients. He was worried about civilian casualties. "This is not what my work is supposed to be," he said.

CHAPTER 13

DINNER

Antakya, Turkey. January 2015.

KHALIL WAS A PLEASANT-LOOKING MAN, ALMOST LIKE A DOLL, WITH a placid expression and dimpled cheeks. As he took a seat across the table, he told me he had two armed men in a car outside, watching the front door. It was a threat, but he smiled and called me *akhi*, my brother.

We were at the Sultan Sofrasi, a restaurant in Antakya. Its street-side entrance opened onto a scene of the kind of hidden, old-style grandeur that underlaid the little city. The clientele was crowded together around white tablecloths under low lights, filling two terraced levels. We were on the top floor, engulfed by the hum of conversation on a crowded Thursday night in January. Munzer sat beside me, and beside Khalil sat a Syrian contact of ours, who had helped us set up the meeting. Khalil was an operative with ISIS who'd been dispatched across the border two months earlier to facilitate the new front in the war against the West. He was working like a grim clerk, sending ISIS members to Europe.

We agreed that if he told me some details of what he was doing, I wouldn't reveal his identity. "There are some things I'm allowed to tell you and some things I'm not," he said, in a voice that was soft like an adolescent's. The waiter came, and I ordered a meal for the table, a traditional assortment of grilled meats. Khalil had once been a member of the Syrian security services, and that's all he would say about it. When the war began, he joined the Free Syrian Army. He commanded a battalion, and for a time he and his men took supplies and salaries from the United States and its allies. He got to know the rebel movement and its various players. A photo from the time, which I saw later, showed him happy as a cat in his FSA uniform, sitting beside some supplies. He took his men to Raqqa and joined ISIS in 2014.

ISIS employed a decentralized military system that operated something like a feudal army, made up of the various groups that had lent it their standards, each with its own level of capability. There were tens of thousands of ISIS fighters across Iraq and Syria who had various degrees of allegiance to the group but worked broadly under the command of ISIS leadership, which could send them resources and reinforcements as needed. A commander's clout was tied in part to the strength of his unit. There was a constant jostling among the myriad factions, which were made up of Iraqis and Syrians and veteran mujahideen who coalesced by nationality, such as the Libyan al-Bittar Battalion, the Saudi-led Green Battalion, and the fearsome Caucasian battalions, led by ISIS's premier field general, the red-haired Chechen called Abu Omar.

A commander's position could be precarious—if you lost men in battle, you also lost power in the ISIS hierarchy. But Khalil had found a way to secure his place. Not long after joining, he gave up control of his battalion and took on a role with ISIS that he described as "security." His job involved assassinations, and he helped to kill ISIS's rivals among the rebellion. I knew a man who ran a rebel group that controlled part of the border, and when Munzer and I called to ask what he knew about Khalil, he flew into a frenzy, demanding to know if we had plans to meet him, and when and where, prodding us to let him trail us so he could kill him. He kept calling about it for days. "He has killed a lot of FSA leaders," he said of Khalil.

The Syrian intermediary who'd arranged the meeting had known Khalil for years. He also knew the man who oversaw Khalil's operation, whom I also had to swear never to name. The intermediary had worked on them for weeks to arrange the meeting, assuring them that Munzer and I wouldn't betray them. Until that last minute, Khalil had worried that the meeting might be an intelligence sting.

Munzer and I had flown down from Istanbul two hours earlier, stepping onto the Antakya tarmac into a crisp desert cold. Munzer, tall and lean in his fur-trimmed coat and skinny jeans, used his first steps out from the plane to light a cigarette. Abu Salah picked us up from the airport in his minivan. As we drove toward the restaurant, the intermediary called to apologize, saying that Khalil had cold feet and wanted to cancel. He and Khalil were together at a café nearby, so I asked Abu Salah to drop me off at the restaurant and bring Munzer to retrieve the pair on his own, hoping he could put Khalil at ease. Munzer succeeded, but when he finally joined me at the table with the two men, he was rattled, whispering that two men in a car had trailed the minivan.

At the table, Khalil laid out the basics of the operation he was running. From a Turkish port city, he worked with traffickers to send ISIS members among the refugees who were stealing off daily all along the Turkish coast, bound for Italy and Greece. He sent them in small groups, he said, in cargo ships filled with hundreds of people: "They are going like refugees." He said these men would help to fulfill ISIS's threat of striking Western countries in retaliation for the U.S.-led airstrikes on the caliphate. "If someone attacks me, then for sure I will attack them back," he said.

Every fifteen minutes, I pulled out my iPhone and typed "all good" into an encrypted chat group; my company had hired a remote team of security advisors to monitor these check-ins and track my location via an app on my phone. After killing Foley, Sotloff, and Kassig, ISIS was down to just one more American hostage, and it was easy to imagine how short the twenty miles to the border might feel if we were kidnapped. I noticed that Khalil was answering calls at similar intervals, saying, "Everything's okay."

The dinner came, and we wrapped pieces of liver and minced beef in strips of pita bread. As Munzer took a bite of salad with his fork in his left hand, Khalil scolded him in Arabic. "You should eat with your right hand like a Muslim, even if you work with the infidels," he said.

Khalil said that his method of moving ISIS members was important to the group because Western governments, along with Turkish authorities, had stepped up efforts to track jihadis returning from Syria, which made plane travel from Turkey risky. A recent estimate had said that more than one-fifth of ISIS members were citizens or residents of European countries. If they returned to Europe in the refugee ships, they could travel home via open land borders that received far less scrutiny than airports. The ships could also land Syrian or other Middle Eastern fighters in Europe amid the confusion of a refugee crisis that worsened by the day. Many observers believed that ISIS needed to keep its fighters in Iraq and Syria to defend its territory and that if it wanted to attack America and Europe, it could reach out to sympathizers there. But Khalil said that ISIS wanted people it trusted on the ground in the West to spearhead its recruitment efforts. And for those who were being sent to conduct attacks, he said, ISIS wanted them to be trained. "We prefer for you to come to Syria and fight with us, and to meet you and trust you," he said. "We trained them for this in Syria."

Suddenly sounding a triumphant note, as if remembering that he was speaking to a journalist, he said, "It's our dream that there should be a caliphate not only in Syria but in all the world, and we will have it soon, God willing."

But he struck a more measured tone as the dinner wore on, complaining to the intermediary about the struggle to keep ahead of Turkish and Western authorities. He had been forced to move his work from city to city in response to Turkish efforts to crack down on refugee smuggling. And he worried about being caught. He'd been told to pose as a refugee himself while in Turkey and to consider finding a regular job as a front.

"We need to smuggle them quickly," Khalil said of the fighters. But traffickers insisted on waiting until their ships were filled well past capacity, sometimes with as many as seven hundred people. The boats capsized sometimes—in a recent wreck, he said, some ISIS members had drowned. Khalil claimed that ISIS had sent thousands of its members to Europe, but as he described the difficulties he faced, I guessed that the number was far lower. The intermediary would say later that he thought it was more like dozens.

Khalil said several times that "the whole world" was fighting ISIS, in reference to the international coalition involved in the airstrikes. He said he hoped that ISIS attacks in the West would break the coalition's resolve, getting the strikes to stop so that ISIS could continue to build its caliphate.

"They insult us and insult our Islamic religion," Khalil said at one point, his voice rising slightly.

"Syria will be visited on them," he said at another, speaking as if there were divine retribution in what he was unleashing.

Khalil and the intermediary went out to smoke. Munzer and I stayed in our seats. The murmur of the restaurant was quieting as diners finished their main courses and the waiters brought toothpicks, fruit plates, demitasse cups of boiled coffee, and small glasses of tea.

At a nearby table, her chair to the wall, a woman sat alone. She wore a business suit and had reddish hair that made her seem possibly American or European. She did not seem to pay attention to us or, in fact, to anything else as she ate silently. I wondered if she was an intelligence operative, or if I was being paranoid.

At a table in a far corner, I recognized a man I'd met on the balcony of the Narin Hotel early in the war. A hard-line Islamist from Syria with a ruddy face and black beard, Nabil was a rebel fighter at the time. With him had been a mujahideen from Tunisia who'd fought in the religious wars in Afghanistan and Chechnya. They'd just purchased a set of walkie-talkies from an electronics store ahead of a planned trip into Syria and were fiddling with them on the balcony. Nabil was a gregarious man, but the Tunisian was wary of speaking with me, and when I asked how he'd found his way to southern Turkey, he silently produced a small, creased map. On it, a small Iraqi town near the border with Syria was marked in blue pen with an *X*. I asked who had made that marking, and he got up and left without another word. I never saw him again, though I later heard that he became a senior member of ISIS.

Nabil and I had stayed in touch. He'd lost interest in the fighting quickly and instead used his connections among extremists to get a foothold in the hostage trade, working as a middleman in negotiations that had freed Western hostages from the Nusra Front in exchange for millions of dollars. On his phone he kept photos of himself posing with suitcases opened to reveal stacks of cash. He always seemed to be involved in a new negotiation. A month earlier, he'd shown Munzer and me a proof-of-life video of two Italian aid workers being held hostage by the Nusra Front in Syria and said that he was working to secure their release.

In the restaurant, I hoped he hadn't noticed us and wondered if he was hoping the same. With him were two men in leather jackets who spoke Arabic with the accent of eastern Syria. Nabil was arguing with them about something, looking uncharacteristically agitated. It was easy to guess that he was in the middle of negotiating another deal, perhaps for the Italian women, who were still in captivity. It was a strange time then, at the start of 2015, when, if you looked closely, you could see the conflict stretching further out into the sea of the world, like droplets of black dye, barely noticeable, turning the water just a shade darker. I mused on how far Nabil had come since I'd first met him in Antakya, fumbling like a child with his walkie-talkie. Now he was sitting in an old tourist haunt in the city of St. Simeon and the apostles Peter and Paul, reaching through his cell phone to European capitals, negotiating with diplomats and intermediaries and families, while outside, Khalil the terrorist was enjoying a postmeal cigarette.

Khalil and the intermediary came back. We finished our conversation, and I paid the bill. "Good," Khalil told Munzer. "Take as much from him as you can. Taking money from infidels is *halal*."

We were all wary of leaving together, so Khalil went first, with the intermediary. They walked through the restaurant's modest door and were gone. Munzer and I waited for a few minutes, collecting our thoughts. We knew that if Khalil had lured us into a trap, it could be waiting when we stepped outside. As if on cue, a van approached the curb as soon as we walked into the night. But it kept on rolling as I stood there dumbly. Abu Salah had promised before the meeting to keep an eye on the door and call me if he saw anything suspicious, but I looked up and down the street and didn't see his van. Munzer called his cell phone, again and again, but it continued to ring.

Getting worried, Munzer and I walked down the street to the Narin Hotel, taking a seat upstairs in the corner of its café. As we sat there wondering what had happened to our driver, Nabil burst in—and this time he appeared to be in a state of bliss, celebrating with his two colleagues. (The Italian hostages would be released not long afterward.) Munzer decided to call Khalil and asked him if he knew what had happened to Abu Salah. What he really meant was, *Did you kidnap him?* But Khalil took on a tone of great concern. He said that his security detail had noted that Abu Salah had driven off shortly after depositing us at the restaurant. "My guys were surprised that he didn't stay and watch the door," Khalil said. He offered to call in a description of Abu Salah to the nearest ISIS-controlled border crossing, in case there had been some mistake. Two nervous hours later, we finally reached Abu Salah, who joined us with a sheepish smile. He explained that his mother-in-law was dying in a hospital, and he'd been up for several days without sleep. He'd pulled into a parking garage and fallen into a deep slumber, snoring through our frantic phone calls.

A month later Munzer and I were sitting on the grass along the seaside in the Turkish port city where Khalil had been conducting his mission, as commercial freighters inched past in the sky-blue waters. With us was Khalil, along with a human trafficker with a careless stubble, who squinted nervously into the sunlight. After our dinner in Antakya, Munzer had traveled to the port city to canvass his smuggling contacts, asking if there was someone among them who was working with ISIS, and they had pointed him to this wary trafficker. He had told Munzer that there was no way he could speak to a journalist, but Munzer had insisted, and the man had decided to place a call to his boss while Munzer waited. Then, with a look of surprise, he handed the phone to Munzer. It was Khalil on the other line. "What are you doing, brother Munzer?" Khalil said. "I told you to call me if there was anything you needed."

So we had traveled down on a Wednesday afternoon to meet Khalil and the trafficker together, sitting in the grass like an odd group of picnickers. I asked the smuggler to tell me about his charges, curious how much about them he knew. He seemed bewildered by it all, aware that he was working for ISIS but lost in the gravity of what he was doing. "I'm sending some fighters who want to go and visit their families," he said. "Others just go to Europe to be ready." He said some fighters were Syrian. He could tell from their accents that others hailed from elsewhere in the Middle East, while still others spoke Arabic poorly or not at all. Some told him they were from European countries, he said, and a few claimed to be from the United States.

After he received the fighters, he put them up in a hotel, waiting for the passenger list for each ship to fill with regular migrants and for the weather to be right. He said he had ten ISIS members waiting to deport as we spoke: "We will send them on the next ship."

The sun was high in the sky. Khalil moved to the side, took off his coat to use as a prayer rug, knelt on it, and began to perform midday prayers. As he lowered his head to the grass, muttering softly, two elderly Turkish men approached. Standing over him with their necks craned, they shook their heads at the confused refugee and corrected him. He had thought he was bowing in the direction of Mecca but in fact was faced the wrong way.

CHAPTER 14

BODIES AND BOMBS

Erbil, Iraq. February 2015.

I FLEW 1,000 MILES FROM ISTANBUL TO ERBIL, THE CAPITAL OF IRAQI Kurdistan, passing by Mosul as it writhed in the grip of the caliphate, with the snack carts clattering aboard my plane. Erbil was the launching point for the U.S.-led war against the caliphate. With ISIS plotting attacks in Europe, stopping them felt more than ever like an emergency. From one of the high-rise hotels that dot the valley city, I hired a translator and a driver to take me and Yusuf Sayman, the photographer, toward the Mosul Dam, on the frontier of Kurdish-controlled territory. As we raced along the four-lane highway in a Kia Cerato, semitrucks rumbled past in both directions. The road wound along the base of Mount Maqlub, whose summit is home to Christian hermitages built in the fourth and fifth centuries. On the other side of the mountain sat Mosul, twenty miles to the southwest. "Wrecking Ball," by American pop star Miley Cyrus, blared on the Kia's FM radio: *I came in like a wrecking ball. Yeah, I just closed my eyes and swung*. I wondered if anyone might be tuned to the same signal on the other side of the mountain, in the heart of the caliphate, listening in on a forbidden receiver.

The driver was a twenty-one-year-old student who spoke fluent English and was pursuing a business degree. He'd intended to take advantage of the commercial boom after the U.S. invasion that had seen international businesses flock to Erbil, drilling oil and building housing developments with names like English Village, along with shopping malls and hotels. Granted semi-autonomy by Iraq's 2005 constitution, the secular and pro-Western Kurdish region had been an outlier of stability in the Middle East, largely free of the sectarian conflicts that plagued the rest of Iraq and many of its Arab neighbors. Since the rise of ISIS, though, the construction cranes had stopped their work as the Kurdish region suddenly found itself bordering an extremist proto-state. If not for the last-minute intervention of U.S. airstrikes as ISIS surged toward Erbil the previous August, the city, home to some 850,000 people, might have become part of the caliphate. I asked the young driver if he thought the Kurds' fortunes would hold. He paused for a moment. "I think so," he said.

I was relieved to be away from Turkey. After Munzer and I had returned to Istanbul from our second meeting with Khalil, he had sent the intermediary who'd arranged our meeting surveillance photos taken of us during our trip, as a warning. Then, after we published our story about Khalil's operation, he invited us back to the border for another meeting, saying he had new information to share. The intermediary had caught wind of this and called with a warning. Someone from ISIS had gone through our previous articles about the group and ordered Khalil to discover the identities of contacts who'd shared information about its recruitment efforts in Turkey. The meeting was a trap.

The *peshmerga* had a 650-mile front line with ISIS. Working in concert with continued U.S. airstrikes, via a command center in Erbil where U.S. and Kurdish officials monitored the battlefield on video feeds from American drones, the Kurds were slowly chipping away at the edges of the caliphate. The *peshmerga* had regrouped from their defeat in Sinjar, the mountainous scene of the Yazidi genocide, and become a key partner in a new kind of U.S. strategy, which had promised a war-weary public that America would defeat ISIS without deploying combat troops of its own. The United States could bomb ISIS from the skies all it wanted, but it needed local allies on the ground to do the fighting.

As we neared the Mosul Dam, which sat about thirty miles from the city, we began to roll through *peshmerga* checkpoints, where guards were scanning the civilian traffic for hidden fighters and bombs. Finally, the driver dropped us in a spot where only military vehicles were allowed to pass, and a *peshmerga* officer picked us up in a Toyota Land Cruiser.

Traveling closer to the front lines, we bumped down roads patrolled by SUVs packed with *peshmerga* and pickup trucks whose beds were outfitted with heavy machine guns manned by soldiers wearing ski masks to fight the cold. We crossed the dam, where the water of the Tigris River sat still and blue, and traveled into a small village called Wana to a street that had just been retaken from ISIS.

There, in the rubble of a small home, three young ISIS fighters lay dead at the foot of a crumbled wall. Sprawled on the ground, their long hair splayed, they had just the wisps of beards, and their eyes were turned skyward. The bodies stank, a smell like vomit, and had holes ripped through them; one was missing part of his chest, another one side of his head. Another was charred from a rocket-propelled grenade. There was the soft, wet sound of cats chewing at the flesh. A *peshmerga* soldier was gagging. He pressed a handkerchief to his face. Then he crossed the street, sat on a curb, put his head between his knees, and spit. He lit a cigarette. "I'd rather smell the smoke," he said.

The rest of his squad gathered around us at the curb. They spoke as if they'd been dispatching demons. "They are like animals, and they don't have brains to think," a lieutenant said. The young fighters had been left behind by the ISIS commander in the village, a sacrifice to slow the *peshmerga*'s advance as the ISIS unit retreated. Someone pointed out that the corpses had no shoes on. The fighters had been wearing only socks so that they could scamper more quietly through the pockmarked streets.

The sector commander arrived in a convoy of pickup trucks and SUVs and swaggered toward me, flanked by a contingent of fighters. A general in his sixties with a thick black moustache, he wore a traditional uniform, a brown tunic over baggy brown pants, and had a rifle on his shoulder. "All the houses here are full of their bodies," he said.

Known as Zaim Ali, or "Leader Ali," Omar Othman Ibrahim was one of the *peshmerga*'s most respected commanders, making his name in their long struggle against Saddam Hussein, a decades-long battle marked by mass executions and chemical weapons attacks at the hands of the dictator's forces. That fight burnished the *peshmerga*'s reputation for ferocity—*peshmerga* means "those who face death"—and they were legendary for the ability of men like Zaim Ali to take advantage of the Kurdish region's mountainous terrain in holding back more powerful forces. But they were fighting a different kind of enemy as they neared Mosul. Zaim Ali drove us to his base, and in the quiet of his office there, he admitted that his soldiers had been shaken by ISIS's extreme brand of warfare: waves of suicide bombers, vehicle-borne explosives, roadside bombs. "It would affect the will of any army in the world," he said. "There's car bombs, suicide bombs; you shoot someone, and he blows up. It's a lot different than in the past. The way of fighting has changed."

Like other soldiers and commanders I would meet in the days that followed across the *peshmerga* fronts, Zaim Ali was unsure of American intentions. Even for one of the country's top commanders, it was hard to read the U.S. commitment. In Washington, the Obama administration was still debating even the number of military trainers and advisors it might send, worrying about the semantics of whether the media and public might consider them "boots on the ground." Zaim Ali said he appreciated the airstrikes—without them, the Kurds would likely be overrun. Yet he was wary of America dragging out a war from afar that required the Kurds to take daily casualties. "You cannot just say that you are at war with ISIS," he said. "If you want to be in a war, you have to be on the ground, face-to-face."

In the corner of the country between Mosul and Syria, home after home had been flattened by U.S. strikes, across village after village. A *peshmerga* colonel, Galal Alenky, showed us the wreckage of a pickup that had been hit by a U.S. strike as ISIS militants, using the machine gun in its bed, fired on him and his men. On the ground were singed ammo boxes and a shredded bulletproof vest. "These places that we liberated—it was not easy," Alenky said. "We sacrificed for them with blood."

The forty-seven-year-old headed a battalion based in the shadow of the Sinjar Mountains, where thousands of fleeing Yazidis had taken shelter from ISIS in the summer. The Kurds controlled the mountains and the villages to its north. ISIS still controlled most of Sinjar town. The clothes and toys that had been cast away by the Yazidis in their panic still littered the dirt along the road that led from the town to the mountains. The *peshmerga* had pushed into the edge of the town weeks earlier, but their attack had bogged down into bitter street fights. Alenky said ISIS wouldn't be rolled back easily. "They're coming from around the world," he said. "And they're not afraid to die. They don't turn back."

America's presence around the front was something like a deity's, everywhere and nowhere at once, amid the rubble and the distant rumble of the strikes. Soldiers tried to divine the Obama administration's intentions. Some wanted it to send combat troops. Others, like Alenky, rejected the idea, saying the United States had sacrificed enough to Iraq. "What we are doing is for us. We do it for honor," he said. But he still felt in the dark about U.S. plans.

The *peshmerga* had recently uncovered several mass graves in the region, in areas newly won from ISIS. They contained victims of the Yazidi genocide.

The first we saw had been exhumed a week earlier. It was in a farming village, and the dirt path to the hole where the bodies had laid was rugged and long, winding past a farmhouse and then off-road through muddy, rock-strewn grass, ending at a quiet shore of the Mosul Dam Lake. It seemed a long way for ISIS militants to have taken their captives—some twenty men plus a woman and child—for execution. The locals couldn't say for sure why they had chosen such a serene place. All they left behind were the corpses, piled together with their hands bound behind their backs and covered with dirt haphazardly. A sixty-year-old man from the village explained how the bodies had been found with "holes in their heads, like an execution." He kicked through the dirt of the grave to reveal bullet casings and faded clothes. The victims, he said, were Yazidi farm laborers. No one had come to identify the bodies.

A second grave sat outside another village in a field beside a poultry farm. The *peshmerga* had found it when the farm's owner, who'd returned when the area was freed, saw dogs pawing the dirt. Although the bodies had been exhumed the previous week, a long pit dug six feet into the ground still bore signs of the ISIS rampage. Possessions of the victims, such as a dusty toy unicorn, remained, and splashes of blood caked into the top of the pit marked a spot where some men had been beheaded. Alenky said that twenty-four bodies had been uncovered there. Small fragments remained: hair, a rib bone, teeth. "Nobody could believe that this would be here," Alenky said.

He arranged a convoy of armed pickup trucks to take us to a grave site that had yet to be exhumed because it was still within ISIS mortar and sniper range. I had spoken the previous night to a man who'd watched the massacre through a pair of binoculars from a nearby village. First he'd seen ISIS militants round up Yazidi men, women, and children at a traffic intersection. The women and children had been dragged away, and then the men were gunned down with assault rifles and buried in shallow graves. A similar scene was repeated later that night. "We could see the men in the headlights of [ISIS's] cars, and we could hear their screams," the man said. The next day, a water truck washed the blood from the street.

Grey clouds reached down toward the mountains around us as we stepped out from the convoy and approached the graves. *Peshmerga* watched for ISIS movements from a sandbagged post on a ridge. The graves were small mounds of earth along a roadside. The fighters who'd escorted us gathered around as I stood there staring at the scraps of clothing and Yusuf paced methodically with his camera, its shutter clacking. Some of the soldiers crouched in the dirt, using sticks to dig for clues about the people inside. So far, only one of the victims had been identified: an electrician and father of three whose ID card had been unearthed. The other clues that the men were picking through were testament only to the carnage: a pair of underwear, shards of bone, a patch of flesh.

"ISIS, they are animals," someone said.

He was tall and thin, sixty-six years old, with a thick, black moustache and a hardened aspect that was both calm and something beyond angry. Under his jacket he wore tan fatigues, and so did several of the young men standing behind him in their woolen caps and scarves. I learned that these men were Yazidis who had volunteered with the *peshmerga* after the genocide. One of them guessed that he had three relatives buried in the graves at our feet. Another said nine or ten. Sinjar town sat just beyond the cloud-touched mountains, and as the *peshmerga* continued their slow march, more sites like this would be discovered. One of the Yazidi fighters said that in his village alone, more than five hundred people were still unaccounted for. As Yusuf photographed and I took notes, the Yazidi men stood silently, staring into the wind, standing straight as rods.

For a while I kept a photo that Yusuf had taken of that moment on a wall above my desk. The photo evoked the swirl of different currents that war brought forth in me: weakness and defiance, revulsion and admiration, nihilism and belief. It is centered on the old man. His comrades stand in a row behind him, and behind them are the mountains and the clouds. All of them stare as one at something beyond the frame. The photo is aligned so that the old man is level. But the world around him is tilted—the road, the white pickup and its mounted machine gun, the mountains, the clouds. It's as if someone took the man from the photo, turned it ten degrees counterclockwise, and put him back in place. This was a feature of many of the photos Yusuf took on our assignments together. To me it was an expression of the countercultural spirit that defined him, which at one point had led him to Avenue C in lower Manhattan, to run a bar frequented by legendary drunks and jazzmen, and at another had led him to join me with his camera in places like Egypt, Syria, and Ukraine. In a world that thought it was up and down, Yusuf saw things sideways. And the way he framed his subjects and their suffering seemed to insist that sideways was reality.

I left Iraq after visiting the graves and returned three weeks later with Ayman Oghanna, a twenty-nine-year-old photographer of British and Iraqi descent who approached his work differently than Yusuf did. He came at the war with ISIS as if it were a personal struggle, and in a way it was for him. He'd been working in Iraq since 2009, through many tough and ugly assignments, and his photos had a haunted and angry quality. They were raw and often up close, seeming to say, *Fuck you. Look.*

Ayman had grown up in London and spoke with an almost aristocratic accent that managed to complement his gruff and scattered personality. He was six-foot-four with jet-black hair and crystal-blue eyes and barreled through life with the haphazard grace of a figure skater who seemed always about to fall. His mother was English, his father an Iraqi Christian from Kirkuk, a Kurdish city south of Erbil. He felt his Iraqi roots deeply and was on a never-ending mission to wrangle a passport from the country's authorities. He was always working on his Arabic. During a previous trip to Baghdad, after several difficult days of work, we had resolved to unwind by getting as far as we could into a bottle of Scotch. I put the bottle on an end table between a pair of chairs, and Ayman called down to the front desk to order ice. There was some confusion, and I heard Ayman repeating himself in Arabic: "Yes! Bring a lot. Yes, I'm sure!" We waited, complaining that the hotel's service had reached a new low. Finally, there was a hesitant knock on the door, and I jumped up to answer it. Before me stood a nervous teenaged attendant holding a great pile of bananas. In Turkey, where Ayman lived, the word for ice is similar to the Arabic word for banana, and he must have mixed them up. The boy had put the bananas on a platter and wrapped them in saran, unsure perhaps how to present them to a guest who wanted so many so aggressively. He held the platter out to me as his eyes moved between the bottle on the table and the two large and sad-looking men.

In Erbil, Ayman and I hired a Kurd in his fifties who once worked as a translator for U.S. special forces, and together we headed to the front lines. I'd arranged an embed with the unit of *peshmerga* specialists tasked with dealing with IEDs. Extremist groups had relied on these devices in prior wars—they were employed expertly against U.S. forces by the Taliban in Afghanistan and al-Qaeda in Iraq and in both of those conflicts had caused most of the American casualties. But ISIS was using them on a scale never seen before, laying them out en masse in a tangle of defensive lines around Mosul and the rest of its territory. It seemed as if it would take an eternity for the local troops to cut through them. In towns and villages that the *peshmerga* had freed from ISIS control, residents returned to their homes only to be maimed by hidden explosives planted beneath a floor tile, or set off by a chain in a ceiling fan, or rigged to explode when they turned on the stove. And ISIS had deployed IEDs across the landscape, burying them in fields and hiding them along roads. The weapons were exploding on soldiers and civilians alike.

The *peshmerga* specialists battling this were part of a small unit of explosive ordnance disposal (EOD) technicians. They were mostly just engineers, I found, who had been trained to build military bases and bridges. Some of the older ones had dealt with Saddam-era land mines. Those factory-made devices could often be disarmed with a switch, but each batch of the new IEDs was unique; many had intricate designs. Often they were rigged with special traps to kill the EOD technicians who tried to defuse them. It was a deadly game, the bomb makers and the technicians each representing an opposing side, destruction and preservation, as they tried to get inside the minds of their adversaries.

At one EOD outpost adjacent to a military base, beyond a rusty metal gate, sat a collection of defused bombs, a library of the tricks and techniques they contained. The IEDs that the specialists had uncovered were often simple and complex at once. They could be made with basic items like paint, fertilizer, kitchen pots, and jerry cans. They could also have sophisticated components, like a cell phone the militants called to trigger the bomb when the specialists arrived or a device that detonated it if moved. The vast territory and resources ISIS controlled allowed it to produce some IEDs on a near industrial scale: the specialists believed there were workshops or factories. One type of IED they'd found often outside Mosul had a shell made from oil pipeline. A thick metal cylinder was cut and welded with precision, with a hole for the fuse drilled on one end. The explosives were packed in so tightly that a captain at the base said it had taken thirty minutes to spoon them out. He thought the packing had been done by machine.

The EOD technicians lived in fear of assassination; I couldn't publish their names or photos with their faces. They also refused to tell me their casualty figures, but they were losing specialists with almost every operation.

Crater after crater lined a road to the front outside Kirkuk, sixty miles south of Erbil, where a *peshmerga* colonel and his men worked to detonate IEDs under an afternoon sun. Pickup trucks full of camouflaged soldiers took care to straddle the median as they passed, wary of the edges of the road. The EOD team had dispatched around forty-five IEDs that day in controlled detonations, showering dirt onto the asphalt. Across a field from the road was a collapsed house where, the previous day, an IED had killed four of their colleagues.

The *peshmerga* had defused or detonated more than 6,000 IEDs since August. Those were the ones they'd been able to find. The colonel pointed to the fields that stretched to a set of hills on one side of the road and the village with the flattened home on the other. "To be honest, we believe that those open fields beneath the hills, and the hills, are filled with IEDs. All those houses are full of IEDs," he said.

The technicians were scanning the fields with old airport security wands. I learned that they had little training from their American allies and lacked modern tools like signal jammers, X-rays, and robots. One specialist recounted a U.S. soldier calling the EOD teams "insane" when he saw how they worked. They scanned for trip wires with laser pointers. Even their metal wire cutters were dangerous. Most professional EOD technicians used plastic or ceramic ones to avoid short-circuiting the bombs. Those were available in the United States for $20 on Amazon, but the colonel told me they'd been unable to find them in Iraq. They were using what they could buy at the local hardware store.

Six months into the U.S.-backed military campaign, the colonel and his men had a single Mine-Resistant Ambush Protected (MRAP) vehicle, which had been donated by Italy. After crawling into the fields with the airport wands and attaching the explosive charges to the bombs, they would crawl into the MRAP, unspooling wire behind them like kite string. Then, protected by the hulking vehicle, they detonated the bombs. It was painstaking and dangerous—and they were clearing only the bombs along the roadsides so military vehicles could reach the slowly receding front lines. Soldiers winced as stray dogs trotted through the fields around them.

Three hundred yards or so away sat a small cluster of houses, and when a man pulled up in a car and entered one of them, a technician shook his head. "We told them not to come back yet, but they never listen," he said.

The next day we accompanied the colonel and his team on an emergency call on the front lines, bouncing in the back of a pickup truck as the men fastened the straps on their helmets. The *peshmerga* had just taken a village called Mullah Abdullah. Smoke rose from pools of oil that had been set ablaze to obscure the view of U.S. aircraft. The *peshmerga* unit that had regained the village wandered the streets in a post-battle daze, their adrenaline subsiding. Beside a house at the center of the village was a sedan packed with explosives and covered with a tarp. Soldiers watched warily as the colonel and his officers approached the car. I began to take big steps back, wondering if someone with a remote detonator was waiting to kill the EOD team. A few minutes passed, and Ayman walked up to see what was happening. Then he was running toward me, waving with both hands. "Move back, move back," he yelled. "They're poking it with a stick!"

We retreated about a hundred yards. Soon there were *peshmerga* around us. One of them turned to me. "Sir, do you think we're back far enough?" he asked, thinking I was an American soldier. *I'm not the one who can help you*, I wanted to scream.

We moved back and back and back some more. No distance seemed great enough. Finally, I stood with some soldiers on a porch about a half a mile away. The colonel and his team did their controlled detonation, and the air cracked with such force that it knocked the wind out of me. The windows of the house behind me burst, and from the direction of Mullah Abdullah came a shower of debris.

———·———

The situation was even worse on the war's other front lines. The Iraqi EOD team based at an interior ministry compound in Baghdad was considered one of the world's most experienced; its members had worked alongside American experts all through the occupation and then continued on their own. When I met them at their headquarters, I found them dejected and demoralized, their equipment in need of replacement and repair. The technicians were struggling to manage the frequent car bombs that ISIS was sending into the capital, and a bell rang at regular intervals, calling out teams to address suspected IEDs around the city. A lieutenant told me that the scale of the IED threat was leaving much of the disposal work to be handled by amateurs among the Iraqi military and Shia militia. "Unfortunately the whole place has become a front line. And we have to work fast," he said. "We don't have time to clear everything."

The officer in charge of the EOD division said his teams across Iraq were overwhelmed. He criticized America for not doing more to help, saying that the technicians were relying on robots and other tools that the United States had given them a decade ago. "It's not just people. I don't have enough equipment," he said. He had hosted some EOD workshops for Shia militia to fill the gaps, he added, "but it's not enough."

"I've been in the field so long and still can't consider myself an expert. These people have been coming to the field in just the last year," he added. "We are familiar with IEDs. But the difference is the number and the quality and the amount of explosives they pack into each. It gets bigger and bigger."

The Shia militia had helped to fill out the government's lines, rushing into battle with Iranian advisors and turbaned clerics. I traveled with them to a neighborhood they'd recently won in Tikrit, Saddam Hussein's birthplace. Searching for EOD technicians there, I learned that their definition of one was anyone willing to do the job. A former police officer told me he'd taken a one-week course in Baghdad, and "after that I had to go out in the field to learn." Another young fighter working to disarm the IEDs said he'd had no training at all. One militia officer, a retired Iraqi general, said his men tried to smell for explosives and that when they suspected there were IEDs along a road or in a home, their first response was often to try to detonate them with bullets or grenades. Otherwise the amateur specialists just walked up to the bombs and winged it. I asked him how he could allow his men to take such risks. "We have to," he said. "We are in a crisis right now."

In Anbar province, west of Baghdad, Ayman and I embedded with a militia called the Badr Brigades that was said to be among the most professional. When I told the soldiers that I was interested in meeting their EOD technicians, they told us to follow them on foot down a war-torn road. We walked between burned-out buildings and decapitated palm trees. Eventually, they informed us that we were standing in the middle of an IED minefield. There were no EOD technicians to be found, but one of the soldiers pointed to a mound of earth beside us. It was topped with a bright green set of Shia prayer beads. He didn't realize that the bomb could be set off by the vibrations from our footsteps. Felled power lines and copper wire were strewn about our path. "Don't ever step on the other side of this road," another fighter said. Later, elsewhere in Anbar, the commander of another militia guided Ayman and me with confident strides down a bridge where his own amateur technicians were working. I glanced down and saw that they'd missed at least one IED. The toe of my boot was a few inches from one of its pebble-sized pressure triggers.

CHAPTER 15

PASSPORTS

Istanbul, Turkey. May 2015.

BACK IN ISTANBUL, I THOUGHT OF IEDS EACH TIME I STEPPED OFF the sidewalk and onto the grass of a crowded promenade along the Bosporus, where I sometimes jogged. The city buzzed with the start of the tourist season as visitors from around the world wandered the streets: a European couple posing with a selfie stick, a stocky American in a Red Sox hat, a pack of Thai tourists trailing a flag-wielding guide.

One afternoon, at a café near central Istanbul's Taksim Square, Munzer and I had tea with a former member of ISIS who had worked in its media department but said he'd recently defected. He was trying to make a living in the war-fueled underworld that now extended to Istanbul. He said he had a friend in Raqqa who'd found a stash of dozens of passports belonging to ISIS's Western members. He wanted to sell the documents, but after Munzer and I told him we didn't pay for information, he agreed to give us a photo of one passport for free. It belonged to a twenty-five-year-old American named Sam Neher.

Back at my apartment, I looked Neher up online. As far as I could tell, he was at school at the University of Michigan, happily pursuing a medical degree. I found his student email address and sent him a message, telling him how I'd come across him. His reply arrived a few hours later. "My only connection to Istanbul is I've been there on vacation. How did you get this email?" he wrote. "I'm a bit weirded out."

We spoke by phone the next day. Neher said he'd taken a trip to Istanbul with his girlfriend in December 2014. They visited the Hagia Sophia, the historic mosque whose dome defines the city's skyline, and wandered through the Grand Bazaar, the covered market that has drawn tourists and pickpockets alike since the fifteenth century. Then Neher checked his black travel bag—or "man purse," as he called it—and saw that the pouch where he kept his passport was empty. He trekked out to the massive U.S. consulate on a hill in Istanbul's suburbs, reported the passport stolen, and received a temporary ID. From there he continued on his trip, considering the passport incident "just a blip."

Curious about what had happened to Neher's stolen passport, Munzer and I began to search for answers. As we did, we heard versions of the same story that the former ISIS media man had told. A rebel claimed his battalion had captured dozens of passports from an ISIS office, and he too agreed to show us a photo of one of them. This time, the passport belonged to a twenty-one-year-old Minnesotan, who told me he'd had his passport "nabbed" by a thief on a Barcelona beach. A Syrian activist sent us two more photos that were making the rounds. One showed the passport of a college sophomore in Boston who had just helped bring a championship to her varsity rowing team. The other, once again, was Neher. "There are a lot of people who would pay a lot of money for this stuff," the activist said.

None of these people were connected to ISIS—and I guessed that the claims to the contrary were just a scheme to trick spies and unscrupulous journalists into buying the information. At the same time, I thought that what had happened to Neher's passport offered a unique window into the refugee crisis that ISIS was working to weaponize and the blurring of identities that went with it. Just as there was no real international push to end the conflict, there was no plan to deal with the exodus it had created, which was pushing the global number of refugees to levels unseen since

World War II. The migrants drowning in the Mediterranean were one symptom. The booming market in stolen passports was another—one that also showed the Syrian conflict's unusual reach.

Munzer and I took a taxi to Aksaray, the smuggling district where he'd spent his first days in Turkey, just a twenty-five-minute walk west of the Grand Bazaar. We found it packed more than ever with Syrians. Refugees crowded around a fountain in the main square; word of mouth told them that if they waited there, they might find a smuggler who could help them reach Western Europe. Passage on the deadly sea route was running between $2,500 and $6,000, and to pay it, many Syrians, along with Iraqis and migrants from forgotten places like Afghanistan and Eritrea, were parting with everything they had.

We knew a veteran human trafficker, Samir, who worked from an office in Aksaray. Migrants holding ragged suitcases and cheap orange life jackets milled about the building's entrance. We found him sitting, as usual, in a brown leather jacket behind his heavy wooden desk as assistants tended to the migrants who filtered in and out, writing their names on the ship registers and taking wads of American dollars and Turkish lira. Samir was a tall, gaunt man with the hungry smile of a hyena. He seemed to enjoy the visits Munzer and I paid him, especially when we brought whiskey. A Syrian refugee himself, he'd started in the business by canvassing the parks and streets of Aksaray for the established smugglers. Now he was a powerful operator, working under the protection of the Turkish mafia. He arranged boats to Europe from the Turkish city of Izmir, 250 miles south, sending his clients down from Istanbul on special buses that departed from a park near his office. The story going around about Samir was that someone close to him had drowned on one of his ships. Every time I asked about it, he would drop his brash demeanor and tell me quietly that it was a story for another day.

Samir had found another way to get migrants to Europe that was far more expensive than the journey by boat but also much safer. It involved getting clients with fake or stolen passports onto commuter planes. To make the scheme work, Samir needed Western passports—and there were thousands to be had for him and the city's other traffickers.

Samir took out an iPad, pressed the screen a few times, and turned it around to show me. On it was a vast digital marketplace for stolen passports; with a finger he scrolled through them. Occasionally, a refugee's headshot had been pasted beside the info page to see if it was a good fit. One balding Syrian had a doppelganger in a European passport. "The same, eh?" Samir said.

When he found a match for a client, Samir arranged a complicated scheme that allowed migrants to use the passport at airports in Turkey and Greece, where they boarded planes bound for wealthy European countries like Norway and Germany. The venture was more expensive than the sea route, costing up to $17,000, and more difficult to pull off. It often involved traveling between various cities and changing documents in mid-air, depending on which passports might work in which airport security lines. When Syrian refugees arrived in their target country, they surrendered to authorities and requested asylum. It was worth the money and the struggle, Samir said, to reach Europe safely.

A machine that scanned passports and tested their validity sat on a corner of his desk. When a passport is reported stolen, it gets flagged in an international database kept by Interpol. But border authorities receive an alert only if they check the passport against this database, and often they don't. Samir and the other traffickers worked with colleagues around Europe who acted like an advance army, probing every airport for weaknesses. Smugglers like Samir were buying the passports from criminals who stole them in Istanbul and across Europe. Sometimes people with U.S. or European passports even sold them, Samir said, since replacing them was relatively cheap. "It's easy for you to get another passport," he said. "But for Syrians, if they have the passport, it's holy like the Quran."

Syrians were dying by the crowded boatload trying to reach Europe's shores, but a Western passport offered a chance at salvation far removed from the dehumanizing journey by sea. With a passport like

Neher's in hand, a Syrian whose own identity had been shattered in the conflict could take on a new one, for a few hours at least, and board a plane.

The passport schemes were another way to see how the boundaries of the conflict were fading. I could sense it in Istanbul, as the Turkish government careened toward dictatorship, the security services were riven by infighting, and sources whispered that ISIS had established cells across the country. The first ISIS attack in Turkey was still a couple of months away, but as I walked the streets of my neighborhood, I imagined how it might change with violence—how the cheers from the basketball court, the happy bustle of the dog park, the laughter of kids on swings could in a blink become a distant memory. I wasn't the only one. My Turkish neighbors confided that they, too, were gripped by a rising unease, and I knew that the Syrians living in the country could feel it too. Many had already given up on returning home. The threat was just too great, whether from the regime and its airstrikes, or from ISIS, or from other militants. Europe offered hope: a chance to get a job, continue an education, move on with their lives.

While my U.S. passport gave me the freedom to travel almost anywhere, a Syrian passport was extremely restrictive, with the United States and most European countries requiring entry visas that were all but impossible to obtain. One afternoon in Samir's office, I found myself sitting next to a bulky Syrian who kind of looked like me. He had a friend sitting next to him, who pointed out that a simple handoff could change the man's life: "You want to share your passport with this guy so he can go?"

The friend, who was also Syrian, spoke in fluent English with a northeastern accent. "Call me Joshua," he said, when I asked his name. He said that his wife and daughter, both U.S. citizens, lived in Connecticut. He had called the United States home for more than fifteen years before getting deported after a brush with the law, landing in his native Damascus just before the war. He recounted the horrors he'd witnessed there with disbelief, and he was nervous about the journey ahead, which would find him crammed into the hold of a rickety ship, praying not to die. "I have no choice, man," he said.

At a restaurant in the city center, Munzer and I met the Syrian man who had concocted the story that the passports of Neher and the other young Americans belonged to ISIS fighters. He'd never even had the actual passports in his possession, he said—just photographs of them, like the ones on Samir's iPad.

"I know this one," he said, when I showed him Neher's.

He was rail-thin, with cigarette burns on his dress shirt. One day in the spring, he'd gotten his hands on a cache of the photos, each showing a different stolen Western passport. He sent the photos to some activists who worked around the border, and pretty soon they were being marketed by entrepreneurs, like the former ISIS media man, as alleged foreign fighters. Their images became something like trading cards—sent from smartphone to smartphone across borders and cities. Thousands of Westerners were believed to be with ISIS, and the value of information about them was rising. Governments didn't know for sure which of their citizens had slipped into the war and worried who might be coming back.

The thin man attributed the passport scam to desperation. Everything in Syria was for sale, not just information—from artifacts and oil to factories, carted away piece by piece—and people were doing what they could to manage as citizens of a country that no longer existed. He'd been a successful engineer before the war. Now, he conceded, he often spent his nights sleeping in the park across the street. "I wish I could use my passport to go to another country," he said. "If I had money, I would buy a stolen passport and do it directly."

Soon after, with Samir's help, we tracked down Neher's passport. It had never left Istanbul and sat in the hands of another trafficker. He wouldn't meet me, worried about being seen with an American, but he agreed to see Munzer. At one of Aksaray's cafés, he put the passport on the table and let Munzer leaf through it. The trafficker said he'd bought it from another smuggler for $700.

He showed Neher's passport to some colleagues at another table, trying to figure out where it came from, and someone placed a call to the man who'd plucked it from Neher's travel bag. The thief entered the café about an hour later and produced an iPad that he'd stolen earlier that day from a tourist near the Grand Bazaar, one of his favorite haunts. "I can take everything, from people and from shops," he told Munzer. "If you want to buy anything expensive, just call me, and I will steal it and sell it to you for half the price." Whenever he managed to steal a passport, he sold it to smugglers. So did other thieves in Istanbul and elsewhere, well aware of the rising value of a Western identity.

The trafficker said he'd had trouble finding a buyer for Neher's passport so far—he was still searching for the right face. Once he found him, he added, "I will send him to Europe."

I called Neher in Michigan to let him know his passport's fate. "I suppose if it can help the refugees, it's not all bad," he said.

CHAPTER 16

ARTIFACTS

Southern Turkey. June 2015.

MUNZER AND I WAITED AT A RESTAURANT TABLE I'D RESERVED, smoking in the pleasant air of a late-May evening. Mohamed, the former oil smuggler, had come to town, and he arrived in a button-down shirt and leather jacket. He was with a friend, Talib, and as we ate, they explained why they'd come to Istanbul: to sell an ancient statue that Mohamed had procured. Talib was a veteran trader in illicit artifacts and had agreed to introduce Mohamed to potential buyers in exchange for a percentage of the sale. The buyers they had in mind were Turkish, but they were sure that once a deal was completed, the statue would make its way to Europe, where it could fetch more money.

Syria was disintegrating. Its towns and cities were destroyed, its people were leaving, and, piece by piece, it was losing its history. Western countries were barring Syrian refugees, but buyers there were creating a market for looted Syrian antiquities. As masses of desperate Syrians languished in camps on the fringes of the West, antique coins and statues and other valuable artifacts from Syria were appearing in the homes and private collections of the wealthy. In Europe and America, as people tried to ignore what was happening in Syria, men like

Talib and Mohamed, the trafficker Samir, the hostage negotiator Nabil, and the ISIS operative Khalil were going about their work, each in his own way dependent on the Western market. Throughout our dinner, Talib stayed engrossed in his Android phone, which chimed constantly with WhatsApp alerts. Contacts around Syria and Turkey were sending him photos of new items on the market, asking his opinion of their value and trying to gauge his interest. He gave off a sense of wonder, almost joy, as he explained some of the objects to me. In the glow of his screen, he had the aspect of a veteran tomb raider sifting through a treasure chest.

Soon after, Munzer and I traveled south to meet with Talib and other members of his underground trade. I wanted to learn more about what I considered to be one of ISIS's greatest strengths: its ability to use the desperation surrounding the war in Syria to make itself stronger. The trade in artifacts seemed to embody that—and unlike with the oil trade, it was buyers in the West who were providing much of the demand. The sale of illicit antiquities was an important revenue stream for ISIS, which was facing economic pressure as it fought military campaigns on multiple fronts and U.S. strikes targeted its oil refineries. ISIS wasn't the only group doing this—everyone from the Nusra Front to the Free Syrian Army used artifacts to raise funds—but it was the most effective. It was organizing its own teams to dig through historic sites and granting licenses to others, effectively legalizing the trade in the territory it held and taxing it.

We visited Talib in a border town. "Come," he said, and led us into a bedroom.

On the floor was an old carpet, rolled up and grimy. Talib unfurled it, releasing the smell of earth into the humid air. Inside the carpet was an ancient mosaic, and as he stepped onto it, a fine white dust covered his bare feet. The dust covered the mosaic too, obscuring a scene by an unknown artist from antiquity. "Put some water here," Talib said, clicking the trigger on a spray bottle. "It will become clear." First a man's face appeared on the stones. He wore a crown and sat upon a throne. Talib sprayed water to the right, and there was a soldier leading a prisoner with bound hands. The king held his palm above the prisoner, passing judgment. "First look at his eyes," Talib said, his bottle still clicking. "You will think they are real and they have souls."

Looters had found the mosaic in Syria, in the floor of an ancient villa that the passage of time had seen buried underground.

Tall and athletic, with intense brown eyes, Talib crouched down to scoop up some stones that had come loose from the mosaic, dropping them into a plastic bag. When he began dealing in stolen antiquities, in 2003, he was hoping to make a better living under a dictatorship with few options for ambitious men with no ties to the ruling elite. Now he was a veteran of a trade that had exploded with the chaos of the war, using the money to support his extended family.

An untold number of people had joined Talib in a booming black market. Many of the newcomers had no interest beyond making money, but Talib was enamored with the history of the ancient objects he traded. Known among his colleagues for having an expert eye, his phone buzzed with newly arrived photos each time we met. People asked him to come and "talk" with their artifacts. "Falso," he would say, his voice rising, when he saw a forgery. If he liked a piece, he called it "fantastic," drawing out the word in English for effect.

His mosaic had been looted from Apamea, a city in northwestern Syria with vast ruins that were under rebel control. Talib said he bought it for $21,000 from a dealer in Syria and hoped to sell it for $30,000. He guessed it might change hands once or twice more from there—and that its final destination, like its original one in ancient times, would be a rich person's home.

Munzer and I spent over a month traveling along the border to meet people involved in this illegal trade, from the grave robbers and excavators who stole the artifacts to the middlemen and dealers who sold them. They told us that many of their artifacts were likely to eventually make their way to Western buyers, believing that unknowing and unscrupulous buyers in Europe and America were at the top of the market, the demand fueling everything that happened beneath them.

"We have been living in a war for more than four years, and people will do anything to feed their kids," said one middleman on the border, guilt ridden about his role in bleeding Syria's history. "I don't care if the artifact is coming from [rebels] or from ISIS. I just want to sell it."

In order for traders to sell antiquities, diggers around Syria worked daily to pull them from the ground. The digs ranged from backyard affairs by heavy-handed amateurs to skilled excavations. One man, a thirty-six-year-old Syrian, worked near Apamea with permission from a local rebel group, rolling a bulldozer over acres of land to turn up small artifacts or uncover clues that might lead to a greater score, such as an ancient burial cave. Inching through the chambers and reaching into tombs, he felt exhilarated. He might discover jewels that wealthy citizens of past empires had taken to the grave. Often, he said, "there are only bones."

On a warm evening, he and a colleague sat on the floor of a living room near the border and served tea as they waited out the last hour of the Ramadan fast. They were part of a team of six that split any money they made. They could go for weeks without a payday, sweating "for nothing" in the sun, the digger said.

"We feel bad because we are stealing our history and selling it for a cheap price," added his colleague. "But we have become homeless and jobless."

Another digger seemed motivated less by the potential profit than by the sense of possibility the work gave him in such hopeless times. "I dig because I like it, and if you start digging, then you will like it also," he said.

He said he and his fellow diggers had a name for themselves: "brothers of the sand."

For ISIS, the antiquities trade served twin goals. They wanted to erase pre-Islamic history in the areas they controlled. They also wanted to make money. One activist on the border sent us videos that he said came from a dig in Deir Ezzor province, which was still an ISIS stronghold. The videos showed workers in well-dug excavation pits near the Euphrates River, chiseling around artifacts and brushing them clean. The camera paused on old documents from a 2009 excavation suggesting the workers were in Dura-Europos, an important archaeological site that ISIS had looted extensively.

When I emailed the videos to Mark Altaweel, an archaeologist at University College London who had worked extensively in Syria, he was shocked by the professionalism. "This is like a proper excavation here. It's what we do!" he said. "These are people who have done this before."

A former museum worker from Deir Ezzor said he was struck by the extent of ISIS's antiquities operations when he saw them up close. When we met him at a café in Sanliurfa, in southern Turkey, he explained that his prewar job had involved restoring antiquities, taking him to museums and archaeological sites around the country. When the war started, he made rebel groups maps of places to search for artifacts and helped them dig. He cringed at the looting, he said, but hoped the money would pay for things like weapons and schools. When ISIS overran much of Deir Ezzor the previous summer, it offered him an ultimatum: work with us or die.

The first thing he noticed were the machines the extremists owned: metal detectors and treasure hunters that scanned the ground for buried objects. There were also bulldozers, hydraulic diggers, and boxes of dynamite.

ISIS allowed civilians with the know-how to dig on their own, granting them special permission and charging a 20 percent tax. The man said that it also employed special teams to target high-value sites. ISIS had asked him to decipher engravings in rocks that it believed were clues to ancient burial sites, a common local myth. "I told them I'm not a magician," he said, but he went to work. Eventually, he escaped to Turkey.

He gave me caches of photos of artifacts. Middlemen sent them from smartphone to smartphone, trying to find buyers. Some of the artifacts in the photos were fakes. Others were real, experts told me, and several of these objects had appeared on websites suspected of selling illegal antiquities. Many of the looted artifacts from across Syria had been uncovered only recently—and unlike those stolen from collections or museums, no one even knew they were missing.

In Antakya, a former lawyer and his business partner, a former car salesman, were the kind of middlemen who didn't have the funds to buy antiquities themselves. Instead, they used photos like those in the cache to line up buyers, aiming to take a commission. "This work became hope for people, because if you know someone with an artifact, and you help him sell it, then you can both earn some money," the former car salesman said, sitting in a small courtyard as canaries chirped in a cage. The business made it easy to see how, amid the desperation of the war, someone could take a series of steps, each of them logical or at least graspable in its immediate context, and end up, in one way or another, doing work that served ISIS. The former car salesman's partner, the ex-lawyer, said he was trying to earn enough to smuggle his family to Europe. "I don't want to keep watching my kids grow here and not be able to do anything for them," he said. "When I have enough money, I will stop this business. I will quit, I will break my phone, and all my contacts, and all my photos."

The pair told me they'd met Western buyers before. When a deal was in the works, they said, each side had the antiquity in question appraised by its own expert. Then they negotiated the price. The two men acknowledged that they didn't have much leverage. "In the end they know the Syrians will accept a low price, because we just want to sell it," the former lawyer said.

The lure of a potential payday got the better of them as the afternoon in the courtyard wore on. They took out a Ziploc bag full of old coins they said came from Syria, letting me dig through it. Then they asked if I was a buyer in disguise. I assured them I was a journalist, but the former car salesman took another stab: "Are you sure you don't want to buy something?"

———·———

The difficulty of establishing the provenance of looted Syrian antiquities, whose illicit origins were being obscured by middlemen like those in front of me, helped with trading them in the West. "There's almost no way to verify these things," said Altaweel, the University College London archaeologist. "How can you know when and where these things were acquired? It's just what the dealer tells you."

Expensive items could also be sold directly to collectors. "It's all about who is connected to whom," Altaweel said. "It's a very personalized trade."

To be traded legally, an item typically needs an export license from the government of the country where it was found or documents tracing its history to a private collection. But archaeologists and other critics of the legal antiquities trade—some of whom believe that artifacts shouldn't be bought and sold at all—said it had long been plagued by doctored paperwork. And tracing an object's path became harder the more it changed hands.

A veteran Syrian dealer who specialized in antique coins said it was common for them to be traded openly in the West. On top of being easy to smuggle, a coin dug up in Syria could have conceivably been found anywhere. He named a host of cities that minted coins in antiquity—Lyon, Antakya, Athens, Rome. "There is no proof it is coming from Syria," he said.

Other classical artifacts commonly found in Syria could likewise have been uncovered someplace else. "It's easy to make papers," the dealer said. "It's impossible to stop this business: in Europe, in the United States, in all the world."

Michael Danti, an archaeologist who spent twenty years surveying and excavating in Raqqa before the war, was directing a project, backed by the U.S. State Department, to document and track looted Syrian and Iraqi antiquities. "Almost all of the material we've seen is offered to people in Europe or to Europeans in Lebanon and Turkey," he said. "From there they ship it to places like Greece and Bulgaria, and they move it deeper into Europe."

Danti said long-established criminal networks handled much of the trade. High-value antiquities drew more scrutiny but were still being sold, he added. "Either trusted dealers will move them to North America or Europe or known buyers will acquire them directly," he said.

One day, as we visited Talib for dinner at his home, he became excited. There was a new item on the market that he badly wanted to see. It had fallen into the hands of a Turkish dealer who often came into possession of Syrian antiquities more expensive than Talib could afford. Talib decided to pay him a visit and invited Munzer and me to join.

We left early in the morning in Abu Salah's beat-up minivan, driving northeast through the mountains along the border until we reached the city of Gaziantep. The Turkish dealer—a gruff man in a pink polo shirt and jeans—then joined us in the van. He directed us out of the city as his partner followed us in a white sedan.

The man didn't seem to believe I was a journalist, but he was happy to have an American along for the ride. His best client, in fact, was an American, he said. He described the client as a man of about fifty who visited a few times a year with a translator. He said he worked for an American company; when I later researched the company, I found that archaeologists had long suspected it of dealing in conflict antiquities. "He is a really good guy," the Turkish man said of his American client. "And he pays a lot of money."

He took on the tone of a salesman at Istanbul's Grand Bazaar, claiming he'd never sell a fake to an American because this would be against Islam. He said the item we were headed to see was beautiful and repeated one of the few English words he knew several times: "Guarantee."

He added, in Turkish, "I swear on Obama's life."

We rolled for miles down a road with nothing but brown grass on either side, arriving finally at an isolated villa. The man and his partner led us inside. Talib sat on the floor of an airy den with windows that looked onto a mountainside. The man's partner brought in a small bundle covered in a white sheet. Talib unwrapped it eagerly. "Slowly, slowly," the partner said.

Inside was a copper statue about eighteen inches in height. It showed what appeared to be a deity from ancient Greece, with laurels in his hair and winged sandals on his feet. Talib traced his finger over veins that ran down the statue's arms.

He held it in his hands as if it were an infant, and then he brought it to his face, pressing his nose against its stomach and inhaling deeply. He was trying to sense the integrity of the patina—the green coating that comes with age—smelling for traces of paint that would tell him it was fake. Satisfied and glowing with a quiet intensity, he pulled a magnifying glass from his pocket and inched it over the statue, his right eye pressed against the lens. The room was silent.

Later, on the ride home, Talib said he thought the statue was authentic—and a "fantastic" find. He had in mind a buyer who lived in Turkey, he said, and for the right price, he could likely arrange a sale. I asked what would happen to the statue if it ended up in his buyer's hands.

"Direct to Europe," he said.

CHAPTER 17

BREAKING POINT

Sanliurfa, Turkey. August 2015.

ONE DAY IN EARLY JULY, AT AROUND 3:30 P.M., A SEDAN DRIVING past an empty school in downtown Raqqa exploded.

The car was hit by a missile from an American drone, becoming a heap of smoldering wreckage in an instant. Whoever had been in the vehicle was obliterated. So were the driver and passenger of a van driving behind the sedan, and a local delivery man, and a father and his young son who had been passing on a moped.

ISIS militants arrived soon after and ordered the small crowd of bystanders not to photograph anything. Then they picked up the pieces of the person or people who'd been inside the car, deposited them into a duffel bag, and sped away, leaving the dead civilians on the street.

American bombs were falling with increasing intensity on the caliphate's towns and cities. ISIS members were tying sheets and tarps between buildings to block the aerial view of the streets, and they were doing more than ever to blend in with civilians.

ISIS worked hard to keep civilians trapped in its territory. They were a revenue stream, thanks to the group's infamous tax regime, and could be used as human shields. It issued orders against leaving, killed some people who tried, and kept its territory ringed by checkpoints. It cost what some families considered a fortune to pay a smuggler to escape. Others looked at the sad situation of refugees in Turkey and decided that, if they had a job and a house, they were better off staying put. The U.S. airstrikes were just another thing they left to fate.

The attack outside the Raqqa school was recounted to Munzer and me by a twenty-seven-year-old Syrian who lived in an apartment across from it. He'd been at home when the explosion sent his mother and sister scrambling, screaming and crying. "I heard the bombing sound and I thought our building was hit," he said. "I cannot explain the feeling."

He met us, along with one of his neighbors, at a shopping mall in Sanliurfa, the city near the Turkish border that was receiving the majority of refugees from ISIS territory. He was in town to visit family; he still had a construction job in Raqqa. It was a crazy thing to be able to sneak across the border and a short drive later be in an air-conditioned center of modern commercialism, with Levi's and Burger King and a movie theater that played the latest Hollywood blockbusters.

He explained that when people fled Raqqa, ISIS often took their property in retaliation. As U.S. airstrikes intensified, a number of ISIS members had moved into his building and were now his neighbors. "They are living among us," he said.

"[The missile] hit the target, but the people around the target were affected," added his neighbor. "I saw the kid lying on the sidewalk, and I felt I couldn't walk."

The Obama administration had sold the American public on a certain kind of war. It was meant to be guilt-free. Keeping in line with that aim—and with no NGOs or journalists on the ground in ISIS territory to challenge the narrative—the United States insisted that its air attacks almost never killed civilians. As Munzer and I sought out victims and witnesses of those attacks, we saw that this was obviously not true.

Over the course of a month, we documented about a dozen cases where U.S. strikes had killed civilians but the official U.S. line was that only ISIS members had died. We knew there must be many more, and even U.S. diplomats privately told me the numbers were much higher. One man recounted how his father and mother were killed along with his two brothers, his sister, and her two children in one U.S. strike in July. A sixty-seven-year-old man described seeing "whole families" killed in another U.S. attack. One son lost his aging father; another lost his mom. A twenty-eight-year-old mother was sitting with her three children on their rooftop in Raqqa when a U.S. airstrike hit a nearby bridge. She saw something like a flash, she recalled, and a wall crumbled onto her kids. "It's like a moment, a second," she said. "I couldn't move; my tongue couldn't speak."

Rushing the children to safety through the suddenly chaotic streets, the woman saw someone carrying the body of a neighbor, his insides showing. She spent the next week at a cousin's home, where her three-year-old son refused to leave the bathroom, thinking it was safer from airstrikes. Then they fled to Turkey. As we spoke in a home near the border, the son sat timidly in her lap. She said that he was too scared to go outside.

In the port city of Iskenderun, a two-hour drive from Antakya, I met Talha Amouri outside the hospital where his two-year-old niece Nariman was on life support. She'd been at home in northern Syria one recent night when a U.S. missile streaked down from the sky. Talha was outside, and the explosion knocked him off his feet. He dug through the wreckage for hour after frantic hour, pulling out members of his family. He found five of his nieces—ages eight, seven, six, five, and three—dead. But Nariman clung to life, her arms locked around her mother, who had also survived. Nariman was rushed to a hospital near the Turkish border and then to the one in Iskenderun, where she lay beneath a web of tubes and bandages.

In addition to killing Nariman's five sisters, the strike had also wounded her pregnant mother, who suffered a miscarriage, and her older brother, who was recovering in Syria, according to doctors, witnesses, and relatives. They said three civilians were also killed in a house nearby: a fifty-five-year-old woman, her twenty-one-year-old son, and her seventeen-year-old daughter. The strike appeared to target a makeshift weapons depot near the homes that was used not by ISIS but by a rival rebel group.

I sent all the details I could gather to a public affairs officer from the U.S. military, who admitted that the coalition had conducted a strike in the vicinity. But she said the U.S. military had determined there were no civilian casualties. As proof of this, she cited aerial photos taken the day after the strike, saying they showed no evidence of destroyed houses.

Confirming that Nariman's home had been destroyed was as simple as calling a U.S.-backed rebel fighter in the town, who got on his moped, drove to the blast site, and sent me some photos of rubble. Like many houses in the village, the Amouris' had been small and made of concrete, making the wreckage hard to notice from the sky.

As Munzer and I sought out victims around southern Turkey, we realized that many people had no idea who had hurt them. Various nations were bombing Syria at once, and America's obfuscations about civilian casualties only exacerbated the bewildering chaos. Soon Russia would join Assad in attacking opposition towns and cities, showing far less concern than the coalition did for minimizing civilian harm and sometimes seeming to intend it, adding the power of its air force to the destruction.

With summer moving toward fall, the refugee crisis, already four years in the making, began to take on the feeling of an exodus. It seemed as if Syrians were realizing en masse that the country would never be put back together again. The number of migrants making the journey from Turkey to Europe was skyrocketing, with a record number of Syrians applying for asylum in EU countries. Munzer and I would call our friends and sources in southern Turkey and find that they were gone. Abu Salah, who had driven us up and down the border in his minivan, texted Munzer a shaky smartphone video that showed him piloting a small speedboat toward a Greek island off the Turkish coast; sometimes the traffickers gave discounts to passengers who agreed to captain these craft. As Abu Salah steered through a foggy dawn, his fellow migrants serenaded him with an Arabic take on "For He's a Jolly Good Fellow," their voices rising above the hum of the motor and the lapping of the waves.

The decisions to leave seemed sudden, but they were the result of years of suffering. I remembered all those times I'd heard Abu Salah and his wife screaming at each other on the phone, the stress of watching their children grow up in a refugee camp overcoming them. It was the piling on of misfortune, as unforgiving as the march of time. I knew a rebel commander, a defected colonel, whose battalion had U.S. backing and plans to bring the people engineers and a steady supply of bread. Their cause was hopeless; they were losing. We had dinner at a restaurant in Antakya, where he was a refugee. With him was a friend, who told me that one day early in the war, a tank had fired outside his house in Damascus. Tanks stink like rust and brown exhaust and grease, and the sound their canons make when they fire is an abomination, ear splitting, screeching. The tank fired right next to the house, when his son was three or four, and at that moment the boy had stopped talking. Years had passed—silence, suffering. At the schools in southern Turkey, the teachers tried to shuffle the boy to special ed. They gave no thought to psychological care, the man said. He threw his hands up: *What am I going to do?* This was one window into the breaking point many refugees were reaching. Eventually the colonel had enough and quit the war and moved his family to Germany. He had connections, so his family got visas, and they arrived in Germany legally, by plane. Most Syrians couldn't get visas to Europe, so they were going on the boats.

Western governments were becoming alarmed as they realized that the surge of new arrivals made them impossible to vet. At the same time, it was dawning on some that the refugee crisis was not just collateral damage from the war effort run by Assad and Moscow and Tehran but part of their strategy. Assad had lost control of about three-quarters of the country, and by making those areas unlivable, it was easier to regain control. The people fleeing were almost exclusively Sunni, meanwhile, meaning that each departure helped a government bent on promoting Shia-Alawite dominance accomplish its goal. And the refugee crisis was destabilizing many of the same countries that had united in support of the opposition. The more Muslim migrants poured into Western countries, the stronger far-right populist and isolationist currents there were becoming, promoting hostility not just to the newcomers but to institutions like NATO and the European Union. A terrorist attack on their own soil would only help them make their case.

Assad's jets bombed schools and hospitals and markets and homes. His forces carried out sieges that choked off food to opposition-held areas. Munzer and I called one man in northern Syria who described a recent attack from a barrel bomb—a crude device that was exactly what its name suggested, explosives packed into a barrel and dropped from a helicopter, relatively useless for attacking military targets but good for terrorizing civilians. He described the explosion as "like the sound of the god of death." Two-thirds of his village had already cleared out because of the almost daily attacks.

From a rebel-held Damascus suburb, a Syrian journalist described three recent massacres he had witnessed. In one, the government bombed a marketplace, killing more than one hundred people. Most of the dead were women and children. "I saw people turned to pieces," he said. Six days later another attack leveled an apartment building, and two days later an airstrike killed ten more civilians in their homes. A young mother in Daraa described how airstrikes had destroyed her family's home, and a Syrian photographer in the coastal province of Latakia recounted pulling bodies from the rubble of a market that was bombed. A man in Aleppo said government forces had fired a rocket into an apartment building, killing four people and wounding fifteen. "It's a scorched-earth policy," he said.

In Aksaray, orange life vests hung from shop stalls along the crowded streets. One vendor told me that his cheaper vests could only keep a man afloat for a few minutes and billed his more expensive versions as "guarantees." Syrians crammed into the parks by the dozens, waiting for the nightly buses the traffickers arranged to take their clients to the coast. Families carried black trash bags stuffed with their possessions. Munzer and I found one man sitting with his wife and two daughters on a park bench beside their bags and life vests. They'd been in Turkey for two years, ever since a massacre by government soldiers in their village near Damascus: first the village had been bombed, and then soldiers had executed residents whom they suspected of rebel sympathies. Some were "beheaded like chickens," the man said. "They want to empty the country."

He said the family wouldn't travel together, so that if the boat sank, they wouldn't all die at once. He was going first. His daughters seemed panicked about his departure. Buses idled at the edge of the park as Turkish policemen watched. The government had decided it was tired of hosting so many refugees and had eased up enforcement on the human traffickers. Another night, as Munzer and I sat in the office of Samir, the mafia-backed Syrian smuggler, a cop burst in. Samir jumped up from his desk, pulled out a wad of cash with a look of annoyance, and put it into the man's hand. The cop gestured for more, but Samir ended the transaction by sticking his middle finger in his face.

CHAPTER 18

DEATH COMES TO YOU

Sinjar, Iraq. November 2015.

THE YOUNG SOLDIER PAUSED TO TAKE A SELFIE ON THE BATTERED street. The *peshmerga* had just cleared ISIS from the town of Sinjar, but as his comrades fired bursts of celebratory gunfire, Azhar Khalaf Shamo wasn't smiling. He was a Sinjar native, a Yazidi, and he knew this street—he stood in front of what had been a family-run store. Now the entire block was rubble and metal scraps, like all the rest. "It's totally destroyed," Shamo said. "No place looks like before."

Sinjar had been ISIS territory since the young ISIS field officer known as Okab, or Eagle, stormed it a year earlier in the surprise attack that initiated the Yazidi genocide. Freeing Sinjar was meant to mark a turning point in the U.S.-led campaign to roll back the caliphate. The *peshmerga*, feeling redeemed, rolled through the town in a convoy of tanks and pickups, honking. I was walking with a column of *peshmerga*. U.S. airstrikes had been pounding Sinjar for days, and the soldiers stepped around collapsed buildings and downed power lines. An officer told them to keep to the middle of the street for fear of IEDs hidden in the jumbled roadside. The street was webbed with tangled wires. "Don't touch them, don't pull them," a soldier shouted.

Shamo was a Yazidi volunteer with the *peshmerga*. He looked dazed. He'd lost seven siblings to ISIS's rampage. At least 3,000 Yazidis were still believed to be in ISIS captivity. Childhood memories lingered as he walked: where I saw a pile of rubble indistinguishable from the rest, he saw a corner store where as a kid he'd bought ice cream. He stopped at another pile, the home of a man who'd seized the chance to take a Yazidi woman prisoner on the day ISIS arrived. "This was our neighbor," he said.

"I just came here to ease some of my pain," he continued. But the closure he'd hoped to find by returning as part of the liberating forces was proving elusive. "Yes, it is liberated. But how can we come back?"

That night, I joined a group of tired reporters at a hotel in Dohuk, the Kurdish city closest to Sinjar, and found myself wondering if the momentum of the war might finally be shifting. The road through Sinjar had been a key supply line for ISIS, linking Mosul and Raqqa, and disrupting it would set ISIS back on other fronts. Sinjar was also a symbolic victory for the *peshmerga* and their American allies. Kurdish officials had even promoted a hashtag for the battle: #FreeSinjar. With the battle won, the coalition would turn its attention to Mosul, preparing a major offensive to take the city where the caliphate had started.

I woke up the next morning and grabbed my phone to check the weather and learned that ISIS had launched a massive terrorist attack in Paris overnight. Militants had carried out coordinated strikes across the city, killing 130 people in a series of shooting rampages and suicide bombs. It was the deadliest attack in France since World War II and by far the largest ISIS attack in Europe, making it clear that they had opened up a new front. One of the assailants, who had come to Europe from Syria on a refugee boat, intentionally left a Syrian passport at the scene before he detonated his suicide vest. The attack boosted Europe's anti-immigrant and Islamophobe politicians as they rose in the polls, while in America, which was gearing up for the next presidential election in 2016, Donald Trump would soon call for a ban on Muslim visitors and immigrants as Obama warned people not to "turn against one another."

———·———

Even that morning, as I watched the news play out online, I could see the backlash. France announced that it would ramp up airstrikes in Raqqa in retaliation, with its president vowing to be "unforgiving with the barbarians." I knew that, from strongholds like Raqqa, ISIS leaders were planning their next assault; I also thought of the civilians who'd suffered so much from airstrikes already. I packed my rucksack and crossed the Iraqi border into Syria, where I rejoined the YPG, the Kurdish militia with whom Yusuf and I had embedded two years before. I visited the static front lines outside Raqqa, and I spent a night in a town near the Turkish border that the YPG had recently won from ISIS. As I drifted in and out of sleep, periodic gunshots rang out in the darkened streets, one to the west, another to the east, and I imagined assassins, revenge killings. The next day, at a community center, I met a mother and her eleven-year-old son who'd just escaped from Raqqa. They described the terror of the airstrikes and of evading ISIS militants as they snuck away to safety. The woman asked me to extend a plea to Western governments on behalf of the friends and family she'd left behind: "Be merciful to the people of Raqqa."

I drove to the border gate and looked through the fence to the spot where, from the Turkish town of Akcakale, I'd once watched traders wheel their laden carts into the caliphate. In the basement of a building near the customs office, there had been an ISIS prison, where civilians were held just a stone's throw from safety, within shouting distance of the Turkish border guards and life in a NATO country. Above the stairs that descended into this underground prison, the jihadis had scrawled a warning: "Forbidden to enter."

At the bottom, a dusty chair sat in darkness behind a heavy desk. An ISIS guard once kept watch there, but now the prison was empty. The only sound was dripping water, and the only relics of the terror inflicted on the captives were the messages on the walls. One had met new arrivals at the desk: "Death comes to you. God is great."

The largest room in the basement was reserved for those who were to be beheaded. Qurans were stacked atop a radiator—prisoners were told to read them as they awaited their fates. Another directive was graffitied outside the door: "Do not approach."

The prisoners were kept in small rooms down the hall. They scratched and penciled cryptic phrases onto the concrete walls. "Ask forgiveness from God," read one. Said another, "God also has mercy."

Some had written their names. A few kept tallies of their time there—one stopped at forty-six days. Others left only phone numbers. The digits appeared on wall after wall.

By the light of a cell phone, I wrote the numbers down in my notebook.

When I returned to Istanbul, Munzer and I began to call them. Most of the lines were dead. But a soft-voiced man answered one of them. "How did you get this number?" he asked.

We met him soon after in Sanliurfa, the Turkish city across the border from where the prison sat, sipping tea in the courtyard of our hotel.

The man, twenty-six, said he'd been brought to the prison with his father in the spring of 2014. They'd worked together as vegetable vendors before the war but turned, in their desperation, to smuggling cigarettes. ISIS militants caught them and put them in one of the concrete rooms. It remained vivid in his mind. "I can never forget it," he said.

He sipped his tea anxiously. He remembered thinking he would die in the prison as he added his own number to those already on the walls. Another prisoner told him, "If they kill you, maybe someone can tell your family you were here."

His hands trembled as he spoke. Though he'd survived the prison, he worried that ISIS was monitoring him and was afraid to discuss it. He pressed his face into his hands as memories returned. Each day began when the guards stirred the dozen or so men in his small room awake. Often they beat the prisoners, and then they made them pray. There were lectures on ISIS's fanatical version of Islam. The prisoners were fed just once a day, a small meal in the evenings. They knew there were other men in different rooms suffering the same fate. "When we were being beaten, they heard us, and when they were being beaten, we heard them," he said.

The prisoners were rebel fighters, amateur smugglers desperate to feed their families, and men who had violated ISIS's draconian codes. They feared the room with the Qurans. "Every day they woke me up, and I thought maybe it would be my last," he said.

Finishing his tea, he remembered that it was about a month into his time at the prison when his father's name was called. Days later, a guard pulled him out too. The guard explained that his father had been told to work with ISIS and refused. He'd been led into the room the prisoners feared, given a Quran to read, and killed. Terrified, the son pledged allegiance to ISIS, promised to stop his smuggling, and was released. Soon after, he fled to Turkey, where he was piecing together menial work, still haunted by the prison and his father's fate. "I feel guilty," he said, "because they killed my father but released me."

CHAPTER 19

DEFECTORS

Sanliurfa, Turkey. January 2016.

OKAB, PERHAPS LOOKING FOR A CHANCE TO UNBURDEN HIMSELF, began to share pieces of his story.

Munzer and I were still in Sanliurfa when we met him in our hotel's courtyard. The former ISIS field officer known as Eagle spoke for hours, describing how his conscience had been jarred by the massacre in Sinjar and the long process that followed to free his mind from ISIS. Rather than a clean mental break, it had been like a struggle to wake from a nightmare.

Men like Okab were filtering out from Syria as dissent quietly spread in the ISIS ranks. Many found themselves in Sanliurfa, the closest Turkish city to Raqqa, where the modern malls and hotels mixed with ancient religious sites. Legend had it that when the king Nimrod cast Abraham into fire, as some Islamic traditions tell it, he landed in Sanliurfa, in the spot now known as Abraham's Pool, where the flames were transformed to water. In the shadow of a thirteenth-century mosque, you could feed sacred fish and visit a cave said to be Abraham's birthplace. Civilians were arriving in Sanliurfa from ISIS territory regularly, and ISIS members were rumored to be among them. Then there were defectors, who were something in between.

After our first meeting with Okab, Munzer and I sought out more defectors, in Sanliurfa and around the border, to learn about a hidden community that was scattering around the globe—inside Iraq and Syria, in Turkey, and, in the cases of some foreign fighters, back at home. They lived in the shadows, fearful of retribution from ISIS on the one hand and of arrest on the other. They'd been part of the same group that tortured and beheaded civilians in the basement prison near Akcakale, that massacred Yazidis and took women as slaves. Now they were saying they wanted to move on. As they reclaimed their minds from the grip of fanaticism, they were left to wonder how they could have taken part in such atrocities. "Maybe you think they are bad people because they joined ISIS. But for me, they are my brothers," Okab said that first night in the courtyard. "Because the same thing that happened to them happened to me."

Okab had been a university student in Raqqa, smoking cigarettes and chasing girls with his classmates, before radicalizing gradually through the civil war—until ISIS's hard-line vision began to seem like a pillar of order amid the chaos. By the time ISIS took control of Raqqa, in the summer of 2013, he was a rebel fighter who'd lived through two years of extreme violence. The bloodshed had subsumed his family, his cousins and siblings killed or kidnapped by the Kurdish YPG, an ISIS enemy that Okab, like many Syrians, considered an Assad ally. ISIS offered him the chance to fight them both and pursue his desire for revenge.

He was also drawn to the brute simplicity of its draconian Islam—cutting off the heads of murderers and the hands of thieves, lashing lovers for premarital sex—at a time when it seemed there was little order or logic to be found elsewhere. The militants put him through their indoctrination courses, which instilled an unexpected radicalism in his mind. He had been living as an infidel, far from God, he learned, and obeying

ISIS would bring him close. He was soon marching eagerly toward a violent death. He fought in dozens of battles, gaining a reputation for fearlessness.

"I cannot explain this feeling, but they teach us that God is waiting for you, and you must go to him. So go and don't be afraid of death," he said. "And we wanted to die. Because when we die, all the hard things in this life will end, and we will start again."

This mind-set was gone by the time he returned to Raqqa after the massacre in Sinjar. As he made plans to leave ISIS, though, he began to reconsider. Syria was destroyed, his family had unraveled, and his time with ISIS had tarnished him in the eyes of many of the people he knew. *If I leave*, he wondered, *what will I do?*

He clung to darker urges too. As an ISIS commander he had status, a weapon and a car, a house and a salary. He was a respected fighter; if he left he would be just another refugee. He also felt responsible for a relative who'd been kidnapped by the YPG in retaliation for his work with ISIS. And he still wanted revenge.

Okab made a decision he would later find hard to justify: Though he had seen the worst in ISIS, he would continue to fight Assad and the YPG under its black flag.

Other defectors experienced similar confusion, recalling a winding mental process filled with the same uncertainty that had led them to the group in the first place. ISIS's rise to power had given it unique appeal at a time when rival rebel groups struggled to give their fighters weapons and salaries. One twenty-seven-year-old fighter from Deir Ezzor said he had little love for the group when he joined but saw few choices as a fighting-aged male living in its territory. "I knew that they are criminals," he said. "But it's very hard to live your life in Syria, especially in ISIS areas, if you don't join them."

ISIS gave him a house, a car, and a monthly salary and paid for his wedding. He too fell under the trance of extremism and, like Okab, found himself in the middle of a massacre. He took part in the killing, he said, and refused to reveal more. The guilt drove him to defect—but he felt stained by his crimes. He canceled plans to flee to Europe after he began worrying that other refugees would recognize him and alert the police. So he remained in limbo near the border in Turkey. "There are many people who want to defect," he said. "But how can they survive?"

Potential defectors also had to worry about getting caught. ISIS members were often prevented from traveling without permission, and many fighters were isolated in military camps. All were closely watched by the same secret police who terrorized civilians into submission; several defectors said they feared ISIS could find them wherever they hid, even in Europe. We met a Syrian in his thirties who'd worked for ISIS's secret police, tasked with monitoring his comrades. Reserved and imposing in a leather jacket and jeans, he said he'd received regular reports from informants about potential defectors: "Spies came to me many times, saying this person or that person wants to defect."

He was supposed to pass the information to his superiors but eventually began to keep it to himself, he said, as he too became disillusioned.

Another defector, twenty-eight, found that the best way to move on from ISIS was to keep fighting. He joined a rebel group that battled both ISIS and Assad, turning his gun on his old friends. "I thought ISIS would be able to fight the regime if they built their Islamic state, because the regime is a state, and only a state can fight a state," he said. "But they are just like the regime. They told the Syrian people that if you are not with us, then you are our enemy. And they committed terrible crimes."

Still another defector, a twenty-six-year-old Syrian living in Sanliurfa, described how time after time he'd worked to pull himself from ISIS's radical mind-set only to be sucked back in. When ISIS first descended on his native Deir Ezzor, he'd fought against it as a member of a rival rebel group. Then, after ISIS won, he was captured and given an ultimatum: fight with us or die. Soon he was at war with his old allies.

When he wasn't fighting, he attended indoctrination courses taught by foreign instructors. After years of war, he found himself drawn to the sectarian hatred they preached. "Every day, I would wake up in the morning, go to pray, sit with ISIS members and start talking about how we will kill all Shias and Alawites after we finish our fight with the [rebels]," he said.

During short breaks to visit home, his family would plead with him to leave ISIS and press him with evidence of its crimes. He would be swayed. Then he would return to his military camp and feel his mind swinging back the other way. "We only talk to each other; we don't watch the media," he said.

By the time he spoke with us in Sanliurfa, he'd been living there for three months. Sipping tea, he said he rejected ISIS. Yet he still fixated on the idea of sectarian revenge. "Shia and Alawite civilians, if they don't convert to Sunni Islam, we must kill them," he said.

He paused. "I'm twenty-six, and I was always changing my mind," he said. "But what if I tell you about kids inside ISIS?"

Mohamed, the smuggler who'd trafficked in oil and artifacts, was helping to care for a middle-school-aged boy who'd been rescued from ISIS in Syria. He invited us to his home to meet him, and we found that the boy didn't consider it a rescue at all. Despite the support that Mohamed often expressed for ISIS and his business ties, he didn't want the boy to have anything to do with the group. He thought efforts to recruit children into jihad were wrong. The boy had attended ISIS's indoctrination courses in Raqqa and still considered himself a loyal member. He wanted to return and fight for them. "I'm not too young," he said. "Everybody can go to jihad, young people and people more than one hundred years old."

The boy sat cross-legged on a living room carpet, looking younger than his age, as a television in the corner relayed updates from the war. One day the previous summer, after the boy arrived in Turkey, Mohamed had taken him to a beach, hoping to win him over with the sight of young women clad in bikinis. The boy had taken one look and said he wanted their blood to turn the sand red.

In the living room, when the subject turned to school, the boy said he was doing well and hoped to be an engineer one day. When the conversation turned back to ISIS, he said he hoped to slaughter anyone the group determined was an infidel, even from among his neighbors and friends.

"Not all of them," Mohamed prodded him.

"No, all of them," the boy replied.

"Say at least that *you* don't want to kill them, but that maybe ISIS will kill them," one of Mohamed's relatives said.

"No," the boy insisted, staring deliberately. "I want to."

In Sanliurfa, on another cold night, Okab chain-smoked beneath a heat lamp's orange glare. He wore a sweater and a soft expression that belied his reputation from the battlefield.

Munzer and I pressed him to explain again the most problematic part of his story. As he told it, he'd been stuck in his contradiction in Raqqa—knowing he should leave ISIS yet continuing to fight for it—when he received what he saw as a grim chance to make amends. One of his superiors offered to give him a gift: a Yazidi slave. He accepted, telling himself he could offer her safe haven.

"I just wanted to protect one Yazidi person at that time," he said.

The woman was so ill from the sexual brutality she had endured from her previous captors that he rushed her to a hospital. She was also traumatized by what had happened to her family—her husband killed in front of her and her two young sons taken away for indoctrination in children's camps. "I tried to help her feel better," Okab said. "But how can a woman who had this happen to her forget?"

By the time Okab escaped to Turkey to tell his story, the woman couldn't be reached, making it impossible to say how she felt about her new captor or what happened to her in his custody. In Okab's telling, he didn't touch her during the months they lived together in Raqqa, and though he knew she could never fully trust him, he believed they became friends. Over hours of interviews, he expressed horror at what ISIS had done to the Yazidis and in particular at the enslavement of Yazidi women. "I was telling people they are human," he said. "It's *ha-*

ram"—forbidden—"to rape them and sell them and treat them like this. But their only answer was that they are infidels. They don't understand human language."

At the same time, the quest he described to protect the woman was part of a story he was telling himself—one in which, despite all the wrong he had done, he remained the hero. He recalled telling the woman about his own experience in Sinjar and his thoughts about defecting. "I needed to find someone to talk to about this, because I felt I would blow myself up if I didn't," he said. "She was the only person."

From Raqqa, he began to set his sights on the border with Turkey, he said, hoping he could find a way to smuggle them both to safety. As he told it, she refused to leave without her two sons, of whom she'd heard nothing since they were separated in Sinjar. He asked about them at children's camps, careful not to raise suspicions, but turned up nothing.

I later learned that a small circle of Okab's family and friends had known of his plight with the Yazidi woman and that some had tried to dissuade him from helping her. "We asked him to be careful and to forget the woman, because they might be killed together if ISIS caught them," recalled one of them. "But I think he wanted to help her in order to atone."

In the end, what I found true in Okab's story was his realization that, after all, he was not the hero he wanted to be. One night, fighting back tears, he recounted how he was still in Raqqa, debating his next step, when he received permission from ISIS to travel to Turkey to get treatment for an old battle wound. He took the trip, telling the woman he'd return for her. But he didn't. While recovering from surgery, he said, he'd received a warning from a friend in Raqqa that ISIS had discovered his dissent and that he risked being arrested if he returned. He stayed put and never heard from the woman again.

He'd learned that he couldn't right his wrongs. The relative who'd been kidnapped by the YPG was released without his help and now refused to speak to him. As for the Yazidi woman, Okab knew she was probably still enslaved. And as for himself, he said, all he hoped for was to find a way "to live a normal life."

CHAPTER 20

FOREIGNERS

Berlin, Germany. March 2016.

THE MEMORY STICK WAS BLACK WITH LIME-GREEN TRIM AND WHITE letters that read, "Transcend."

I held it in the grey light of a Berlin morning that seeped through my window in an old hotel. Then I buried it inside my suitcase.

The suitcase sat beside me in a taxi as I rode to the airport through a late-winter haze. I handed it to a clerk at the check-in desk and drifted through the departures hall in a crush of sounds and faces. As I waited in line at a duty-free shop, a group of high school students stood in front of me. They were American too, boys and girls with headphones and zits, their voices high-pitched. They were buying boxes of chocolates.

I had traveled to Berlin to meet Leo, the Syrian refugee from New Jersey who'd been my companion in the summer of 2012. He had left Turkey in early 2013 for Germany and applied for asylum. He picked me up from the airport in a 2003 BMW sedan and drove me to a café, where we sat in a corner and smoked hookah.

Someone had sent Leo a cache of ISIS personnel files that were leaked from the caliphate. They contained the names of hundreds of the foreign jihadis who gave the group its unique global reach. The files offered an unprecedented look at the identities of these foreigners, who often operated under nicknames and kept their faces hidden behind masks. Their stories were told in the minutiae of bureaucratic forms that asked their names and birthdays, blood types and marital statuses, countries of origin, dates of arrival, educations, and work histories. The forms also contained emergency contacts—and many of the younger jihadis, not much older than the high schoolers at the airport, had put their moms.

From the café, Leo and I moved to the small, pleasant apartment where he was raising his new family. His two-year-old son watched cartoons as his wife prepared a Syrian dinner. She was from Damascus, and they'd struck up a relationship online, after he arrived in Berlin, still living through his iPad. He'd helped her get a visa, and they'd been happily married since.

On a laptop, Leo helped me sort through the thousands of pages in the cache, and I copied them onto the memory stick. They were intake forms that new ISIS members had filled out when they arrived in Syria, as ISIS gathered strength in 2013 and 2014, their personal data logged into computers by the clerks of an aspiring state. The forms were matter-of-fact in their bureaucracy, as if joining ISIS were as normal as starting a new job. One question asked applicants to check a box indicating whether they wanted to be a suicide bomber.

A Saudi student who'd been studying in Kentucky put in the notes section that his visa to the United States was still valid. An Indonesian businessman said he had six children and an O+ blood type. Most were first-time jihadis, like a chemist from Toronto, a chef from Istanbul, and a Palestinian Swede who'd been working at an electric plant. There was a bookseller from northern England, a driving instructor from Tunisia, a sports trainer from France, an Azeri trader, and a mechanical engineer from Germany. An Egyptian surgeon said he'd fought previously with insurgents in the Sinai desert. An Uzbek man said he was a veteran of the war in Afghanistan and listed "mafia" as his profession. Some of the forms belonged to well-known jihadis, such as Douglas McCain, a onetime aspiring rapper from Minnesota and the first American reported to have died fighting for ISIS. His form said that he arrived in Syria in

March 2014 and listed his nom de guerre as "Abu Jihad al-Amriki." Others had stayed off the radar. A few weeks later, during a counterterrorism raid at an apartment in Brussels that police said was connected to the Paris attacks, a police sniper would kill Mohamed Belkaid, a thirty-five-year-old Algerian who until that point had been unknown to authorities. He opened fire with an assault rifle the moment police opened the door. His form said that he reached Syria from Turkey in 2014 and had asked to be a suicide attacker.

U.S. officials believed that more than 38,000 foreign fighters in all had traveled to Syria and that ISIS had between 19,000 and 25,000 fighters of all nationalities in its ranks. They were like members of the fictional death cults that come with the apocalypse—the "army in tennis shoes, tramping," who haunt *The Road*, Cormac McCarthy's grim vision of the future. "Yes," his protagonist says, "they were the bad guys." They were also mirror images of our modern world, men and women at ease in it and part of it. The files on the memory stick captured them as their old lives dissolved into the new, after they had traveled to Turkey through airports like Berlin's, met with guides like the smuggler Abdulrahman, and crossed into the caliphate.

In Istanbul, I took my suitcase from baggage claim, got into a cab, and was sped home along the Bosporus. For years the suffering of the places I visited had seemed to recede on these drives, as the salty air rushed through my window, but now the sense of separation was gone.

In my kitchen, the radio played news of another attack: a suicide bomber in the Turkish capital had killed 37 people and injured 125. I was sad but not surprised; the violence was starting to feel normal.

That was what I'd learned about violence and what unnerved me: not how extraordinary but how normal it could be. And I thought ISIS understood this—that violence was just as at home anywhere as it was in Iraq and Syria, that people just needed a push. I'd been abducted once, in eastern Ukraine, by the separatists who'd plunged the region into a senseless war, and what frightened me most about my captors was how, behind their weapons and masks, they were so ordinary. I was blindfolded, and as we slowed to pass through their own checkpoints, I heard them cock their guns; they were just as rattled as I was, wary even of their allies. They brought me to a shed and had me stand with my palms against a wall. My heart was racing, and as my legs began to falter, someone put a sympathetic hand on my shoulder and offered a chair. They were unsure what to do, hurt me or help me, as if the picture were flickering—between friend and enemy, war and peace.

Sometimes I could close my eyes and feel the pull and crush of a world gone wrong: the surge of a crowd as it pushed toward police, the pulse of adrenaline as I raced down upturned streets. Gunshots cracked the air, and tear gas burned like the future, sanitized and sick. My body armor pressed against my chest. My face was punched, my arms bound behind me. I heard the roar of duct tape unwinding as a blindfold wrapped around my head. And these memories blended with the images of America I saw online—the rioting crowds, the fevered rallies, the militarized police—which gave me the same clenching in my throat and tingle in my spine. There were bodies in the streets of Europe; there were helicopters hovering above my balcony. There was the boom of another attack, and my apartment swayed slightly.

Munzer and I dug through the forms on the memory stick. We called the emergency contacts listed in them, reaching people around the world: friends and siblings, moms and dads.

The mother of a Saudi man who was twenty-six when he joined ISIS in 2013 recounted, in a sad, tired voice, how he'd been studying computer engineering, with a wife and baby daughter at home, before abruptly deciding to go to Syria alone, telling his parents he was volunteering at a hospital there. When he later admitted that he'd joined ISIS, his father cut off contact. But his mother kept trying to convince him to come home. "I tried to stop him many times," she said, "but I couldn't."

She last heard from him in early 2015, when he called to say he had remarried and asked for her prayers. "We haven't heard anything about him since," she said.

A man in Tunisia, whose younger brother, an unemployed baker, had gone to Syria in November 2013, had resigned himself to having a sibling in ISIS. He remained in touch with his brother, who had reported doing well for himself with ISIS and having multiple wives. He sent home $500 a month and promised to buy the family a house the next year if he was still alive. The man said his brother had never been religious and had joined ISIS because it seemed like a good chance to make a living.

"He didn't go to college, and he tried to get a visa to move to Europe, but he didn't have any luck. He was just smoking weed and doing drugs," he said. "We refused this idea [of joining ISIS] at the beginning, but now we don't ask him to come back. We just say take care and send us photos of your kids."

One reason ISIS asked fighters for their contacts was so it could send home word of their death. It considered this good news.

A former trader from Saudi Arabia left the number of a friend when he registered with ISIS as a suicide bomber in February 2013. The friend recalled their last conversation. "He asked me to say hi to his parents and friends, and he asked me to tell all the people who know him that he is happy, because he is going to heaven in a couple of days, and he cannot wait for that moment," he said. "I don't want to talk more about him, because he's in God's hands now. But I just want to say that it's a big mistake that people are coming from across the world to fight and die in Syria."

A Saudi man who'd been studying abroad in the United States joined ISIS in October 2013, listing his contacts as his mom and dad. About a year and a half later, his mother said, she received a call from a man she didn't know. "The caller was strange—he was happy, and he thought he was giving us beautiful news," she recalled. "He told me, 'Congratulations, your son has won.' I asked, 'What did he win?' He said, 'He gained martyrdom for God.'"

The caller said her son had died fighting "infidels" in Syria near the border with Turkey, not far from where he'd first entered the country and filled out his form. "I have been depressed since he left us for Syria," the mother said. "I haven't had the taste of sleep for a long time."

The documents were the last traces many foreign fighters left before they disappeared into Syria. Munzer became obsessed with them, drinking beer and chain-smoking in his apartment as he called the numbers through the night.

One woman in Sudan thought it was her missing son calling when Munzer reached her from his Turkish number. "I miss you; I always pray for you. Please take care, my dear—why didn't you call me for two years and four months?" she said, the words spilling out. "I love you."

Munzer was quick to correct her, and she recounted how her son had left for Syria without saying good-bye. He had called from Turkey only to tell her he was joining ISIS, and she hadn't heard from him since. "I wish I had wings to fly to Turkey and stop him from going to Syria," she said.

She called Munzer back three times in the days that followed, begging for updates about her son. At one point she convinced herself that he was an ISIS member posing as a journalist. "Please give him back to me," she said, weeping. "I don't believe you—I think you were with him, and I think something bad happened to him. Tell me if he is still alive or not."

———·———

We published an article about the documents, and afterward someone reached out as part of his own family's search for answers. Ahmed was a twenty-five-year-old writer from Toronto with a secret connection to the conflict. His cousin had been the subject of a missing person's report since the summer of 2014, when he left Canada after telling his family he was taking a vacation to Turkey. He'd emailed his mother a selfie from some ruins there and disappeared.

Ahmed had contacted us to say he was in Istanbul and ask if his cousin's name was among those in the forms. He sat on the couch in my office with a glass of whiskey as Munzer searched the cache. His cousin was there. His form showed that he'd joined ISIS shortly after he last contacted his parents, crossing the Turkish border into the Syrian city of Jarabulus.

"Fuck," Ahmed said.

Many of ISIS's foreign fighters had been drawn to its promise to create a new world, and their families were a link to the past some were eager to cut. Ahmed's cousin put on his form that he wanted to be a fighter. It added that he was single and was a student before coming to Syria. It listed his date of birth, his hometown, and his mother's first name. When he came to the section for a contact at home, though, he left it blank. The notes section said that he left his passport and cell phone at the arrivals desk.

Ahmed said that he and his cousin, who was two years older, had been close once. Ahmed had looked up to him—he would pull him away at family gatherings to listen to hip-hop and drink beer. He took him to his first strip club. He'd been a funny and freewheeling high schooler, popular with girls, the person who took over the dance floor at weddings. "He was the guy who, when he starts dancing, everyone watches him. My dad would tell me, you need to dance like him," Ahmed said. "So he was a party animal until he started becoming conservative."

Ahmed's cousin had first become interested in Middle Eastern politics when he went to college. He became religious and then increasingly hard-line. Eventually Ahmed unfriended him on Facebook in response to his radical posts. Ahmed, meanwhile, moved away from religion as he pursued a writing career, and the two had lost touch by the time his cousin made the trip to Turkey.

"But there was a time when we converged," Ahmed said.

He thought for a moment. "To me, if he joined ISIS, he's a murderer, a committer of genocide. He's the closest thing we have today to a Nazi," he said. "And he put that he wanted to be a fighter. He said that he wants to kill people. He didn't say he wants to be a fucking teacher or something."

He paused. "If he was sitting here in front of me, I'm not saying I would shoot him. I would probably feel sympathy for him again," he said. "But two years have passed, and on a conceptual level, I wish he was dead."

Later, using the new information about his cousin, Ahmed began to search online. After his cousin first went missing, Ahmed had tried to find him on Facebook again, but his cousin had deleted his account. When Ahmed read the form, though, he realized that his cousin, like many fighters, had given himself a nom de guerre. He plugged it into Facebook and searched again. This time he found him. The profile photo showed his cousin posing with a machine gun, with a Salafi-style beard and aviator sunglasses, and ammo belts hanging from his neck.

Munzer and I checked with an ISIS-linked source who said that, as far as he could gather, Ahmed's cousin was alive and well. I asked Ahmed if he wanted to find out more, but he wasn't sure. "My mind is racing," he said.

His cousin had written a post two years earlier as his family searched for him, his father even flying to Turkey, traveling along the border, retracing his son's steps. "We come to slaughter you—I swear to God we will show you hell," the post read. "There is no solution except jihad. May God help us get to your necks."

PART III

MOSUL

CHAPTER 21

COUNTERTERROR

Kalak, Iraq. Thirty miles east of Mosul. October 2016.

AHMED THE BULLET HAD A SECRET HIDDEN IN HIS PHONE. IT WAS A photo of the major: naked, unconscious, and smeared with blood.

Ahmed giggled. "I haven't shown these to anybody," he said.

He swiped a stubby finger across the screen. Another photo showed a top-down view from the turret of the major's Humvee. He was slumped in the passenger's seat. A rocket-propelled grenade had fractured his skull and buried shrapnel in his head, shoulder, and chest. No one was supposed to see the man who would lead the coalition's charge into Mosul this way. A third photo showed him supine on a stretcher, a white bandage tight around his forehead. His expression blank, his eyes closed, his chest pale and concave, he was a picture of human frailty. "Our security deleted all the photos from my phone," Ahmed said. "But I found a software to bring them back."

Ahmed was a veteran machine gunner in the major's battle convoy. He fired .50-caliber bullets from the turret of an armored Humvee, but that wasn't how he got his nickname.

The major, Salam Hussein al-Obaidi, was Iraq's most renowned ISIS killer. He was trained by U.S. commandos at a secret base in Jordan early in the Iraq War. He then spent years working alongside them as a "breacher" in the night raids that tormented ISIS's predecessor, AQI. He'd gained his fame, though, just the previous spring by leading the offensive to recapture Anbar, the sprawling province west of Baghdad. The RPG attack he survived there only increased his stature, though it also left him with numbness in his arm and a jagged scar on his head.

With the frantic efficiency of a marauding colony of fire ants, Major Salam and his men had set up a forward operating base in some houses of an abandoned village called Kalak thirty miles east of Mosul. When he commandeered civilian homes like this, he called them his "hotels." The battle plans were not yet finalized—in fact they were changing daily—but as I settled in at Kalak with the photographer Warzer Jaff, the soldiers there seemed certain that Major Salam would be the first among the thousands of troops waiting to attack Mosul to set foot inside it. I'd spent months preparing for the offensive, traveling with Jaff to the front lines around northern Iraq, speaking with U.S. military planners, and working to secure an embed with Major Salam and his battalion, after learning that they would be the main attacking unit. Soldiers and militiamen at checkpoints all along the 230-mile drive north from Baghdad had rushed over to take selfies and shake his hand.

Ahmed's photos cut through the major's aura and stripped the war back to its core.

Ahmed was in his thirties but looked older, with weathered features, a black moustache, and a round belly. His moods shifted between wide-smiling exuberance and gloom. On this day he was on the sunny side. He wore a grey T-shirt that said "American Sniper," a backward cap, and a necklace of turquoise beads. During the Iraq War, because Iraqi special forces such as Ahmed and Major Salam were the closest allies U.S. troops had, their enemies hated them intensely. So when militiamen kidnapped Ahmed from a checkpoint in Baghdad one day, they didn't just torture him. They put a circular saw to his forehead and tried to peel off his face. Then they put a hood over his head, shot him five times, and tossed his body in a garbage dump, thinking he was dead. Ahmed survived, though, and was found by an elderly man, who carried him to a hospital. When he recovered, he had gained his nickname—The Bullet, for what couldn't kill him—and he returned to his turret.

Horror stories were common with the men in the major's crew, though they didn't always see the horror in them. Ahmed shared his casually. On a city block in Anbar he'd been in his turret when his Humvee came upon a white SUV, the kind Iraqi officers drove sometimes. It wasn't until the vehicle got close that he saw the driver's long hair and beard. Ahmed unleashed the .50-cal, which nearly severed one of the jihadi's arms. He jumped down to finish the job with his pistol, but the jihadi burst from the car and took off down the street, the wounded arm flapping at his side. Another time, he had just poked his head into his turret when a sniper's bullet, fired from a home nearby, hit near his forehead. All that stopped it was the turret's reinforced glass. "I went crazy on the house and destroyed it," Ahmed said. "I didn't even care if there was a family inside."

After U.S. soldiers left Iraq in 2011, the local units they had worked with in the Iraq War were variously broken down, politicized, shuffled, and reorganized. Yet Major Salam and his men were still more or less in their original state; they were relics of the old war, like ISIS, even as they led the charge in the new one. They still went by the name that their American mentors had given the battalion back in 2005: the Iraqi Counter-Terrorism Force, or ICTF, the initials emblazoned on the sleeves of their black uniforms and the turrets of their black Humvees.

Ayad, a thirty-one-year-old ICTF veteran, looked like a retired linebacker, physically imposing but not quite in shape. He wore a baseball cap with a T-shirt and jeans when Jaff and I met him one night, before our trip to Kalak, outside the guarded compound in Baghdad where we were renting rooms. The Tigris River was stale before us across a four-lane road. Two blocks behind us was the upscale district of Karrada, buzzing as families strolled amid a halogen-lit blur of restaurants, clothing shops, and fresh-juice stands. On what used to be its busiest stretch, a smell like a burnt match lingered. In the summer, 281 people had been killed by an ISIS truck bomb there, and it was as if the sudden surge of death had been seared into the atmosphere. The truck rammed a building that ran the length of a city block. Shops lined the ground floor then, and apartments filled the four stories above, all of it now a blackened husk.

With Ayad we got into our hired driver's sedan and rolled through the wired aggression of downtown Baghdad after dark. Military police in blue-and-black fatigues stood with their machine guns in the shadows of the streetlights. Checkpoints were illuminated against the night's haze. Concrete blast walls wrapped around homes, topped with glass shards and razor wire. Teams of security guards perched on many rooftops. Entire blocks had been cordoned off by gates of reinforced metal, where a knock would be met by the creek of a sliding hatch and a pair of wary eyes. The prison-yard claustrophobia had written itself into the city's DNA. Every layer of fortification and barricade testified to an old escalation of violence. A local could point to each as a marker in the story of Baghdad's tragic recent history, like reading the rings inside a fallen tree.

I saw the golden glow of the Babylon Hotel approaching. A thirty-six-story ziggurat, surrounded by a high wall, it was an island of light in the darkness. This was a bastion for the foreign and local elite: bankers, businessmen, powerful sons, and war profiteers who dined along the sweeping pool in the courtyard as tumult churned through the streets. "This is where the thieves can be safe," Ayad said. The sedan was descending into a tunnel that marked the hotel's gate of entry. Signs on the walls said in English, "Remain in your car." A stoplight on the ceiling clicked between green and red. Guards led bomb-sniffing dogs down the sides of the sedan, and then we parked in an underground garage and walked upstairs to the hotel's entrance, where Ayad deposited his handgun with a guard before we stepped through a metal detector. We passed beneath the lobby's vaulted ceiling.

In the courtyard, the pool's aqua water shimmered with the rays of submerged lights. We walked down a footpath to a table beneath some palm trees and ordered cheeseburgers from a waiter who didn't speak Arabic. I felt we were simultaneously in Baghdad and anywhere. At a table nearby, a group of young men were smoking hookah and sipping small cups of coffee. With trim-cut designer clothes and carefully toned muscles, they affected a nightclub sort of toughness. I looked back at Ayad with his T-shirt and extra weight. He had probably lost track of how many people he'd killed, but Iraq's best soldiers tended to look ordinary. War was not something they went to but a life they lived, and they came as they were, leaving it to others to preen and play tough guy. He saw the same everyman quality in the U.S. special forces soldiers he'd spent years fighting alongside. "The Americans I know are good people," he said. "None of them are from rich or powerful families. They're just regular, middle-class guys."

The food came, and I asked Ayad when he became a soldier. More than a dozen years earlier in 2003, as soon as he finished high school, he'd signed up for the new Iraqi military that the United States was building. My mind scanned back to my college dormitory. My lone memory of the invasion was set in a common room there: a blue carpet, a block couch, and a TV on a wooden stand. The TV showed a news broadcast with a rolling shot of a clear blue sky, through which U.S. bombs were falling. Following the war became like paying passing attention to a Yankees game muted on a screen above a bar. I rooted for America, which was all I felt my country asked of me. Ayad had passed a lifetime of violence in the time since that memory. Recently, the U.S. government had offered him the chance to relocate to the States, but he declined. "I feel like America is my second home, even though I've never been there," he said. The war was all he knew, though, and he believed he had more work to do. The men in Major Salam's orbit seemed to be caught in a loop: each new conflict that erupted was also the one they were fighting already. Ayad said he would continue for another ten years. He also said he wanted ten kids. To me those numbers said,

As long as it goes and as many as I can. He and his wife had just had their first child, a boy. They named him Adam, because the name was beyond the tribalism that plagued the country. Someone called Adam could be a Sunni or Shia Muslim or a Christian or a Jew. It predated violence. In Turkey, it was just the word for "man."

The battle for Mosul, 250 miles to the north, was about to begin. Ayad was running security for a convoy that Iraqi special forces were sending up from Baghdad—the one that would take Jaff and me to Kalak, where Ahmed the Bullet shared his photos with me. When we requested a spot on it, Ayad said to be ready to leave the next day.

Jaff and I were standing on the side of a highway on the edge of Baghdad. My clothes and body armor were packed into two duffel bags at my feet. Flatbed trucks thundered past one after another, sending gusts of crisp morning air swirling over us. Strapped on the truck beds in pairs were the Humvees of the Iraqi special forces, painted in their trademark black. The four-ton vehicles bore the signs of past battles with their armored shells pocked by bullet holes and dented from bomb blasts. The reinforced glass on their doors and windshields had cracked and clouded. The soldiers, likewise battle worn, were perched on and around the Humvees in their black uniforms, some in ski masks and others with their faces open to the sun, as placid as gargoyles as Iraqi flags thrashed in the headwind. Interspersed among the flatbed trucks were the hulking mine-resistant vehicles known as MRAPs, bulldozers, tow trucks, fuel rigs, and school buses, all of them painted black, along with trucks laden with food, bottled water, blankets, and generators. Ayad had found us a spot with two soldiers traveling in a pickup, which emerged from the convoy. I threw my bags in the rear and climbed into the back seat.

It would be a two-day drive to the outskirts of Mosul at the convoy's plodding pace. Twenty minutes down Highway 1, though, we saw the first signs of the war. A landscape of farm fields and palm groves gave way to rows of low-slung homes and shops that hugged the roadside. The buildings were charred and crumbled; metal gates were ripped like paper; car frames were twisted and seared. I had first passed through this area not long after the Iraqi military freed it from ISIS, two years prior, and nothing had changed. The destruction continued for mile after mile: sunken bridges, severed radio towers, toppled power lines. As the sun began to set, the convoy stopped for the night outside Tikrit, at an Iraqi military base called Camp Speicher. In 2014, ISIS had captured more than 1,500 cadets from the base and executed them in a field nearby. As the pickup rolled through the gates, I recalled a visit to one of the mass graves where the cadets had been found—the smell of the decomposing corpses, a sickly kind of sweet, the sound of a militiaman crying, and a patch of daisies rising from the earth.

Back on the highway the next morning, the convoy slowed as soldiers scouted for ambushes. The sky darkened to black in the distance before us, as if a tropical storm were approaching. It was the smoke from oil fields that had been ignited in more recent fighting and still burned uncontrollably. The smoke cast a pall over the horizon and sent a haze rolling over our heads that dulled the sunlight. We paused on a stretch of highway that cut through another ruined town. Children emerged from battered buildings to gawk at the soldiers, who had exited their vehicles, looking ahead at the ominous skyline. An old woman shuffled forward. She had a faded tattoo in the shape of a cross on one of her cheeks and was squinting so hard I thought she might be blind. She was chanting things like "God bless you" and "God protect you" at the soldiers as people often do when faced with an advancing army. A soldier looked at her and asked, "Where are we?" We returned to the vehicles. Instructions came on the radio to pick up speed along the curve ahead, because an ISIS mortar team was monitoring the approach of the convoy, and bombs were falling there.

In the afternoon, we reached a floating bridge spanning a narrow stretch of the Tigris. We were thirty miles south of Mosul, outside the city of Qayyarah, where part of a U.S. Army battalion was stationed at the ruined airport, looking out onto the oil fires, and surrounded for miles by dirt so fine that the soldiers called it "moon dust." The vehicles lined up to pass one at a time over the bridge, and I got out to walk across it. The sky straight above seemed to mark the oil cloud's edge. To the right, it was black for as far as I could see, the cloud's reflection turning the water below it menacing, swamp-like. To the left, the sky was blue. There the water looked fresh and inviting. From the river the convoy traced a rough arc beneath Mosul for three more hours, heading north and west, until it arrived at Kalak.

Kalak had been freed from ISIS, but none of the residents had returned. The one-story homes were full of dust and broken glass. Only faded memories remained, such as a child's ripped drawing taped to a wall. It was nearly dark, and Major Salam and his men snapped into action with the speed of veteran invaders. First, engineers checked for explosives in the handful of houses where the soldiers planned to stay; then the soldiers swept and mopped the floors. Outside the largest home, where I put my bags, there was soon a vast container of water for showers and a generator. A soldier began to work the wires behind the walls to set up electricity. Another was in charge of Major Salam's flat-screen TV and the satellite dish he used to get cable and Wi-Fi. There was shouting and rumbling in the streets as other soldiers rolled the Humvees off the flatbeds and began to get them battle-ready.

Inside the home was a set of stairs that led up to the roof, which, like rooftops all around Iraq, residents used in the hotter months to lounge and sleep. It was flat and bordered by waist-high concrete walls. The view stretched across fields to an incline about a half a mile away, where a small factory marked the start of ISIS territory. Kalak sat astride Highway 2, giving Major Salam and his men a straight shot into eastern Mosul, but first the ISIS-held towns along the way would have to be cleared. The sun was setting, and the soldiers lit a massive fire beside the home to keep mosquitoes at bay. For long minutes Major Salam stood alone and still in the glow of the fire, his palms pressed against the top of the concrete wall, staring out toward the heart of the caliphate.

CHAPTER 22

ARMIES IN THE NIGHT

Khazir, Iraq. Twenty-two miles east of Mosul. October 2016.

THE INVADERS WERE ASLEEP ALONG A RIDGELINE, STRETCHED OUT IN their bedrolls. Their tanks and Humvees waited beside them in the darkness. When dawn broke and the *peshmerga* rolled their vehicles into the ISIS-held villages in the valley below, they would fire the first shots of the offensive for Mosul, but a quiet had settled on the night's last hours. I could hear the fading echo of a fighter jet high above and the distant rumble of an airstrike.

From the rows of sleeping soldiers, a footpath cut uphill through dead weeds to a small house lit dimly by a porchlight. Soldiers who couldn't sleep were shuffling off their worries inside. The battle plan called for the *peshmerga* to clear the last ring of historically Kurdish land, to the north and east of Mosul, that was still part of the caliphate, before the ICTF would lead the assault into ISIS's strongholds. So with Major Salam impatiently waiting in Kalak, Jaff and I had embedded with the *peshmerga* for the battle's opening salvo. It was supposed to be a secret, and we, along with several teams of journalists who'd joined the unit with us, had promised not to publish news until the battle began. But the men in the house said the enemy knew they were coming. They discussed rumors that ISIS had moved four hundred fighters into the string of villages they were about to attack. "That valley is full of ISIS ambushes," one said, and the men felt there were eyes on them already. "Their sniper teams get really close at night," said another.

The attack from Khazir would be carried out by a joint force of *peshmerga* and Kurdish military police. Some of those who planned to join the assault, though, were just volunteers, like a thirty-six-year-old man who sat alone on the porch, staring into the night. He had a handlebar moustache and a scar on his face from an untreated shrapnel wound. "I'm not getting anything from the government to be here, and I don't want them to give me anything," he told Jaff and me. "I'm bringing my own bullets, my own uniform, my own gun."

He wanted to be part of history. Mosul covered 70 square miles, and the coalition had ground the ISIS defense lines to a ring of towns and villages that surrounded it. As the soldiers in Khazir prepared to push toward Mosul from the east, more fighters were mustering all around the cordon, waiting for the signal to begin a coordinated assault meant to mimic a noose tightening. There were the *peshmerga* as well as the various factions of the Iraqi security forces, ragtag groups of Sunni Arab tribesmen, Shia militia who were backed by Iran's Islamic Revolutionary Guard Corps, small Yazidi and Christian battalions, and the neo-Marxist YPG blocking supply lines from Syria. Many of these groups had fought one another before and believed they would do so again one day—but they had agreed to put aside their differences, for a little while at least, and band together. At the same time, as American pilots floated by in the warplanes overhead, some of the world's most elite soldiers were hidden among the ranks of the anti-ISIS alliance. America, Britain, Australia, France—all these and more had sent small units of commandos embedded and disguised as local forces, advising their movements, launching computer-guided mortars, and calling in airstrikes. Some American special operators had also spent the war stealing behind enemy lines to carry out arrests and assassinations on classified missions.

When the ISIS emir Abu Ayman al-Iraqi had told the Syrian rebel commander Mohamed Zataar, during their 2013 phone call, that in the next war America would rely on local troops—"They won't send anyone whose name is William or Benjamin. They'll send people named Ahmed and Mohamed and Abdullah"—he had missed a key nuance. The men named William and Benjamin were still there, in the shadows and above the clouds. It was still America's war, even as it was also the war of the Syrians and Iraqis. By 2016 Abu Ayman was dead—as he had predicted, Zataar had outlasted him—killed by one of the drones or pilots in the clouds. Yet his promise of total war remained in my mind: "Either you cleanse us or we cleanse you."

Hoping to get a few hours of sleep, Jaff and I left the house and walked down to the Land Cruiser we'd rented. I sprawled out in the back seat, and he stretched out in his sleeping bag on the ground, snoring. In *The Forever War*, a book about the Iraq War by the journalist Dexter Filkins, Jaff had played a starring role, working alongside Filkins, then a *New York Times* correspondent in his forties. The pair carried on in the heart of the civil war, and Jaff, in the book, was all bravado and aggression. He hailed from a big Kurdish clan, had done hard time in the Kurdish resistance, and seemed unfazed by the danger they faced—Filkins likened him to the cool-blooded detective played by Clint Eastwood in *Dirty Harry*.

Jaff was a man who would not be rushed through a meal, and Filkins relates a scene in which they receive a hostile welcome from fellow diners at a kebab house in a tense town north of Baghdad. "We walked in and Jaff said something to the owner, and then we headed toward the back and sat down. And everyone in the restaurant was staring at us," he writes. "Under my breath, I suggested to Jaff that perhaps we ought to leave. Jaff didn't say a word, but reached down and unstrapped his Browning 9 mm pistol and laid it on the table in front of him. Then he ordered his kebab, as if there was nothing amiss. Within a few minutes, everyone got back to minding their own business."

I admired the way Jaff had worked his way through a bureau of powerful and sometimes jealous journalists to make his own career. He'd become an established photographer and a U.S. citizen and bombed around Manhattan with his wife and daughter in a red Mustang with "PESHMRGA" on the license plates. The man who accompanied me for the battle in Mosul had mellowed as a husband and dad, no longer chain-smoking or toting a gun, but he still had a vibe that said *I don't answer to anyone, and none of this scares me*.

When the Twin Towers fell, I was in third period at high school, twenty miles to the east on Long Island, and after the students whose parents worked in the towers were called one by one to the principal's office on the loudspeaker, we were sent home early. Standing at Ground Zero on September 11, Filkins saw a transformation coming. "My countrymen were going to think this was the worst thing that ever happened, the end of civilization," he wrote, explaining that in the places he'd worked, such death and destruction was, if not commonplace, then not extraordinary—a cyclone in India, an earthquake in Turkey, decades of war in Afghanistan. "I don't think I was the only person thinking this, who had the darker perspective. All those street vendors who worked near the World Trade Center, from all those different countries, selling falafel and schwarma. When they heard the planes and watched the towers they must have thought the same as I did: that they'd come home."

It was hard to be in Iraq during the ISIS war and not feel the repercussions of that moment: in the security-choked streets of Baghdad and in soldiers marked by more than a decade of fighting and in civilians who had lived through all of it. I wondered how the terrorist attacks that ISIS was carrying out might affect the American mind-set all over again, and I wondered too about the other countries ISIS was targeting. After the attacks in Paris, there had been more: sometimes, as in Brussels, there were operational links to ISIS, while other times, as in San Bernardino, California, the attackers were only inspired by it. The forces of nativism and populism were rising in Europe, and with a presidential election less than a month away, Donald Trump was within striking distance in the polls at home, capturing better than anyone the unease that people were feeling.

ISIS had mastered the use of social media to amplify every attack, whether carried out by one of its fighters or by anyone at all with ISIS sympathies, turning even lone wolves into extensions of its global reach. Within this strategy was an evolution: while Osama bin Laden's al-Qaeda had focused on sophisticated, high-profile operations, ISIS embraced the ordinary. Shooting up random office parks and driving trucks through crowds were the kinds of attacks that made it seem like anyone could be a threat. They were designed to get people to turn their suspicions on each other. And I felt it happening, in conversations with people around the world, often total strangers, who would let out their anxieties when they found out where I lived and worked. Or there were conversations like this one, over email with a friend from home: "Frank had a baby, Dan is president of a company. . . . Know I said I wanted you home where it's safe—but in a few weeks not sure that will be the case. It's really getting weirder and weirder and I'm not sure when the weirdness will start to become legitimate fear for your own safety."

To me it was an open question whether the forces that ISIS had helped to set in motion could be stopped with its defeat, but as the Mosul battle commenced, these were the stakes. The Kurdish fighters at Khazir were calling the offensive the *final battle*, and local soldiers across the anti-ISIS alliance often spoke of the war in the context of this greater upheaval, saying they were the world's front line against the militants. None of them were saints, and each force was there to pursue its own geopolitical interests; yet they also saw themselves as foot soldiers in a global struggle.

A coalition victory in Mosul would signal the end of ISIS as a landholding force in Iraq and set the stage for the isolation and eventual loss of its remaining territory in Syria. ISIS had once controlled as much as 40 percent of Iraq, and that number had been whittled down to 10 percent, with at least 1 million civilians still living in Mosul. Raqqa, by comparison, had around 200,000 residents and could be won more easily once its supply routes from Iraq were cut. ISIS had been preparing its defenses in Mosul for more than two years—digging tunnels, planting IEDs, and filling trenches with oil to burn for cover from airstrikes. A defense analyst had told me that at least 5,000 ISIS fighters remained in the city, and it was clear that they would use the population as human shields. The previous day, I'd asked Munzer to message a former ISIS commander to see how he thought his old comrades were feeling on the other side of the battle line. "Mosul is the human and moral reservoir for ISIS, and the strategic link between Syria and Iraq, and they depend on Mosul," he had replied. "It has a great significance in the hearts of the fighters. They will fight fiercely."

Below the ridgeline, the airstrikes thundered with increasing intensity, and the Land Cruiser gently rattled as I drifted to sleep.

The sun was about to rise when the rumble of the departing *peshmerga* vehicles woke me. I sat up in the back seat and saw Jaff standing beside the window, rolling up his sleeping bag. We started the engine and fell in with the advancing caravan as it rolled into a valley down a snaking dirt road. The armored tanks and Humvees were at the head of the caravan, and behind them a line of vehicles stretched for half a mile. The *peshmerga* were pouring toward the front lines with everything they had: white Toyota Hilux pickups, SUVs, buses, sedans, motorcycles. The sun had started to rise over the hills behind us, washing the procession in a soft yellow light. As we bounced along the road, I could hear machine guns firing. On the horizon, trenches of oil and pyres of tires were burning as ISIS sought cover from airstrikes. The caravan paused, and I stepped outside and strapped on my body armor and began to walk along the line of vehicles as *peshmerga* fanned out through fields of parched grass. A compact man in green fatigues and a skull-and-crossbones face mask walked among them, speaking English into a radio. He was an American soldier, feeding information back to his post. "All right, brother," he was saying as he passed.

I returned to the SUV, and we rolled a little faster than before, moving toward a town called Bartella, where the smoking oil and tires had created a deep, dark fog. The crack and rumble of the airstrikes drew closer. A bomb exploded on the right side of the convoy, shooting a geyser of dirt into the air. I thought for a moment that one of the airmen had made a mistake but realized that the blast was from an ISIS mortar. More began to explode around the convoy. I cursed myself for coming in a vehicle so vulnerable to shrapnel and put on my helmet.

As we drove deeper, the mortar fire increased. It meant, I knew, that militants were likely watching us in the distance somewhere. Mortar rounds are bombs launched into the sky from a portable tube; the weapon has exceptional range, and it's hard for targets to make out where the bombs are coming from. Attackers usually work in teams; one watches the target with binoculars and calls back the results to the other, who fires more bombs, in a game of trial and error. As the mortar teams harassed the caravan, the pilots overhead tried to kill them, but the militants were using the smoke for cover—hiding, reappearing, firing, and sneaking off again.

We rounded a bend, and a mortar hit just short of our vehicle. Then another hit very long, smashing into the rocky slope of a hill behind us. At first glance it looked like a bad shot, but we were being bracketed, the mortar team using the hill to calibrate its range. We pulled into a ditch and ducked behind the vehicle for cover. The mortars, the harassing machine-gun fire: these were the maneuvers of an insurgent army in a tactical retreat. It felt too easy. The *peshmerga* continued to roll past, pouring their men toward the retreating battle lines, the vehicles kicking up dirt around us—old pickups with machine guns mounted in their beds, two men with assault rifles astride a dirt bike, holding each other tight, a commuter bus packed with grim-faced soldiers.

CHAPTER 23

COMMANDOS

Al-Qosh, Iraq. Thirty miles north of Mosul.
October 2016.

IN OCTOBER 2015, JOSHUA WHEELER, A THIRTY-NINE-YEAR-OLD DELTA Force master sergeant, led a team of Kurdish commandos on a mission behind ISIS lines. They lowered down into a guarded compound in a Black Hawk helicopter and began taking fire immediately. By the time the operation was over, some twenty ISIS militants had been killed and sixty-nine prisoners had been saved. Wheeler, though, had been shot dead, making him the first U.S. soldier to be killed in the ISIS war. U.S. officials, to maintain the narrative that no American soldiers were involved in combat operations, distorted what had happened, saying that Wheeler had not been meant to engage with the enemy, that his role on the mission was unusual, and that something had gone awry.

In June, four months before Jaff and I joined Major Salam for the Mosul offensive, we had traveled to Iraqi Kurdistan to learn what really happened to Wheeler and what troops like him were really doing in the war. Knowing the Americans would never speak to us, we instead met with members of the little-known group of elite Kurdish commandos whom Wheeler and his unit had been training and fighting alongside, including a captain who was firing his automatic weapon alongside Wheeler just before his death.

We found that U.S. special operations forces were far more involved in the fighting than Americans had been led to believe. They worked with local troops like the Kurdish commandos to perform kill-or-capture missions, call in airstrikes, carry out sniper attacks, and pound ISIS positions with artillery. The Kurdish commandos were called the Counter-Terrorism Unit (CTU), and one of them described the work they were doing with Wheeler and his comrades as "removing ISIS members from the field." Since that trip, Jaff and I had been prevailing on Aziz Ahmed, a young Kurdish intelligence officer, to let us see the CTU in action. In October, a few days after we joined the *peshmerga* for the opening assault of the Mosul offensive, Aziz called to say that our request had been granted—but only if we joined the CTU immediately. With Major Salam still waiting to start his attack, we agreed.

We sped our Land Cruiser to a small village thirty miles north of Mosul, in the shadow of the Zagros Mountains. There we found some fifty men in green fatigues and red berets standing at attention in the yard of a sympathetic farmer. A commander addressed them in Kurdish in a voice inflected with a laryngitic squeak. "Listen up. This is not the first time you guys are doing this. You know your roles and you're well trained," he said. "Just remember to be aware of your surroundings. They will throw everything they can at you. They have car bombs, tunnels, IEDs. And they are looking for every chance to attack us. Remember that. Whenever we stop, that gives them a chance to attack. Remember the discipline of your training. Don't be lazy. Don't open the windows of your Humvee. Don't say I need to go and take a leak. You have everything you need."

A pair of soldiers leaned on one another's shoulders as the commander spoke. Somehow in that soft fall breeze, I was reminded of a pregame speech at a high school football game, my mind moving, for a few pleasant moments, to the quiet innocence of an athletic field somewhere on Long Island. But the commander's words were like a madman's, the danger of the task conveyed in his simplicity: Don't stop, don't pee. Fear this enemy. Kurdish flags in red, white, and green flapped from the vehicles parked outside the gate. There were Range Rover Defenders, armor-plated Ford F-350s, a tactical air control vehicle with its tall antenna, a dozen Humvees. A neighbor peered over his fence.

In the morning the men would launch an assault to punch through ISIS lines, driving a wedge into ISIS territory that would let regular *peshmerga* forces fill in behind them. As the CTU fought their way southbound toward Mosul in a small convoy, they'd be all but surrounded.

The commander began to call out the order of battle. Humvee one would be outfitted with a DShK heavy machine gun. He called the names of its five-man crew, and they raised their hands. Humvee two would have an autocannon. Next in line would be the snipers, and then the EOD engineers, and then a PKC machine gun, and then more vehicles with more heavy weapons. The speech was done, and the men began to make their preparations—a soldier carefully placing a machine gun in its turret, the officers removing the ranks from their sleeves.

I walked over to the Humvee that would occupy the eighth spot in the convoy, where a thirty-three-year-old captain named Saeed was readying the antitank missile launcher mounted to its turret. I would accompany his crew into the battle on my own, since the unit's commander had agreed to surrender just a single spot in the Humvee, leaving Jaff to trail behind in an MRAP. Standing erect, with his beret cocked to the side, Captain Saeed greeted me in English and smiled warmly. He had become a *peshmerga* fighter when he was seventeen and was one of the first to sign up for the CTU program in the midst of the ISIS emergency.

I asked about the American commandos he sometimes fought alongside. "That's secret stuff. I don't want to talk about it," he said. "Right now my profession is the rockets. That's what I do."

As the man who defended the convoy against suicide car bombs, Captain Saeed knew he would have a busy day. His weapon, called a BGM-71 TOW missile launcher, fired rockets attached by a thin metal wire to a console in his turret, allowing him to direct them toward his target with a joystick. TOWs were designed to stop tanks and were the best defense the convoy had against the armor-plated car and truck bombs. ISIS sometimes sent the vehicles straight at Captain Saeed. The militants were successful once, he said, ramming his Humvee and detonating a blast that sent it two stories into the air. The blast killed his driver and knocked him unconscious. "When I came to, I couldn't feel one side of my body," he said. "I grabbed my arm, because I thought it was severed, to take it to the hospital so they could reattach it."

The arm, in fact, had only been dislocated, and Captain Saeed had returned to his unit the same day.

He said, "All of us have considered the day when we're going to be killed. And we have a goal. And for the goal it's worth spilling any amount of blood." He wasn't just talking about defeating ISIS. He was a hard-line Kurdish nationalist—a man who, though he knew it fluently, refused to speak Arabic. He saw pushing ISIS off Kurdish land as a prelude to drawing the boundaries for a new Kurdish state; what territory they took he did not intend to be leaving. The CTU was run by the chief of the Kurdish intelligence services, Masrour Barzani, son of the region's president and its most aggressive advocate for independence. Captain Saeed ticked off the atrocities and injustices that had been perpetrated against the Kurds across the decades. To him, independence was the only way to make it right.

"We don't care about death," he said, and I knew it wasn't a boast. "To die for President Barzani, for Kurdistan, is normal. Because Barzani wants a Kurdish state. To die for a goal that big is worth it."

Darkness fell on the field, and the men readied their vehicles, their floodlights illuminating the night. Jaff and I huddled with Aziz, the young Kurdish intelligence officer, making the kind of grim negotiations that arose often as we worked to insert ourselves into the war. The CTU had never embedded a journalist before, and the commander wanted to bounce me from the attacking convoy, since putting me in Captain Saeed's Humvee meant displacing the highly trained soldier who should have been there. Jaff, for his part, was livid that he'd been relegated to an MRAP in the back. It was something we should have been running from anyway, but instead we stood there and argued heatedly. Eventually Aziz, who was educated at the Royal Holloway university in London, told Jaff he was stuck with the MRAP but let me keep my spot. "We don't have control over anything out there," he said in his posh British accent. "You're going to be completely surrounded. It's fucking dangerous."

Jaff and I walked between two rows of idling vehicles. Atop one of the Humvees, three soldiers sat together, the one in the middle playing a music video on his phone, their faces lit by the glow of the screen. We came to a pair of armored dune buggies. They had windshields of bulletproof glass and roll cages outfitted with machine guns and floodlights. The two drivers standing near them wore sleek black helmets cut above the ears. One had a bandana covering his face. The other wore a medical mask. I asked about the purpose of the buggies, and the man with the bandana said, "If ISIS runs away, we can catch them."

Across from the buggies was a massive armored vehicle that the Kurds had made themselves. It looked like a cross between a tank and a battleship, with two heavy machine guns mounted on top of it. Four men peered down from the edge as I approached, waving like sailors anchored at port.

The troops arranged their vehicles into a caravan to head to the front lines, and Jaff and I got into the Land Cruiser to follow them. I steered it into line as the unit rumbled through darkened villages. Bystanders stopped and waved when they saw the men passing, the vehicles rolling slowly. A child scampered in the sidelong glare of the headlights.

The soldiers stopped outside a town called Tel Skof at a great berm that stretched for miles through fields that farmers had stopped working. For about two years this had marked a boundary with ISIS. Jaff and I had been there before and knew that on the other side stretched a no-man's-land and then, just in rifle range, an ISIS berm that mirrored the one the CTU men now parked their vehicles behind. Regular *peshmerga* were stationed along the berm. I could also see a few Western soldiers camped on their own, their bearded faces lit by a small fire. I backed the Land Cruiser against the berm and pushed back my seat.

———·———

The alarm on my iPhone was set for 4 a.m., and when it blared, I stepped out into the darkness and changed my shirt, cleaned my hands with sanitizer and put in my contacts, then grabbed a bottle of water and brushed my teeth. I heard the rumble of the heavy engines starting along the berm. Headlights flashed on. The unique sound of Kurdish filtered through the chilly air, a variation of an ancient Iranian dialect preserved by the isolation of the mountains: *Ew kata bash. Beyanee bash. Hello. Good morning.* I put on my body armor and stuffed my notebook into its front pocket.

I left Jaff sleeping in the Land Cruiser and walked along the berm until I found Captain Saeed standing beside his Humvee in his red beret. An airstrike cracked and shook the ground, and scattered cheers rose. I used my flashlight to scan the Humvee's roof: binoculars, a fire extinguisher, a pair of assault rifles.

Captain Saeed climbed into his turret, and I slid into the back. The turret's manhole was cut above the middle of the roof, and Captain Saeed hung down from it, sitting on a thick strap that came under him like a swing, the toes of his boots touching the seat beside my thigh. I craned my neck to look up through the turret. It was that spectral time when night is brushed with the first shades of day, and a gibbous moon still shone. Captain Saeed was staring up at the brightening sky, as if meditating.

Kurdish nationalists like him, just as Syrian rebels once did, sometimes likened themselves to America's revolutionary patriots, ready to die for their vision of a new country, and he seemed in that moment like a figure from another time, though I couldn't say whether it was in the past or the future. On the one hand he was an anachronism, with the migrant crisis and the dissolution of global boundaries making the idea of statehood difficult to imagine in the pure way that he saw it. On the other perhaps he was a harbinger of a time when new territory would be carved from the world's disarray. Either way, I knew the world was built by zealots like him.

The rest of the team took their seats in the Humvee: a boyish driver whose helmet almost covered his eyes, another soldier in the back seat behind him, and a man who introduced himself in broken English as Ahmed in the passenger's seat. Captain Saeed gave me a set of noise-canceling headphones. When the men gave the signal that he was about to fire his weapon, he said, I should take off my helmet and put them on.

Sixteen Humvees lined up and rolled through a gap in the berm. *Peshmerga* watched as we passed, waving and filming on their phones. The hellish roar of a surface-to-surface missile battery cut through the air behind us. The convoy moved slowly through the dead fields, pausing as an armor-plated tractor swept the ground for IEDs. Plumes of dirt shot into the air as the devices detonated. Between each explosion was the mechanical rumble of the vehicles and the slow creak of our turret, as Captain Saeed turned it with a hand crank, scanning. The driver leaned toward the windshield and peered through the murky pane.

As the Humvee rocked and rumbled, I began to drift to sleep. The sky had turned a bright blue, and the sun was heating the metal shell around me. As I dozed, an alarm vibrated on the fitness tracker on my wrist; it was set for 7 a.m., still synced to my schedule at home. Briefly I imagined the night table beside my bed, the soft light through the curtains, and the warmth of my fiancée. It grew hotter in the Humvee as the sun continued to rise, and I began to sweat beneath my armor.

The first gunshots sounded from one of the vehicles at the head of the convoy, and our driver cast his eyes about worriedly. We rolled forward, dry reeds scratching at the Humvee's shell. Captain Saeed kept rotating in his turret, a predator on the hunt. There was a quiet to the proceedings, as if we were sneaking on foot, as we approached the ISIS berm. We paused for a long while inside a little dip in the landscape, and an armored bulldozer rolled past us. A large explosion sounded ahead, followed by more gunshots. An airstrike hit to the left, then the right. It chilled me to imagine what the pilots might have seen creeping toward us. I received a text from Aziz saying that some American special forces were trailing our convoy in armored pickup trucks, calling in the airstrikes. Then the convoy passed through the berm, into ISIS territory.

Something rocked the Humvee. The driver and Ahmed looked at one another, unsure what it was. The chatter on the radio grew louder. Ahmed cocked his assault rifle, and Saeed did the same with the sidearm strapped to his leg. Ahmed reached back and checked that my door was bolted.

My eardrums pulsed twice, and then again, to the sound of nearby airstrikes. It felt like a long-present static had been cleared from my head. Captain Saeed had his iPhone charging from the cigarette lighter near the driver, and it was ringing in the tone of an old rotary phone. In the hand that cranked the turret, he held a lit cigarette. Through the thick film of my window, I saw a dragonfly land on a reed. A mortar hit beside us. There was a set of three airstrikes, and smoke rose behind a hill. I wondered if the strikes had hit the mortar team and if the convoy was being used as bait, flushing out the ISIS ambushes.

To the right of the Humvee, something was burning, creating a cyclone-like cylinder of smoke. Mortars continued to explode around us, and each time, Ahmed instinctively reached for his gun. The heat was pulsing in the Humvee. I thought it must be noon, but my watch said it was only 9:20. The air seemed to be thickening. As we rolled forward, I again felt myself being rocked to sleep as the Kurdish crackling on the radio, the dated ring of Captain Saeed's phone, and the thud of the mortars seemed to blend into nothing more than a dream.

I awoke to the boyish driver staring with binoculars out his window. We were close to some farm buildings, with tractors and trucks parked in a field. The men thought they'd seen one of the vehicles move. They worried that any of them could be a car bomb ready to suddenly hurtle toward us. The driver put the binoculars down, and we crested a hill. Bullets began to fly at the Humvee from a village, where black smoke from burning tires was billowing. In the fields below us, shepherds were tending to sheep as two boys waved white flags vigorously. Ahmed pointed to two beds on a hill, where the shepherds must have slept at night. "Arabs—like animals," he said.

It was around noon when we passed another village, to the Humvee's left, the soldiers taking note of every parked car. Bullets were flying from that direction. Three mortars thudded one after another into the dirt, approaching the Humvee in a line. The driver yelled up to Captain Saeed, asking if the armor on the vehicle's ceiling could withstand a mortar blast. Bullets began to smack into the Humvee, each time sending dust rising inside. Thick rounds from a heavy machine gun were coming at us from a compound about one hundred yards away, chirping around Captain Saeed's head. The convoy's gunners returned fire.

There was another explosion, and the chirping sound from the bullets intensified. In the Humvee we fanned ourselves and dripped with sweat. A frantic voice on the radio warned that an armor-plated truck bomb was headed the convoy's way. The soldiers in the Humvee strained to look out the windows. Then they saw it, coming right at us from the direction of the compound. They pointed and yelled and called out to Captain Saeed as he cranked the turret's handle and faced his weapon toward the vehicle, which was trailing a long tail of dust, picking up speed. As it neared, I saw the soldiers rip off their helmets and put on their noise-canceling headsets, but it seemed crazy to do that with the truck bomb so close. Instead I put my head down and jammed my fingers into my ears. There was a deafening shriek as Captain Saeed fired; I felt it in my head as a burst of white light. A powerful explosion rocked the Humvee. The soldiers erupted in cheers. With a joyful expression, the man beside me flashed a thumbs-up. Then, as if with the flick of a switch, his expression turned deadly serious again. He flung open his door, sending sunlight into the Humvee, and I could see a geyser of smoke rising from where the truck had exploded, about thirty yards away. He ran to the back of the Humvee, grabbed another missile, and handed it to Captain Saeed, who reloaded the weapon.

For the next hour or two, the battle continued, with both sides firing frantically. ISIS sent two more car bombs that, like the first, were destroyed before they reached the convoy. I was covered in the dust and grime that had been jarred loose inside the Humvee, and beads of sweat dripped from the brim of my helmet. Eventually, I looked out my window and saw that bulldozers had appeared on a hill beside us, each flying the bright Kurdish flag. They looked as formidable as a herd of elephants. They began to push up berms, creating a defensive cordon around a patch of dirt about the size of a football field. This was where the men planned to camp for the night.

The Humvees rolled in and took up positions behind the berms, their weapons pointing outward. We were near a village called Fel Fel, seven miles from Mosul. *Peshmerga* were rushing to cement control of the wedge of territory the CTU had cleared, but here we were at the tip of a peninsula surrounded by a hostile sea. As the troops stepped out from their vehicles for the first time in nine hours, mortars rained down from the south, east, and west. The bombs smashed into the earth outside the little enclave, but the berms offered the illusion of protection.

I stood to stretch my legs in the fresh air and took a selfie with a soldier who thought it was cool to have a foreigner there. From the center of the cordon I could look out in all directions. The Humvees were spaced every ten yards or so along the berms. Black smoke rose up all along the horizon, an easterly wind bending the plumes sideways. Captain Saeed's Humvee was set back on an incline to give him a better view in case he needed to fire his weapon. He sat cross-legged on the ground beside it, talking casually with some of the men about the day they had passed. My bag was in another Humvee, and I walked over to a group of soldiers to ask if anyone knew where to find it. Someone pointed to a vehicle near the berm. I had stepped about fifteen yards from those soldiers when a mortar crashed into them with a burst of shrapnel and a metallic surge of heat. I felt the heat on the back of my neck as I careened forward. When I caught my balance, I ran my hands over my body to see if I'd been hit. Then I heard the sound of moaning. More bombs came crashing down as the mortar team realized they'd hit their mark.

Soldiers were scrambling for cover inside the Humvees, and someone pulled me into one with him. There were four of us crowded in the front seat as I sat like a child on the lap of the man who'd grabbed me. The Humvee faced toward the blast site, and I watched through the foggy windshield as an injured soldier wandered through the settling dust, blood dripping from a gash on his head. Another was laying on the ground, his stomach gashed, bleeding to death. A third was carried by his comrades with one foot severed and the opposite leg shredded. The injured man was set on the ground, and medics rushed to him. Jaff walked over and handed someone the tourniquet from his med kit. Then he snapped a photo. Mortars were still raining down, and the soldiers beside me in the Humvee put on surgical masks. One pointed to the sky as he handed a mask to me. "Chlorine," he said. ISIS had been lacing some of its bombs with chlorine gas, and the soldiers were wearing the masks just in case.

Jaff and I spent the night in the back of an MRAP crowded with soldiers, seated on a bench, as airstrikes boomed one after another. The mission had been a success, but it was also sobering to see how even some of Iraq's best-trained and best-equipped soldiers had been slowed by the guerilla defense. And in this battle, the open fields made it easy for the coalition pilots to see ISIS positions and hit them with airstrikes. That wouldn't be the case in Mosul, where ISIS could take cover in the rows of buildings and among the civilians trapped there. The night sky seemed to rip open as a helicopter gunship roared nearby, helping to keep whatever was moving toward us at bay.

CHAPTER 24

"MOVE SLOW, NO BLEEDING"

Topzawa, Iraq. Six miles east of Mosul. October 2016.

JAFF AND I WERE BACK IN ERBIL A FEW DAYS LATER WHEN MAJOR Salam called to tell us to get ready for his assault. He'd spent almost two weeks waiting impatiently, like a boxer stuck in his dressing room, at the cluster of houses in Kalak where Jaff and I had left him. Since the Kurds had finally rolled ISIS back to Mosul's outskirts, the ICTF was ready to go. Major Salam sent an officer to retrieve us at our hotel.

Jaff and I were sitting in the garden after dinner, drinking a last round of beer, when Captain Zardasht, a Kurd who'd been with the ICTF from the beginning, walked in from the darkened street. He had the air of a man engaged in a battle that only he and his comrades could see and wore a jacket to hide his uniform and rank, wary of what threats might lurk even among the hotel's languid clientele. He joined us at the table, looking like an apparition in the scene of normalcy.

"I'm tired. You know why? I have twenty-eight wounds in me," he said. A scar sliced down the middle of his balding head. He told me he hoped to move to America with his wife and kids one day, but I guessed that he'd been saying that for years without realizing how much time had passed. When I asked the ages of his children, he paused. He didn't know.

He drove Jaff and me to Kalak, and we waited in a daze of semisleep until the battalion's black Humvees were lined up to leave the cluster of houses they'd briefly brought back to life. The brooms, bedding, satellite dish, and generators were all packed into the vehicles. They would leave behind only swept rooms, piles of empty water bottles and Styrofoam boxes in the yards, and tire tracks in the streets. Jaff and I climbed into the back seat of one of the Humvees, and I let my body sway with it as the convoy departed, shaking lightly as the engine churned, breathing the smell of diesel and dirt, the dust drying my eyes and coating my forehead above the bandana I'd wrapped around my nose and mouth.

The thick pane in my window had become cloudy over time, but in the middle was a perfect circle of clear glass. It was like peering through a cottage door into some haunted fairy tale, the yellow lights of the vehicles moving through places that had become nowhere, their people driven away by the war and only these soldiers there to witness the silence of the last hours of the night. The war-faded men were nothing like the picture of soldiers that would have come before to my mind's eye. Some were fat, some gaunt, some very old, and just a few were fit in the manner of American soldiers. Ahmed the Bullet had a large belly. There were no noticeable muscles on Major Salam's thin frame. There was no physical training, just moving and fighting. There was something almost glamorous in the way U.S. combat troops maintained their physiques, but they were part of a volunteer army that deployed overseas to what, at their cores, were wars of choice. For the ICTF, the war was at home, constant, and everywhere. They had a unique kind of hardness—Captain Zardasht with his skull-slit, Ahmed the Bullet with his reattached face, Major Salam with a jagged Frankenstein ridge along his head. The Humvees crossed a bridge over a river and drove on through swirls of dust, their Iraqi flags flying. They passed a checkpoint where a soldier stood alone in the dark, warming his hands in a detritus fire.

———·———

Beyond that soldier was an empty house. Major Salam stopped the convoy there and called his deputies inside for a briefing. They would leave soon to attack a village called Topzawa, which sat along the path to Mosul's eastern gate. Rather than standing over his men and barking orders, he reclined, catlike, on the floor and calmly laid out the battle plan, a touch of gray in his buzz cut.

"Gunners, JTACs, everyone—you have to work together. EODs, this is flat desert. From now on I want you in front so you can clear the way for us. I want space for the tanks." He continued on like that, looking up with alert brown eyes at the dozen officers standing around him. "We're not in a rush," he said. "We're not in a rush at all. The most important thing is no casualties."

An airstrike hit in the darkness, pulsing the eardrums of the soldiers and rattling the windows in their frames. "Now we are starting the offensive," he said.

On the porch, Ahmed the Bullet pulled on a pair of fingerless gloves and began to strut and banter with his comrades, getting loose before a day behind the .50-caliber machine gun in his turret. His briefing finished, Major Salam walked over to me. His natural intensity seemed all the more powerful for being concentrated in his compact, five-foot-eight figure. "I will say this in English. They will send women at the convoy, they will send little kids at the convoy," he said. "No matter what, you cannot leave the Humvee. Even if there are one hundred ISIS dead bodies around the vehicle, you must stay inside. Okay?"

The Humvees were lined up in formation, facing west, toward the battlefield. They shuddered and snorted as the drivers switched on their ignitions. Some of the soldiers pulled on their skull-faced ski masks; one wrapped his head in a black-and-white keffiyeh. Others were shadows of their American mentors in their baseball hats and sunglasses. Like the ISIS militants who themselves were readying for battle in the distance before them, the ICTF men seemed at the same time like a tribe of ancient warriors and an elite and modern army, both anachronistic and cutting-edge, a glimpse of the future and a window into the past. They stepped up into the vehicles in crews of four and five and set off as the sun rose.

———·———

I sat in the back seat of a Humvee near the center of the convoy. Ammo boxes were stacked beside me, and around them was a clutter: assault rifles, gas masks, a rocket-propelled grenade, a case of water bottles, a cardboard box of potato chips. Hanging from the turret beside me was Abbas, a gruff twenty-something from Baghdad, whose stocky legs balanced on a stack of ammo boxes because he was too short for his feet to reach the seat. Jaff was in the passenger's seat, beside the husky driver. A wiry soldier sat behind Jaff, keeping watch out his window.

The Humvees crept in a long column through dirt fields as engineers in an MRAP searched for IEDs. His voice crackling on the radio, Major Salam commanded the convoy from the first Humvee's passenger seat. Topzawa sat near Highway 2, on the route the ICTF planned to take in eastern Mosul.

Our Humvee creaked as it rolled. Ahead, through the windshield, the soldier with the keffiyeh swayed in his turret. He was called Bis Bis, another one of the original ICTF soldiers, stocky and balding with an antagonistic demeanor. He wrapped the keffiyeh around his shoulders and leaned back in the turret, tilting his head skyward.

The three soldiers in our Humvee were much younger, relative newcomers. Abbas said to the driver, "I'm gonna take the flag and put it on the gun." The driver handed him a green banner bearing the likeness of Imam Hussein, the Shia martyr. This was a sectarian marker that most older ICTF soldiers would never use. The younger men still preached the inclusive mantra U.S. troops had founded the special forces upon—one that said they were an antisectarian force building Iraq for Shia, Sunnis, Christians, and Kurds—and perhaps they believed it in their own way. But standards had slipped, and the flag the young men were flying gave their assault a sectarian tinge.

The driver told me he had idolized the ICTF growing up during the American war. They were the baddest Iraqi soldiers around, storming into hostile neighborhoods on kill-or-capture missions. "People used to be scared of them. There used to be songs about them, and whenever they would go into a neighborhood, you knew there had to be something big," he said.

He'd joined at the end of 2011, as the Americans were leaving. There was the open question of what would happen to the special forces and to the rest of the Iraqi military with them gone. He weighed around 230 pounds when ICTF recruiters walked into the army camp where he was training. "They didn't want to take me," he said. He prevailed on an ICTF colonel, who told him he'd give him another shot in three months. He spent that time running, doing push-ups, and skipping meals, and when the colonel returned, he'd lost fifty pounds.

Over the last two years, sitting sometimes for fourteen hours a day in his Humvee, unable even to open the door to pee, he'd gained back most of the weight. The grind of street battles was unlike the specialized missions for which he'd been trained. "This is not our job, street fights. We entered into a dirty kind of war," he said.

The convoy's gunners test-fired their weapons. Our driver checked Facebook on his phone. On the horizon were the low-slung buildings of Topzawa, encircled by a seven-foot-high concrete wall. The ISIS militants defending the village caught sight of the convoy and opened fire with mounted machine guns. Dirt puffed up around us. I heard the by now familiar chirping sound as bullets flew around the turret, the gunners aiming for Abbas's head. "Be careful, Abbas!" the driver yelled as bullets hit the Humvee. Abbas let loose with his machine gun, the shots echoing inside the Humvee's metal shell.

The Kurdish commandos of the CTU had held their positions in the fields and fired on ISIS from afar, but Major Salam got on the radio and ordered his drivers to move forward. They advanced amid a shower of mortars and RPGs. Abbas was firing his weapon madly, the gun dripping oil as cascades of scorching bullet casings fell into the Humvee. "Abbas! Be conservative with your ammunition!" the driver screamed above the din. "We haven't even gotten into the village yet!"

An airstrike hit so close that everyone jumped. A bullet streaked overhead with a metallic zing. "A sniper," Jaff said. The Humvees picked up speed, each isolated in a dust cloud. Fifty yards from Topzawa's outer wall, they broke their column and fanned out. Abbas skidded on his ammo boxes as the Humvee bumped and rocked.

"Abbas! Abbas!" the driver screamed as more bullet casings flooded the floor. Taking the lead from the soldier next to me, I periodically gathered the spent casings, threw open my window hatch, dumped them out, and slammed it shut again.

Sparks flew from the second story of a school where ISIS had positioned one of its heavy guns. Dust billowed inside the Humvee as something exploded in front of it, and the ground seemed to ripple. There was an ear-splitting eruption as the Iraqis fired from a tank. "They are firing at you—be careful!" the driver shouted to Abbas, whose phone had been ringing nonstop. Finally, during a brief lull, he stopped to answer it. A worried aunt was on the line, crying. Like many of the battalion's soldiers, Abbas had been lying to his family about the extent of the danger, but his aunt had seen reports of the increasingly deadly Mosul offensive on TV. Ducking down into the Humvee, Abbas told her he was miles from any fighting. "I swear to God, nothing is going on," he said. "Everything is okay."

As the fighting picked up again, a soldier in a baseball cap stepped from the Humvee beside us and, with his assault rifle, sprayed bullets toward the town. Still fretting about ammo, the driver saw that a box of it had fallen from another vehicle and made a mad dash out to get it. On the radio, Major Salam ordered the men forward again, and our driver pulled up to the village's outer wall. Terrified civilians were huddled in the streets and houses beyond. Major Salam's Humvee rolled up alongside us, and his voice crackled over a PA system with a robotic drone. "We don't have any problem with you guys. Put a white flag on your house, and you're going to be safe," he said. The gunners watched over the wall as civilians inched out from their homes. An airstrike hit a building behind them with a crack like thunder, shaking the ground. Sirens blared from Major Salam's PA. "The plane is not going to hit you," he said. "Come toward me."

Families began to clamber over the wall. The soldiers stepped out of their Humvees, their weapons drawn. They had been attacked before by ISIS members hiding among such crowds, and their faces seem pained as they repressed the urge to help. They ordered each man to lift his shirt and spin, to see if he was strapped with a bomb. One after another the villagers continued to make their harried escape—an old man with a wrinkled belly, a look of terror on his reddened face, a teenager with a laptop case. "Take off your shirt! Take off your shirt. Undress!" the soldiers cried. "Don't come closer! Don't come closer! Take off your shirt!"

Two elderly women emerged, struggling to carry an infirm man between them. The soldiers watched in horrified silence. "Go and carry him," an officer finally said, and someone threw his rifle on the hood of a Humvee and ran forward with his arms outstretched.

An armored bulldozer smashed a hole in the wall. Soldiers stepped through it with their weapons drawn. Topzawa was a small town, and the soldiers fanned out to secure the houses, starting on the ground floors and working their way to the rooftops. Small children peered down at me from behind a brick wall. I saw a man looking nervously from a doorway with a toddler at his ankles and followed a pair of soldiers as they entered the home. Inside, a handful of adults huddled with a gaggle of dazed and dirty children. A woman approached me, thinking I was a soldier. "Do you know if they released the prisoners that ISIS had?" she asked. Her father had been opposed to ISIS, she said. He'd been taken from the house one day and never heard from again.

"We were like prisoners," she said. "If we had breakfast, then we worried about lunch, and if we had lunch, then we worried about dinner."

There were still gunshots sounding in the town, but the children seemed not to hear them. I stepped outside and saw a commotion across the street. A shirtless man was cowering on his knees, his hands bound behind him by zip ties. Soldiers huddled around him. When I approached, one of them held a suicide belt out to me. They believed it was the man's; they had found it in a home nearby. The device looked like a large, limp fish, with dozens of ball bearings packed together and saran-wrapped around the charge, glittering like scales. On the bottom, a liquid explosive the color of bile oozed behind the saran. I felt sick looking at it, imagining the device pressed beneath a shirt, flush against the skin of a belly.

The man's name was Habash. He insisted that he wasn't with ISIS, emitting a childish whine as he looked at the soldiers' feet. "I didn't do anything," he said.

Someone slapped him on the forehead. "Just shut the fuck up and keep your head down," he said.

Another soldier, still wearing a skull mask, approached him. "Lift your head," he said. "Let me see your face."

Habash looked up at him.

"Did you cry?" the soldier asked.

"Yes," Habash said.

He lowered his head again.

One of the soldiers said that Habash had taken off running in his rubber sandals when the ICTF entered the town. "Why run away? Why not hold a white flag like everyone else? And then he has a suspicious family name. And look at his beard and the way his moustache is shaved."

A heavyset man stepped from one of the houses and approached the soldiers cautiously. "This guy has nothing to do with anything. I can sign for him," he said.

"Do you want to leave, or do you want me to handcuff you and put you next to him?" one of the soldiers replied.

Looking down at Habash, the soldiers seemed to be trying to restrain the desire for revenge. One flicked cigarette ash on him. Another wiped it off. One gave him a cigarette. Another took it from him.

Finally, a lieutenant pulled Habash up by his hair. "Come here," he said.

He took him to the center of the street, saying, "I'm going to shoot him." He reached for his pistol. The other soldiers, Jaff and I, Habash—all of us only stood there dumbly. Three of the children watched from the doorway across the street. The lieutenant paused. Then he holstered his gun and put Habash in the back of one of the Humvees.

As the sun set, with the village secured and its residents emptied into temporary camps, Major Salam commandeered a beautiful villa, well-appointed and sparkling clean. "Sunni family" was written in graffiti on an outer wall, possibly put there in hopes of staving off trouble when ISIS invaded. While a few of the men worked to rig the house for electric and set up Major Salam's satellite dish and flat-screen TV, the battalion's cook served a dinner of soup and rice to the soldiers outside. As they ate, families emerged periodically from the nearby fields, dragging suitcases through the dirt and waving white flags. One of the soldiers gave a cigarette to an old man in a white prayer cap. Others remained wary. "In situations like this, I wouldn't even trust my own father," one said. He recalled a close call in Ramadi: "A bunch of families approached us. All of a sudden, three guys from inside the crowd opened fire."

After dinner, Major Salam stretched out on the patio in front of the villa. He cracked a Red Bull, his favorite drink. Habash, uncuffed, was brought before him, along with another man who said he was his brother. Major Salam sat them down and, with an easy air, began to question them.

"Why is your beard like this?" he asked the brother.

"Even the tone of our language, they made us change."

"Why were you armed?"

"They put a pistol in my hand."

Major Salam turned to Habash. It was clear that he was a simple man. When Major Salam gave him a sip of the Red Bull, he squealed and scrunched his face. Major Salam asked what his job was.

"I'm in charge of the generator here," Habash said proudly.

"Dude, stop, stop," the brother hissed. "Don't talk too much. You're gonna make it worse."

Finally the two men admitted that they had been working with ISIS. But Major Salam was feeling benevolent. He set them free on the condition that they would get the generator working, so the villa would have electricity.

When they left, I asked how he thought the day went. "We moved slow, but there wasn't any bleeding," he said.

CHAPTER 25

BASE CAMP

Bazwaya, Iraq. Three miles east of Mosul. October 2016.

THE FOLLOWING MORNING A COLD WIND BLEW AS WE BEGAN ROLLing again, leaving Topzawa. We rumbled onto Highway 2, a few miles from Mosul's eastern edge. On the radio a voice said, "There's the possibility of snipers here. So be careful you guys."

We came into denser terrain: the buildings closer together, the road lined with filling stations and convenience stores, all of them abandoned, their metal grates pulled down.

"On the left side is friendly forces," said the radio. "On the right is the enemy."

On the right was a Mosul suburb called Bazwaya. ISIS had pushed a long berm between the highway and the town, and one of the ICTF's nightmarish black bulldozers was working to fill the gaps in it, to prevent car bombs from sneaking through them.

Abbas slid on his ammo boxes, still unable to find his footing.

There were faded billboards around the rubbled storefronts on the left. "On the right there are animals. Nobody shoot at them," the radio said. We rolled past some horses.

One after another on the sides of the road were mounds of melted tires that looked like giant scalps, the rubber pooled, the cords spread out on the pavement. When lit they must have made an image grand in its menace, the pyres like torches, lighting a path through a netherworld of toppled electric towers and crushed houses.

Beneath a gray sky, the gunners slowly scanned in their turrets.

The radio said, "Be careful. There's a car on the right that has a family holding a white flag."

The metal shells of the vehicles rattled from an airstrike.

Gunshots came at us from the right. Again the driver screamed Abbas's name as bullet casings poured into my lap. The convoy paused. Abbas eased up on the trigger and began to probe around a house—a shot on the roof, a shot in the yard, dirt puffing in sync with the weapon's pop. The convoy began to move again, rolling on without resolution.

For two hours the Humvees traveled between the molten tires as airstrikes thundered and the gunners exchanged volleys of fire with unseen enemies. Then the lines of tires stopped, and the convoy reached a set of berms that stretched down the road like cresting waves. Major Salam stopped the convoy there and told the men to wait. He led a handful of Humvees into Bazwaya to secure houses for a new base just a few minutes' drive into the city. As we idled near the berms, I noticed a strange mass laid before them that looked almost metallic in the refracted sunlight. I stepped out, crouched down, and squinted and saw that it was a mangled body. In place of the legs were swollen stumps seared to an alloy-like orange in the heat of a blast. The corpse had a bearded face and a full head of black hair and was splayed in the direction of Mosul, as if pointing the way.

I dug with my hands through dust-covered debris, casting aside the remnants of a family: candleholders, a doll, a cracked tea set. I could hear the troops clamoring outside in their ant-like ritual to make the houses their next outpost, rigging electric, setting defenses. This time it was left to Jaff and me to do it too. We raised a layer of dust that hung like a fog in the sun-lit air in what had been a bedroom, rifling through broken dreams, a smashed armoire, a pile of toys, a red bassinet. Then we dragged out two wooden bed frames.

We set them in another room whose windows looked onto a small parcel of destruction. What had once been a courtyard had its walls caved in and was littered with an incomprehensible mess of wires and trash. Through the yard cut an ISIS tunnel that stretched into Mosul's city limits. Its roof had been reinforced with wood beams and sheets of corrugated metal. Filaments jutted into the air from holes smashed into it by explosions. An entrance to the tunnel was cut into the yard of the house beside us, where Major Salam was staying.

Across from the room's windows, on the far wall, a small plastic mirror hung from a nail. In it, my sun-reddened face, with its overgrown beard, reflected something primeval, a grim colonizer in a stranger's shattered home. I beat the grime from a peach-and-cream-colored comforter and lay down. On a piece of loose-leaf taped to the wall above me was a child's watercolor painting of a river and a tree.

I awoke that night to shouts in the yard. I pulled on my boots and stumbled outside to see a small crowd gathered near the tunnel entrance beside Major Salam's house. The ghosts had stirred; the men thought they'd heard movement. Ahmed the Bullet stood at the entrance with his sidearm. He smiled impishly at me when I approached, as if we were boys playing a midnight game. Below us, Major Salam stood in the tunnel with a flashlight in one hand and, in the other, a torch. He crouched and strained his eyes into the subterranean darkness. Then he set a pile of kindling alight. As black smoke billowed into the cavern, he climbed up and stepped quietly along the tunnel's spine, pausing here and there to put his ear to the ground, listening for a shuffle, a cough.

———·———

Nothing is sacred—to Major Salam it was a mantra. He had learned it on his first mission as an ICTF man. The Americans had flown their Iraqi charges by helicopter to a mosque outside Baghdad and told them that a terrorist cell was based there. The mosque was empty when they entered, quiet and serene. They stepped into its library, where grand bookcases stretched toward the ceiling, filled with aged tomes. "Clear it," an American officer told the Iraqis.

It was a command they'd learned in their training, and it meant to search a place by upending it. They stepped forward in their boots, desecrating the books as they ripped them from the walls. They found nothing. When it was over, some of the Iraqis quit. It was only much later that Major Salam learned that the mission had been contrived—the final test of their training. He considered it the most important lesson the Americans taught him.

Salam's first encounter with the U.S. military had come in the spring of 2003. A recent graduate from military college, he was standing on a corner in a suddenly war-torn Baghdad when he saw a modified U.S. tank rumbling toward him, massive and green, a mine plow with jagged metal teeth mounted to its front plate. "I was shocked," he recalled one night in Bazwaya, sitting not far from the tunnel outside his villa. The men were in one of their impatient holding patterns again, waiting for the order to move into Mosul proper. "I really admired the power of the American army, which I considered to be liberators."

His father had been a member of the Iraqi air force, and many family members had served under Saddam Hussein. They were part of the country's Shia Muslim religious majority, which was repressed by Hussein's Sunni-led regime. But like many Iraqis, the family saw the military as a way to get by under a dictator who seemed as enduring as the summer heat. When Hussein fell, Salam saw the chance to build a new Iraq, and before long he was training under U.S. soldiers for the new National Guard.

One day during training, a hulking American, the biggest man he'd ever seen, pulled him aside. "Do you want to do something special?" he asked.

Not long afterward, following the American's instructions, he joined a crowd of recruits outside one of Hussein's old palaces in Baghdad. A cadre of U.S. troops greeted them at the palace gate but offered no details except that the training program would be long and hard. "Here is a door," one of them said, motioning to the palace gate. "If you're serious, enter. If not, go home."

Most of the recruits turned and left, but Salam kept his eyes on the gate. "All I wanted was to go through it," he recalled. "It was a new life."

Some of the dictator's exotic animals still roamed the grounds when Salam entered the palace. The training began as the occupation of Iraq was descending into chaos, with Shia militia ambushing U.S. patrols and Sunni terrorists massacring civilians in suicide attacks. The hunt was on for the Jordanian Abu Musab al-Zarqawi as he laid the foundation for a brutal new al-Qaeda branch, al-Qaeda in Iraq, which would later give birth to ISIS. As U.S. soldiers combed through hostile neighborhoods in search of suspects, they realized they would need local help.

The Americans at the palace were from the U.S. Army's Special Forces, otherwise known as the Green Berets, which had conducted clandestine warfare and built up local commando units from Vietnam to Afghanistan. They put the Iraqis through a grueling physical and mental regimen. Anyone who questioned them risked being dismissed on the spot.

After two and a half weeks of training, more than half of the men who'd first entered the palace with Salam were gone, having either quit or been sent home. The pared-down group was flown to Jordan; it was the first time Salam had left Iraq. They trained for three more months under Jordanian special forces and elite U.S. troops with names like Mark the Sniper, Cedric, and Dave. It was there that Salam learned they were being molded into a counterterrorism force that would specialize in hostage rescues and high-value target raids—an Iraqi version of U.S. commando units such as the Delta Force and SEAL Team Six. He learned to fire pistols and M4 rifles, to break into houses, to rope-rappel from helicopters, to kick down doors. At the end of training, he was given the role of breacher, and the newly minted commandos were flown back to Baghdad.

They were formed into a battalion, the ICTF, and became the backbone of the Iraqi Special Operations Forces, or ISOF, which quickly gained a reputation among their U.S. allies as the most reliable soldiers in Iraq. Over time, as ISOF expanded to three brigades, the ICTF would officially be called the 2nd Battalion, 1st ISOF Brigade. But its soldiers still referred to themselves by their original name, and veterans of the first training program even remembered the order in which they had entered it, wearing the numbers like a badge. Major Salam was number fifty. By the time they got to Bazwaya, out of that initial class of seventy-six, only eight remained. The rest were dead, or retired, or simply missing, or had left the country.

Lieutenant Harb Abid, a muscle-bound ICTF veteran, was number nineteen. He was old—ISOF leadership was trying to get him to retire. But when I met him in Bazwaya one day, he said that if he stopped fighting, he'd have nothing to do. And he was sure that there would be more war. After defeating ISIS, he said, the ICTF would have to fight the resurgent Shia militia, just as they had alongside the Americans in the past.

He still spoke with warmth about his old U.S. partners. "You have their back and they have yours. If a bullet comes, it's not going to make any distinction," he said. "With the Americans, I fought al-Qaeda, I fought the militia, I fought the people who broke the law. We were all under death threats. We were the most hated people in Iraq."

The partnership came at great risk to the Iraqis. Lieutenant Harb, like many of his comrades, including Major Salam, was forced to live for long months at a U.S. base when AQI and militia fighters began targeting ISOF soldiers and their families at their homes. AQI killed his brother. "I'm not the only one," he said. "People had their families executed because of their work."

Each man carried his scars in a different way. Most days, Ahmed the Bullet was one of the battalion's most energetic soldiers, exuberant and quick with a joke, and he would talk optimistically about a postwar life with his wife and two young sons. At other times he was downbeat, even morose, and lost in a fog. In Bazwaya one night, I heard a ruckus outside my bedroom and found him rustling about atop one of the piles of clutter. He stood up without a word, put on his headlamp, and walked right past me, seeming tormented, like a searching ghost.

———·———

The battalion was still waiting in Bazwaya. I was sitting in the sun in a plastic chair in the destroyed yard behind our house when I heard a buzzing sound drawing closer. It was an ISIS surveillance drone. It hovered wasplike above me as I looked up in my baseball cap and shorts. Then it continued on its journey.

I returned to the bedroom. Ayman Oghanna, the British Iraqi photographer, had joined us, and his gear was strewn around the back of the room. He was working for the BBC as a sort of freelance bushwhacker to deliver footage from the front lines. With him was a Syrian Kurd whom the BBC had assigned to him as a producer and translator, a small and bespectacled man named Jewan Abdi.

Ayman was burning with his usual passion for covering the war, excited at the thought of breaking into Mosul with the battalion. He had an edge matched by no other journalist I knew; he was tall and broad and beautiful and seemed to live more immediately in the world than the rest of us. He felt things like good and evil deeply, and his complete antipathy for even a trace of falseness could make him a social menace. He had embedded with the ICTF several times and provided the introduction to the battalion for Jaff and me. He took the war against ISIS personally and considered the men of the ICTF friends. Later, when their casualties were mounting, he would forget himself entirely and spend his days volunteering in their trauma center. Jewan had turned out to be a perfect companion. He had a reedy beard, a wolflike smile that belied his bookish appearance, and a demeanor similar to Ayman's that said he was not just covering the war but a part of it. Jaff was wary of him and earlier had gone through his backpack. Jewan, he found, was traveling with a pair of hand grenades.

After a little while, Ayman and Jewan returned from a trip through town, both of them damp with sweat, their eyes glowing with the thrill of a find. Jewan had found a camera bag and from it he pulled a camera, a black keffiyeh, a white prayer cap, and an ISIS flag. They'd visited a house that had been used by ISIS as a media center, vacated only recently and apparently in haste, with the gear left behind and the blood from a sheep's slaughter pooled on the floor. Jewan said he would keep the bag because it was better than his own. He wrapped the keffiyeh around his neck, put on the prayer cap, and looked at his reflection in the mirror, flashing his lupine smile. Then he began to nail the black flag to the wall. "Make sure to hang it upside down," Ayman said.

After sunset the four of us made a bonfire, breaking apart the smashed furniture and using it to make a great conflagration in the yard. Jewan had the black keffiyeh wrapped around his head. The stars filled the sky above us, their light clear and bright, unshielded by the nearby city that sat dim in its occupation. Heavy artillery thundered, sending charges unseen across the darkened landscape.

CHAPTER 26

KEY WEST

Qayyarah, Iraq. Forty miles south of Mosul. October 2016.

SMOKE FROM THE BURNING OILFIELDS SOUTH OF MOSUL HOVERED like a sheet of velvet over the landscape, blocking the sky. Beneath the murk that made the days feel like permanent dusk and along a road that had seemed abandoned stood a food stand stocked improbably with vegetables and meat. We stopped the Land Cruiser.

A man greeted us from beside a tabletop grill.

"Are you open?" I asked.

"Yes," he said. "You are welcome."

With the ICTF waiting for orders just east of Mosul in Bazwaya, Jaff and I had traveled to the southern front. We were headed to the American base at Qayyarah, a ruined airfield forty miles south of Mosul that some U.S. soldiers called Key West, where members of the 101st Airborne were stationed. There were no Iraqi special forces here. Instead, patches of territory were run by the army and federal police and factions of the Shia militia, their various checkpoints lining the road. The facades of empty houses along the roadside were scrawled with graffiti that spoke to the paranoid and arbitrary rule imposed by the area's former ISIS overlords: "It is forbidden for the young men of the village to gather around this corner. This is the order of the *Hisbah*."

The roadside vendor's name was Karim. He pulled pieces of kebab meat from a shelf beside his table and ran metal skewers through them. Then he piled scraps of wood into his grill and lit a fire. With one hand he held the sticks aloft over the cinders and with the other he turned the crank on an old metal blower to feed the flame. Smoke billowed up over the meat.

I asked if there was a bathroom, and he led me through a metal gate in the concrete wall behind his stand. It opened onto a home with chickens roaming the yard and a small outhouse. His wife waved from the porch. When I returned there was a small boy with him who watched as Jaff and I sat at a plastic table that had been laid with condiments. Karim served us the meal with mismatched plates and silverware and joined us.

Like many people in his small town, he'd stayed behind when ISIS came and lived for two years among them, mostly locked in his house behind the gate. I asked whether the quiet boy beside him had been able to go to school. "School? There was no school," he said. "ISIS closed everything. There was only roadside bombs and killing."

About three hundred people had remained, he said. Many, like him, had tried to keep clear of the militants, but he knew the ones who'd joined and seemed to forgive them. "Believe me, I don't think anyone was really with them," he said. "If you had no money for food, you would join them. And they're really scary."

The town sat off a highway between two cities, a place where residents could expect strangers to pass them by. But with ISIS came foreigners: Chinese, Pakistanis, Russians, Arabs from other countries. They told the locals they were forbidden to leave. Neighbors were forced to spy on one another. Karim had nerve damage in one of his legs after being tortured when ISIS discovered a hookah that he kept on his rooftop and secretly smoked in the middle of the night. The extreme religiosity of the invaders was used as a front for pillage and rape. They concocted absurd justifications for abducting women—a Chechen fighter walked off with the daughter of one terrified man after forcing a dowry into his hand of three dates. "If you had women in your family, it was a big problem. You just hid them," Karim said. "You think the Prophet Muhammad did this kind of shit? No, he didn't."

In the distance, four Apache helicopters buzzed like wasps through the creeping murk. Karim had relatives in Mosul, surrounded by the coalition's forces and trapped among the increasingly desperate militants. ISIS had been trying to keep residents ignorant of the battle, insisting that reports of the impending onslaught were lies. But he'd been speaking to his relatives on mobile phones they kept hidden, giving them updates.

"We're having a good time," he said to Jaff and me. "Let me get you some more tea."

The boy wandered off, and I learned that he was Karim's nephew. The boy's father had been arrested by ISIS two years before—they accused him of being a coalition spy—and was still missing. The boy still asked about him. "We say he's going to come back soon," Karim said. "Then we take him to the store and buy him a few candies so he forgets."

He flashed a smile of pearl-white teeth. "We are all destroyed on the inside. Don't judge us from the outside," he said. "They showed us hell."

We continued toward the U.S. base, smoke darkening the horizon, as the great oil fires burn without end on the underground reservoirs. I had been close to such fires before and knew that they roared wildly, the smoke roiling, but in the distance they looked frozen, like a still shot of tornadoes touching down from the sky.

We rolled onto the highway, which stretched across the Tigris and then to the military airfield the Americans called Key West beyond it. The airfield had been destroyed early in the Iraq War and rebuilt by U.S. troops during the Awakening. When ISIS overran Qayyarah, it had wrecked Key West all over again. And when U.S. troops returned the previous summer, they built it once more.

We passed overturned cars and decapitated electric towers. I was struck not by the strangeness of the landscape but by how natural it felt. A dog was chasing our SUV, running and barking. In the barren fields I saw that someone had fashioned a blue tarp into a tent. Three federal policemen were sitting beside it, and we pulled over and got out to meet them.

It was midday, but the air was cold without the sun. The policemen approached us with an air of hospitality, one holding a PK machine gun against his shoulder, and we greeted each other warmly. "Come," one of them said. "We can get a better look over here." And we walked up a ridge that looked out onto the fires and admired the destruction.

Jaff and I returned to the Land Cruiser and drove to a pontoon bridge that crossed the Tigris. Then we came to a checkpoint run by one of the Shia militia, just below the American base. The militiamen waved us through, and we drove uphill and entered the airfield.

———

"It was nothing. It was dirt and that was it. Rocks. A bunch of T-walls laying on the ground."

"The men were dead on their feet. We are talking about twenty-four hours on their feet with one hour of sleep. In full kit. All the soldier sees is what's right in front of him. I was just thinking: Oh God, we got to keep these guys motivated."

"The plans looked like scratches in the dirt."

"I did both invasions. This is my fourth tour in Iraq. Fifth overall. I was here in 06–07. In 10–11. The invasion in 2003. And this one."

"Same country. Same desert. Same dust."

He was a U.S. army sergeant first-class from Texas who'd led the detachment of men who arrived at Qayyarah in the punishing heat of the previous summer to build the base from the rubble. These men were not secret commandos—they were grunts, the boots on the ground that Americans didn't want in Iraq and that their president had promised not to send. Their numbers were kept slim enough to avoid drawing too much press interest, and their arrival had received little notice at home. ISIS fighters had quickly detected the presence of their old enemy, though, and sent mortar bombs at them.

"All we had was dirt and dust and rubble," the Texan said. "Vehicles in a circle. The .50-cals on the vehicles and our guns. Steadily we started getting the walls up. We had to man constantly. There was no one to replace us."

The base was up and running, a beacon of order amid the upturned landscape. The front lines had been pushed back enough toward Mosul that the mortars seldom reached the base anymore. Outside, soldiers jogged along the blast walls in black T-shirts that said U.S. Army; it was the first time security was relaxed to the point that they could leave the barracks without their body armor. One man ran sprints with a truck tire chained to his waist, kicking up the fine dust.

In one corner of the base I found a hand-painted sign that read "Rocket City" in big red letters beside an image of a skull with a pair of missiles making an *X* behind it. Three missiles were stuck tail up in the dirt like totems. Behind them sat a massive, armadillo-like vehicle outfitted with advanced HIMARS launchers that could fire six GPS-guided rockets at a time. Beside the vehicle was a staff sergeant from Maryland. He was a balding man of thirty-four who, if you thought about it, was something of a mad engineer, making complex calculations on the computer attached to his vehicle and then unleashing an unearthly firepower. He pushed his button in Rocket City, there was a small delay, and then missiles rained down many miles away. "We've been ranging targets inside Mosul since we've been here," he said. "We've shot everything from VBIEDs to VBIED factories. Headquarter buildings. Pretty much anything we can range."

The Americans liked to use the word "precision" to describe their bombs. The Marylander said the rockets had a range of roughly forty-four miles and could hit within five yards of an intended target.

On the bumper of his vehicle sat a small jack-o'-lantern. It was Halloween. Costume stores at home had sold out of Donald Trump and Hillary Clinton masks; some people, meanwhile, had vowed to turn to violence if the election didn't go their way, while domestic reporters ran stories about militia groups training in the woods, playing at war, and I wondered if people realized what it was they were wishing for. I returned to the barracks, watching as these Americans carried on with their parallel lives.

"You learn to miss anniversaries, birthdays, Christmases, all the holidays," said the Texan, who had a wife and two sons at home.

"I was in high school when the planes hit the towers, and I know it sounds corny, but I just wanted to join and do something for my country," said a thirty-three-year-old sergeant from Erie, Pennsylvania. After basic training, he was posted to Fort Campbell in Kentucky, "and two weeks later I was on a plane."

His first assignment saw him based not far from Qayyarah, securing supply convoys into Mosul. "It was like now. Nobody wants to hear anything about the war. It's been played out."

"The days just kind of blur together," one of the soldiers said. "I'm just trying to survive to the last bit."

"Their black flags are no match for our beating black hearts," said another.

The open secret on the southern front was that the Iraqi military was becoming bogged down. Its forces were much improved from the units that two years ago had run from Mosul but were still not good enough. They were taking too many casualties and were only crawling forward. The plan U.S. officers had made—in which soldiers would advance like the tightening of a noose from all directions around the city—was unraveling. Only the Iraqi special forces were on schedule. This meant that the offensive would be far longer and bloodier than its planners had anticipated. And when Major Salam and his men pushed into eastern Mosul, they would be on their own, with ISIS able to focus on stopping them.

The Iraqi army's Fifteenth Division was stationed at Key West, beside the American base. I walked over to meet one of its generals. He told me the kind of things that military officers say to journalists, that the enemy was on the run, that morale was strong. Then he went outside and sat in a chair before an Iraqi TV camera, waiting to do a live interview.

When we told an Iraqi journalist from the TV crew, who knew Jaff from previous assignments, that we were considering embedding with the Fifteenth, he said it was a terrible idea, whispering so the general wouldn't hear. He'd been out with the Fifteenth, and they'd been thrown into panic by simple mortars. "I leave the camera running and I just take care of the wounded soldiers," he said.

The general got up. As he walked past, the journalist said loudly, "Dude, they are heroes. They're really brave."

Then he went back to whispering. "Journalists have to take care of the wounded? And people are expecting these guys to liberate Mosul?"

CHAPTER 27

"PUT DOWN YOUR WHITE FLAG"

Mosul, Iraq. Gogjali neighborhood. November 2016.

JUST AS HE'D PLANNED, MAJOR SALAM AND THE ICTF WERE THE FIRST Iraqi soldiers to step foot in Mosul in more than two years. Jaff and I joined them in a neighborhood called Gogjali on the city's eastern edge. As the soldiers relaxed after a day of fighting, we walked up to the rooftop of the home they'd commandeered and looked out onto the darkened city.

I heard a dog barking somewhere below. The roof rumbled beneath my feet as a tank rolled slowly by. A set of three explosions sounded in succession, a few blocks away, and more dogs began barking in a chorus. Gunfire cracked, intermittently at first and then in a rush, like a few light drops becoming a torrent of rain.

Downstairs, soldiers were lounging in the living room. One was in the kitchen, making tea. After a while Major Salam burst in, doing his late-night Tasmanian Devil routine. He barked at the men in mock anger, trying to lighten the mood: "Why isn't the water running? I need to take a shower! You dummies!"

As long as the rest of the Iraqi military was mired along the other fronts of the offensive, the Iraqi special forces were on their own in the city. ISIS was counterattacking aggressively, deploying waves of armored car bombs, the pilots seemingly in endless supply. One attack had nearly killed Major Salam the day before. The explosion knocked him to the ground and left three of his best soldiers dead. One of them was among his closest friends, Haider Fakhri, a gentle giant of an officer who was always at his side, whether clearing newly taken houses, as they had been doing when the bomb hit, or drinking Coronas during downtime.

I woke the next morning to a blast that shook me in my sleeping bag.

Jaff and I were lying in a mudroom, the coats of the family who owned the home on hooks above us. The explosion sent broken glass flying. A screw smacked against a wall and spun on the floor.

We dressed and brushed our teeth in the slop sink. The owners of the house returned, and I heard the husband speaking with some soldiers in the main room, trying to sound jovial, as if he were happy to extend this hospitality. The wife entered the mudroom and collected some jackets from the walls without a glance at Jaff and me.

I returned to the rooftop and looked down on the people of the city. They streamed one after another down the street below, some rolling suitcases, others carrying shopping bags full of clothes. An entire neighborhood was emptying. The people were coming from a district to the northwest called al-Samah, where a clamor of explosions and gunshots signaled that Major Salam and his convoy were fighting. The battle had given residents their best chance in more than two years to flee, and they strode beneath the whoosh of outgoing artillery. There was a loud boom, and a little girl in a pink winter hat shrieked, covering her ears. She and her mother broke into a run, still not sure whether they were safe. Teens walked by in skinny jeans and sweatpants, and a fair-skinned boy skipped down the road as if he were on his way to school. Next came a woman in a black headscarf and oversized designer sunglasses.

Some of the men were holding white flags on their shoulders, pieces of cloth tied to sticks and broom handles. There was another explosion, and a woman in a black *abaya* sprinted past.

Jaff and I went down to the street. A family pushed an elderly woman past us in a donkey cart; she was unconscious, with shrapnel wounds. Beside her sat a little girl dressed in pink. "The fighting is all over our houses," a man said. Lines of people continued toward us on their march. Some soldiers along the roadside handed out cigarettes, water, food.

A man who looked about my age, dressed in a polo shirt and horn-rimmed glasses, walked down the street with his wife and two small sons, carrying a single suitcase. I asked what was happening. "They're killing kids! They're killing families! They're doing everything!" he said.

After the ICTF drove ISIS from the neighborhood, he said, the militants had started pounding it with mortars and car bombs. "It's horrible."

His name was Mahmoud. He and his wife were both civil servants, and I realized that I was their first contact in more than two years with the outside world. "We have no phones. No satellites. We have no idea about anything," he said.

Then he asked, "There are no mortars here, right?"

He took a pack of cigarettes from some soldiers and asked for a light.

The two boys beside him appeared shell-shocked. "They're terrified," Mahmoud said. "Psychologically they're not doing well."

"The city's gone. It's been destroyed," he said. "Whatever I tell you about Mosul is not enough. Because it has been two years. No press, no communication to the world. Whatever I tell you will not be enough. All I'm saying is, all I'm asking, is for the world to rebuild the city after this is over. A world city like Mosul is destroyed. No university. No schools. No hospitals."

Behind us, soldiers were loading the displaced onto cattle trucks bound for the camps. "We are going into the unknown," Mahmoud said. Then he climbed into a truck and pulled his family up with him.

I noticed a small man among the crowd wearing jogging pants and a black ski mask. He was an informant who'd been recruited to tell the soldiers who among his neighbors was with ISIS. I asked why he was wearing the mask. "Because ISIS has sleeper cells," he said.

"Will ISIS send fighters among the civilians?" I asked, as behind him a soldier told a man to open his jacket.

"Of course they will," he replied.

I asked an Iraqi colonel how the troops were managing that threat. "We have names in a database," he said. "We have another department up ahead, and we take them there and we check their names in our database. If someone arrives here without any documents, then we suspect that this guy, he pledged allegiance to ISIS."

"Just today," he added, "a car bomb, a guy, a suicide bomber, he picked up a family and he drove them all the way to the Al-Muthana Bridge, and he pushed the button."

Behind him, the people crowded into one of the cattle trucks began clamoring for it to leave. "Just wait," the colonel shouted up to them. "Because they're firing artillery. One might land among you and your family and kill you guys. Do you hear it?"

"Every day is like this," he told me. He guessed that the troops had transported more than 10,000 civilians to makeshift camps in just the last week. "Yesterday, we were taking people until midnight."

Jaff and I walked for a few blocks against the crowd.

A woman was pushed through the dirt in a wheelchair. A man with three small children used a pink bicycle like a packhorse to tote his bags.

"A mortar landed in my living room," someone from the crowd said.

"My neighbor lost his arm," said an old woman. "He is walking over here with no arm."

Jaff and I stood beside a group of soldiers. "Put your white flag down. You don't need it anymore," one of them told a civilian.

A man stepped out from the crowd and approached. As he did, I braced. He was young and fit and had a long, thick beard. He paused when he reached us. Then he asked the soldiers for a cigarette. Someone handed one to him, and his face cracked into a smile.

———·———

That afternoon, as Jaff and I sat at a curb eating lunch, a soldier showed us a license plate he'd pulled off a car. It had been printed in a factory. Beside the plate number, "Islamic State" was written in English and Arabic. From the moment ISIS took Mosul it had been under attack from its many enemies; yet still it had gone to the trouble to create a motor vehicles department, the most mundane of bureaucracies. It was laughable, but on the other hand it was exactly what made the organization so scary. Many of the Iraqi soldiers had mementos like the license plate. When Major Salam returned that night, tired from the day of fighting, he let me play with one of his—a stamp he'd found in the office of an emir from the *Hisbah*, or religious police, with the man's name, title, and seal. I tried to imagine such a man, sitting behind a desk with a pile of documents before him, stamping away as airstrikes rocked the city.

The civilians who fled night and day down the streets had been pawns in the ISIS delusion that it was running a country. If ISIS was going to create a new world order based around a revolutionary state, then it needed citizens. I sometimes called them "caliphate helpers" when I was feeling cynical, but I knew they were really hostages.

I thought of that when I heard politicians talk of punitively bombing ISIS's cities, speaking as if anyone living in ISIS territory must be a supporter or at least not care enough to leave. It was easy to see why someone might think that, and the politicians were only repeating in harsher tones a question that well-meaning friends and family had asked me: If they weren't with ISIS, then why were they still there? The question made sense until you considered the effectiveness of the ISIS police state, and its public executions, and the gnawing, paralyzing fear that any escape plan would be discovered, and the question of, even if you could escape with your wife and kids, how might ISIS retaliate against your brother, your cousin?

At the same time I sympathized with the Iraqi soldiers trying to determine who had been a true collaborator and who had just been going through the motions, trying not to get killed. There were a couple of volunteer American medics working in the neighborhood, two former soldiers who'd come to lend a hand, and they thought Jaff and I were insane to mix with the crowds fresh out of war-torn neighborhoods when soldiers had yet to even pat them down. Over years of covering ISIS, I had realized that this was its special skill—to make you question everyone, the evil and the innocent.

Each burst of a car bomb—the explosions were sharper and more violent than most, as if you could feel the metal box popping—was a reminder of ISIS's ability to inspire fanatical loyalty. The vehicles were outfitted in factories, where heavy armored plates were molded over civilian cars and trucks. I couldn't imagine how ISIS had found so many drivers willing to pilot them. The number of suicide car bombs was far greater than anyone had expected—it was the largest deployment of suicide attackers since imperial Japan used kamikazes in World War II.

The weapon was the reason the ICTF moved so slowly. It dominated every aspect of the battle and was ISIS's answer to the coalition's air power and artillery. Major Salam said that his convoy had had an especially tough time with the car bombs that day. The narrow streets made it easier for their drivers to hide. One of them had stalked the convoy for hours through the streets. "We were like the rat and he was like the cat," he said.

Before the Mosul battle, ISIS had used mostly foreigners for suicide attacks. They tended to be the most fanatical, and in conventional fighting their lack of language skills and local knowledge could make them a liability. In Mosul so far the foreign bombers had hailed from Syria, Egypt, Iraqi Kurdistan, Russia, Dagestan, Chechnya, Morocco, Tunisia, France, Uzbekistan, the United Arab Emirates, and Ireland, among other countries. But local fighters had featured most prominently in the suicide attacks that ISIS chose to publicize. Even as it lost territory, it was trying lay the groundwork for a comeback, hoping to inspire local sympathies that might help it return one day. Iraqis had conducted more than half of ISIS's announced suicide operations, usually car bombings, in the offensive so far, and often they came from the same town or neighborhood in which they died.

ISIS tried to control the narrative of the battle, just as the Americans and the Iraqis did, and glorifying the suicide attackers was part of its media campaign. First it would announce the attack through its Amaq news agency, often with few details aside from the date and time. Amaq would follow that later with an update: the number of casualties and sometimes a video, either shot from a concealed position or by drone. After that its local media offices often dug deeper, revealing the name and personal details of the attacker, especially if he was a local. It might even put out his photo with a breaking-news alert. Later, the attacker might be commemorated in the daily news bulletin on ISIS's main radio station, al-Bayan, or the Statement, which was broadcast from the FM towers in ISIS territory and could also be streamed online. He might also receive a mention in *al-Naba*, or the Tidings, the group's weekly newspaper.

After dinner, Major Salam decided that the battalion should move deeper into the city. The men quickly packed, and as dusk fell the Humvees departed, rolling past the procession of civilians. After about ten minutes, we arrived at a house far more impressive than the others I'd stayed in. It stood out from its neighbors, a large villa surrounded by ornate stone walls. Inside it was elegant and pristine, with new appliances, comfortable couches, and expensive speakers sitting beside a large flat-screen TV. There were two kitchens.

Abu Seif, an aging soldier who was the unit's intelligence officer, pulled out his phone and took photos to send to his wife. Jaff and I ran upstairs to claim our room. He chose a small one, with no windows. I was excited to spend the night in that lovely home, feeling like a kid at a sleepover, and wanted to stay in one of the nicer bedrooms, but Jaff was wary. He liked the windowless room because it was less susceptible to shrapnel and snipers. And he wanted to stay on the second floor, he said, "because if someone comes in, by the time they kill everyone on the first floor, you're alert."

But we didn't stay long; suddenly there was an order to fall back. "Take everything, we won't come back here," a soldier said, and everyone rushed to the Humvees. Major Salam had a bad feeling too, and the Humvees got back onto the road to return to Gogjali. I noticed men and teenaged boys at the entrances to nearby houses, staring at the Humvees. "Some of these people are probably still ISIS and have phones," Jaff said. Some waved as we passed, and others didn't.

CHAPTER 28

ELECTION DAY

Mosul, Iraq. Saddam neighborhood. November 8, 2016.

THE BATTALION MOVED OUT AGAIN THE NEXT EVENING.

A Humvee waited for Jaff and me in the street. I tried to open the back door, but the handle was jammed. "This vehicle got hit by a car bomb," said its driver, an ICTF lieutenant. He reached back and opened the door from the inside. It had been damaged in the blast that killed Major Salam's friend Haider and the others.

We rolled with the convoy down Gogjali's unlit streets. Our headlights were trained on the pickup truck in front of us; a stack of mattresses tottered in its bed. The ICTF was headed to a neighborhood called Saddam—"the center of the city," Major Salam had told me proudly before we departed. The neighborhood had a history of resistance, the lieutenant said. "Even in 2003, it was one of the toughest."

Jaff wore a green bandana around his face as he rocked with the Humvee in the passenger's seat. He shone his flashlight out the window, illuminating the charred husk of a vehicle just like the one we were in. It looked so small, just a crust, compared to our behemoth. Five soldiers from a different Iraqi special forces unit had perished inside the Humvee when a car bomb hit it the previous day. We turned a corner. Another destroyed Humvee was tipped on its side, its armor peeled away to reveal the engine block. A corpse lay covered by a blanket on the roadside. We passed houses with signs spray-painted on them. "House for Sale." "House for Sale." "God is Great—House for Sale."

Black Humvees guarded the entrance to the street where Major Salam would make his base. Jaff and I stepped out and joined him in a two-family house. We were assigned to the second floor. Children's clothing hung from a drying line in the stairwell. In the bathroom hung women's lingerie, and soiled diapers filled a garbage pail. In the kitchen, a frying pan of half-cooked lamb sat on a stovetop. On the wall hung a smiling scarecrow that held a "Welcome" sign, a decoration for fall. I heard birds chirping. In a corner of the living room, canaries fluttered in a cage. I remembered the refugee from Aleppo I'd met more than four years earlier in southern Turkey, who'd been so optimistic in calling home to check on the birds he'd left behind. A soldier approached with a bag of seeds and threw in a handful. In the morning, he said, he would let the canaries go.

Downstairs, Major Salam was yelling at his men. Gunshots sounded from all directions on the streets outside. "If you guys turn this house into a garbage pail, you're going to be fucked," he said. "Keep it clean. These are people's houses. You don't throw your food like an animal. If I see one Styrofoam package on the floor, I'm going to punish the person. If I see bullet shells on the floor, I'm going to punish the person."

"Yes, sir," the soldiers said.

"I want the satellite dish working, because there's a game tonight."

The young soldier who handled the battalion's communications hurried to the rooftop with the satellite. Jaff and I followed him. The concrete walls were about three feet high, and we noticed that he was taking care to keep his head below them. We made our way to the side that faced west, deeper into the city, and peeked over the ledge. Here and there a house was lit by the power of a generator, glowing in the darkness. In America, voters were going to the polls, while Major Salam and his men had arrived at last at their destination in Mosul. In the morning, the rooftop would have a view of the center of the city and the banks of the Tigris.

Later, near midnight, the house grew quiet as the soldiers prepared to sleep. I found Major Salam downstairs in the master bedroom, freshly showered in a tracksuit, sitting on a king-sized bed. A news program was playing on his TV, but he didn't pay it any mind. He was hunched over his iPad, looking through photos.

He paused on one that showed his friend Haider just before the car bomb killed him. They were standing together on a newly won street when an explosive-laden truck appeared, barreling toward them. The picture, taken by a French photographer who was with them, showed a look of determination on Haider's face. He was drawing his handgun and charging toward the vehicle, along with a second ICTF officer, in a desperate effort to stop it before it reached his comrades. The explosion knocked Major Salam to the ground. When he pulled himself up, he found Haider dead, nearly decapitated. The second officer, along with another soldier, also lay dead.

Still holding his iPad, Major Salam insisted that his friend's death carried no more weight than all the others the battalion had suffered. "Leadership to me is being close to your men. The problem is I am close with all of them," he said. "I eat with all of them, hang out with all of them. Haider is like Conan, Conan is like Amjad, Amjad is like Bis Bis. They are all the same for me. Maybe I was closer with Haider, but it's the same."

He took another look at the photo. ICTF cannons thumped methodically outside. "Those are the guys, just seconds before they leave," he said, his voice softening. "Look at their faces, how they're looking for the car bomb. They are true symbols of selflessness. They gave their lives to protect others."

I asked how long he and his men could go on living with so much death and destruction, spending their nights in broken homes.

"We've chosen this life. We've chosen to live like this," he said. He had a wife and a ten-year-old son whom he rarely saw. Before his near-death experience in Anbar in the spring—captured in the bloody photos

Ahmed the Bullet had showed me on his phone—he'd been wondering whether it might be time to move on, he said. "Maybe I thought once or twice about should I keep doing this. Can I continue? But after I got injured it was the other way around. I got so pissed at the idea that I might not be able to finish the job with my friends and colleagues. With this job, you enter a circle and you can't leave it."

He continued: "It's . . . let me try to explain it to you. The two most terrifying nights in my life are the night that I go home—because I feel like a stranger in my home—and the night I go back to my job. Because I will be a stranger too. This job is its own strange world. Everything is about the battle. Just when you think it's over, it starts again. It's a continuous cycle."

I asked what he told his men to keep them going through a grueling war that had seen Iraq threaten to fracture around them as they waged it—the Kurds pushing for independence, the Sunni community torn apart, Shia militia trying to drive the country closer to Iran, bombs falling around the clock from foreign armies.

"I tell my soldiers, you are not fighting for Iraq," he said. "You are not fighting for a flag. You are fighting for your family. And we move up from there. If you are fighting for your family, you will fight for your neighbors, you will fight for your district. Being patriots doesn't start from the top, it starts from your family. The way we feel is that we are preventing the crisis from reaching our families. From reaching our neighbors. From reaching our city. From reaching our province. And that is what makes Iraq in the end."

Mortars began to hit near the house at sunrise. I woke beside Jaff in a storage closet, opening my eyes to a toddler's neon bicycle, a man's tools, a stuffed polar bear. Jaff was still asleep. It was just past 11 p.m. in America, and using the spotty internet connection from Major Salam's satellite, I checked the election results on my iPhone. Ohio and Florida had just been called for Trump. I sat up, glued to my screen like the rest of my countrymen, as the mortars continued to explode.

A BBC crew was staying in a bedroom nearby, and I heard them waking up. "What the hell is going on?" one of them said.

The reactions in my Twitter feed were on the edge of hysteria. The world was coming to an end; the world was being saved. I messaged an American soldier I knew at the U.S. base in Qayyarah, interested to know how the news was being received there. He had deployed several times in Iraq and Afghanistan and was older than most of the soldiers stationed there, with a harder demeanor, and reminded me of the ICTF men. He was restless at the base, and we often exchanged messages about the war and its shifting front lines.

"Interesting," he said of the election result. "Either way, it won't change our purpose."

Soldiers had stayed up through the night, he said, watching the news in the base's control room. "No one wanted to sleep. Our TV screen: drone footage on one half, FOX & CNN on the other."

I found it comforting to speak to an American who hadn't fallen into the delirium at home. I wondered if, when a country was at war for so long but only a select few ever waged it, the rest of society began to go a certain kind of crazy. Some played at civil war while others vowed to flee to Canada as political refugees, and too many Americans seemed to want to pull a bit of conflict into their lives just when so many people around the world were risking everything to escape from it.

"Every time I deploy I do so knowing how much I'll miss at home," the U.S. soldier said. "Knowing I will be forgotten because I have to be, so my friends and family can move on. But the U.S. is still there. The anthem is right, our flag is still there. Corny I know but I don't care, it's been true for my entire life. But at some point you have to go home and when you do, you'll cry that first time touching down. You'll search for ground to hug. She's still there."

"Not corny," I said.

"Well, I know patriotism isn't in vogue. We lose perspective on it," he said. "Good luck."

The Brits were pulling on their flak jackets.

"There are mortars coming in from that direction," one of them said. "Mike! Stop reading about the election."

Jaff and I had arranged to spend the day with Colonel Arkan, an Iraqi commando who'd been trained at Quantico and other elite U.S. military schools and now spent his days calling in U.S. airstrikes. He worked from a different base, and we took a Humvee back to a three-story home in Gogjali. I found him pacing the rooftop in the gleaming sunglasses that, together with his moustache, reminded me of the character Goose from *Top Gun*. He asked why I was late. When I told him about the election result, he gave me a blank look, thinking I was joking.

"That's going to be like Hurricane Katrina hitting all fifty states," he finally said.

Colonel Arkan, thirty-five, was a unique presence on the front lines. Due to his extensive U.S. training, he was the only Iraqi soldier who had "strike authority" on American jets; normally this was the purview of American or European special forces. This meant that when he issued the order, the pilots launched their missiles. "I'm the daddy, and this is my house, and my car, and I have the keys," I once heard him tell an American officer on the radio in his fluent English. His call sign was Archangel.

American voices crackled on his radio as two U.S. choppers hovered overhead and a drone and fighter jet patrolled the sky beyond them. Around us on the roof, which was enclosed by five-foot concrete walls, Iraqi officers manned radios and plotted coordinates on laminated maps. Gunshots and explosions sounded in the distance, where Major Salam was leading the ICTF convoy. "We're dropping bombs on their heads from the sky, and they're driving bombs at us," Colonel Arkan said.

At around 11 a.m., a call came in from Major Salam saying that an explosive-laden dump truck was headed the convoy's way. Colonel

Arkan found the area where it had been spotted on a map and called in the coordinates to coalition officers in an operations center in Baghdad. "Be advised, we're going to continue scanning those areas looking for a possible VBIED," an American voice replied.

But before the coalition's aircraft could spot the truck bomb, it sped at the convoy, which opened fire with its heavy weapons. We could hear it all on the radio, the sudden cacophony from the gunners, the urgent yelling. A massive blast sounded, and the roof shook. The radio was silent. Then Major Salam informed Colonel Arkan that the convoy's heavy guns had destroyed the truck. Colonel Arkan relayed the news to the command center. "Glad to hear it," the American said.

Major Salam got back on the radio. Another truck bomb had been spotted. Colonel Arkan requested another strike. He believed that this second truck would use the same route to attack the convoy as the first, so he was asking for a "terrain-denial attack," or an airstrike to destroy the road. "ASAP. ASAP, baby. I just need it right now," he said.

Long minutes passed as coalition aircraft surveyed the area. Colonel Arkan's customary brashness seemed to ebb. He was anxious, quietly bracing.

Incoming gunfire sounded around the rooftop, and Colonel Arkan ducked below the walls. Civilians were still fleeing through the streets outside, and they froze, trying to determine where the bullets were coming from. An Iraqi officer stared at five walkie-talkies on a plastic table, trying to hold his concentration. "You see all these radios? They might start talking at the same time. I don't want to miss any number," he said, referring to coordinates. "Because you know, if you miss one number, you can shift the whole direction of the airstrike. And you don't want to do that."

The American in Baghdad called back with bad news. There were civilians sheltering in the area where Colonel Arkan wanted the terrain-denial strike. The chances of casualties were high. He relayed the information to Major Salam. "The guys have accepted the risk, and they're going to block the road with whatever assets we have on the ground and hope for the best," Colonel Arkan said. "These are our own people. You can't just bomb everything, you know?"

The pace of battle had slowed considerably now that Iraqi forces were in the city, in part due to concern about causing civilian harm. They knew ISIS hoped to make the battle as deadly as possible for civilians, betting that this would turn the population against the Iraqi forces and their foreign allies. ISIS wanted the population to doubt the motives and the morals of the latest round of conquerors; that way it might be possible for ISIS, after losing Mosul, to retain a foothold as an insurgency. "You don't want to be responsible for unnecessary deaths," Colonel Arkan said. "I'm here to defend them, not kill them. So if I have that open fire show, it's not going to help. And keep in mind we have to rebuild whatever we destroy."

Another request for an airstrike came in on the radio. "Hang on, we have a target," Colonel Arkan said.

There were seven ISIS fighters in a defensive position in the convoy's path. He grabbed a tablet, swiped his finger to zoom in on a map of the area, and called in the strike. Word came on the radio that a missile had hit his target. "Seven dead," he said, snapping his fingers. "Just like that."

CHAPTER 29

COMRADES

Outside eastern Mosul, Iraq. November 2016.

BENEATH HIS CONFIDENT DEMEANOR, COLONEL ARKAN TOOK THE losses hard.

I had taken leave of Major Salam and retraced the route out from Mosul through its eastern gate. I was sitting with Colonel Arkan in the yard of his rear base. It was pitch-black except for a porch light and quiet except for the hum of a generator. He leaned back in a folding chair and thought about his dead comrades. "My old boys, they were good," he said.

In the summer of 2014, when I ran into the black-clad, English-speaking soldier with the Special Operations patch outside Baghdad, Colonel Arkan had been in Anbar as part of a desperate stand by Iraqi special forces to keep ISIS from overrunning the country. His elite unit had been pulled from its regular mission of hunting terrorists on high-value target raids and thrown into the battle. Lacking the intelligence and planning to which they were accustomed, Iraq's most prized soldiers, who'd once fought "shoulder to shoulder" with the Americans, as Colonel Arkan put it, were dying by the dozen. "Five of them from a house-borne IED on Day One," he said. "It was a shock for us. You know, never lost that many people at once. And these are guys that I've been in their homes, with their families, at their marriage parties, been like in every single occasion with them. Family. And then you just lose them at once."

The house had collapsed on the bodies. Colonel Arkan and his men fought for fourteen days, taking even more casualties, to secure the site and retrieve the corpses of their friends.

This was how the war with ISIS had started for the special forces, and it continued like that for more than a year, in battles all over the country. They kept fighting because there was no one else to do it. They were sin eaters carrying the burden of their allies—of the United States, which had started a catastrophic war and then pulled its troops from the country not because the war was won but because Americans were tired of it, and of the corrupt and sectarian Iraqi government the Americans left behind. Eventually they turned the ISIS fight around, regrouping, learning from their mistakes, recapturing Anbar, and now leading the way into Mosul. But the losses were daunting. The offensive was not going as planned. The Iraqi army and federal police were still too weak; the ISIS defenses were tougher than anyone had expected. And the careful way that Colonel Arkan wanted to fight the war was being overwhelmed. The new U.S. administration was vowing to ramp up airstrikes and to loosen restrictions intended to lessen civilian casualties; the more the special forces were depleted, the more the less professional units in the Iraqi military would have to fill in. Already there were rumblings of abuses by these units, by the Shia militia, and even by some members of the special forces—summary executions, revenge killings. As they lost veteran fighters, even the ICTF was becoming more sectarian, as I'd seen when my Humvee charged into Topzawa flying the flag of Imam Hussein. The sins were overcoming them. Looking back on the growing division in my own country, I wondered if the demons the long and tortured U.S. involvement had unleashed in Iraq were making their presence felt there too.

I knew that U.S. military officials considered it a disaster that so many of Iraq's top commandos had died fighting like common soldiers—wasting men like Colonel Arkan, with all his training, who were schooled not just in the American way of fighting but in the fading U.S. vision for Iraq. Colonel Arkan understood their concern but said there had been no other way. "The country needed us. So we did it," he said. "Because the enemy is not gonna stop. And if you move back one step, they're gonna move forward one step. So you hold your ground and you do your best and hopefully you will be the last one standing."

The Iraqi special forces refused to reveal their casualty numbers, so I asked Colonel Arkan about the losses just among his old team, which had suffered no deaths in action over years of carefully planned missions. When the war with ISIS began, he said, "all the guys that I worked with, like my own team—everybody was alive."

In the time since, half of them had died. "Pretty much I have lost every single best friend that I have into this war," he said. "This war hurt us a lot. We're not designed to do these kinds of operations. But because of the ability that we have and the capabilities that we have and the skills that we have, it was falling on us that we have to stop this. You just keep moving, man. You know, you're not fighting overseas or something like that. This is your own house. This is your own family. Your own cousins, your own friends. Your wife, your sister, your girlfriend, your ex-girlfriend. This is who you're defending."

He continued, "That's the thing that people don't understand. The U.S. army guys, they deploy overseas to fight for principles, which is noble. Someone actually fighting for freedom, for justice, you know, for the basic human rights. It's noble. And it's worth fighting for. But compared to defending your family and your own home and your own ground? There is no second-guessing. You just have to push to the last drop you have."

CHAPTER 30

SUSPICION

Antakya, Turkey. January 2017.

After the First there was the Second, and after the Second there is this third war we are experiencing now, piecemeal. We are at war. The world is conducting a third world war: Ukraine, Middle East, Africa, Yemen. It is very grave.

—Jorge Mario Bergoglio, Pope Francis,
December 7, 2016

EVERY MORNING, IN THE PREDAWN DARKNESS, THE PLATOON AT A remote ISIS outpost in the desert of eastern Syria woke to the alarms on their phones. They piled sleepy-eyed into their pickups and drove, keeping their headlights switched off, to an olive farm. There, beneath a canopy of green sheets spread between a cluster of trees to shield them from the eyes of drones and warplanes, they gathered to be guided through *al-Fajr* prayers. It was a beautiful place, surrounded by the quiet of the fields, their weapons beside them and their prayer mats laid out amid the trees. With battlefield losses mounting for ISIS, some of the fighters remembered a promise ascribed to the Prophet Muhammad in one of the hadiths: "Whoever performs *al-Fajr* prayers in congregation is under the protection of God."

The imam who came to the men each morning, sent from the *Hisbah* office in the nearest city, was their only link to ISIS leadership. He would arrive dressed in a black tunic and prayer cap and sink to his knees to face them. When the prayers were complete, the imam would give an hour-long address as the sun rose, leading the men through religious lessons and relaying updates on the battle plans. One morning in November, though, they found their imam unusually excited. There was no discussion of doctrine or strategy. Instead, he delivered news: Donald Trump had just been elected U.S. president. This was a great gift to ISIS, he said. "We have to use this chance."

The imam told the men that Trump's victory had the potential to draw Muslims around the world to the ISIS cause. He told them to go out on their social media accounts and send a message. "Now you have to do jihad in another way," he said. "We have to be smart and call people to join us, and tell the truth to others about Trump."

With orders fresh from the *Hisbah*, imams were giving addresses like this across the caliphate.

One of the fighters gathered beneath the trees that day, a Syrian in his twenties, met me on a cold night in January 2017 to relay the story.

Not long after my conversation with Colonel Arkan on the edge of Mosul, I'd returned to Istanbul. Jaff and I planned to rejoin Major Salam in about a month. The battle in eastern Mosul was slowing, and as Trump's inauguration approached, I wondered how ISIS members saw the new president, who had spoken about the group so often during his campaign.

My Syrian colleague, Munzer, and I began to call our contacts in Turkey, trying to find people who, on election night, had been on the ISIS side. This led us back to Mohamed, the former oil smuggler from the border. We made the familiar flight to Antakya, then drove to Mohamed's house on the edge of Syria.

He had invited a young Syrian defector, Ammar, to join us. Ammar fiddled with a finger ring as he recounted the reaction of the *Hisbah* sheikh near his old outpost in the desert.

Ammar had no opinion of the new U.S. president. "I only know what's going on in Syria," he said.

But he recalled that ISIS's interest in Trump had been intense in the days following his election. Men with video cameras joined the prayer gatherings at the farm. They recorded whenever the imam turned to Trump, and "every day he was talking about Trump," Ammar said.

The speeches delivered to soldiers at the front, like the celebratory social media posts circulated by ISIS and its backers online, were part of the group's extensive messaging efforts. Videos featuring sermons like those Ammar witnessed were broadcast in mosques and public squares throughout ISIS territory, and they were also packaged as part of ISIS's online propaganda. ISIS was eager to show that Trump's rhetoric—from his call for a travel ban against Muslims to his promise that the airstrikes he ordered against ISIS would pay far less heed to civilian harm—meant that ISIS had been right about America and its Western allies. Munzer and I had spoken with current and former ISIS members who said that even as ISIS gradually lost Mosul and faced the destruction of its territorial caliphate, it believed it had won another kind of victory. As one ISIS emir put it, speaking to us over encrypted chat, "Trump announced his hatred of Arabs and Muslims and did not hide it as presidents did before him."

Another recent defector recalled how he'd been finishing his night shift at an ISIS checkpoint in Raqqa early on November 9 when the friend who came to relieve him told him, with a hysterical laugh, "They elected the dog Trump! I swear to God, he will burn the world."

In the days that followed, the defector said, ISIS leaders in Raqqa hailed Trump's win as divine intervention. "They told us that victory is at hand and that God has sent the pig Trump as clear evidence of this," he said. "And they said that now God will make the Americans start fighting amongst themselves, and they prayed to God, saying, 'O God, destroy the oppressors by the hand of the oppressors and let us escape them unharmed.' And we said, 'Amen.'"

I knew that ISIS propagandists would have spread similar messages even if Hillary Clinton had won—just as they did during the presidency of Obama, whom ISIS members referred to, like they did Trump, as an enemy of Islam. I also knew that ISIS felt it could rally around Trump in a way that it couldn't around other American politicians. All but a small fraction of the world's 1.6 billion Muslims despised ISIS and rejected its claim to speak for global Islam. They would likewise reject the idea pushed by ISIS members that Trump or anyone could drive them into the terror group's arms. Yet, in his remarks about Islamic terrorism, Trump had directed his focus on the religion itself, in contrast to Barack Obama and George W. Bush, who took pains to differentiate between terror groups and Muslims.

Sitting with Ammar, I was struck by the idea that he could have been one of the young men firing at the ICTF back in Mosul or shot up by one of its gunners. He took his phone from his pocket and flipped through photos from the front lines. One showed him on a road outside Raqqa, smiling, with an arm around a friend. He'd been wearing a brown stocking over his face, and it was rolled up around his forehead. A sign in the background read, "Don't be lazy. Go to fight." Another photo showed him with a group of fighters at an airfield. They had arrived in their battle convoy and were posing with their weapons, grenade launchers, AK-47s, and machine guns mounted on their pickups. Another showed a young man whose beard looked incongruous around his babyish face. Ammar said it was a friend of his, who was a local emir. I remarked that he looked almost like a child. "Believe me," Ammar said, "he has experience."

I asked Ammar what he did before the war. It was a question I'd been asking since I first arrived in Turkey to help myself imagine people as they were before the violence. His response reminded me how much time had passed. When the war started, he was a sophomore in high school.

He said he still believed in the ISIS cause. But he was dispirited about its prospects. "They taught us that ISIS will stay forever and they will continue to the United States and Europe and all the world," he said. "I wish that would happen. But it's impossible, because all the world is against ISIS."

"But they didn't stop ISIS," he added hopefully. "It still exists."

Ammar had defected a few weeks earlier, leaving Syria and escaping to Turkey. He said he left because he'd been reassigned to another front line and feared that, once posted to unfamiliar territory, he was likely to be ordered to become a suicide bomber. "I was worried they would send me somewhere to blow myself up," he said. "Some people, they support the idea of going and bombing themselves. But my project was to succeed and go to other countries and build the Islamic State."

Mohamed, who'd been listening to our conversation, interjected: "He wants to live!"

For all the ISIS sympathies he'd expressed over the years, Mohamed had always been riled by the idea of the group's leaders using Syrians as fodder for its suicide missions.

The boy Mohamed was helping to look after—who had once vowed to turn the sands of a Turkish beach red with blood at the sight of bikini-clad women—joined us after a while. He was just a year older than when Munzer and I had first met him but seemed to have doubled in size. He wore plaid dress pants and a sweater. He said he still wanted to be an engineer. He also still wanted to rejoin ISIS. "Why shouldn't I support them?" he asked.

"When he grows up, and when he finishes his university, then I will take him there," Mohamed cut in. "I told him he has to finish university first because to be educated in ISIS is better than to be normal in ISIS."

"Yes," the boy agreed.

"After he finishes his studies and gets married and has kids, he can go," Mohamed said.

"You told me first to finish my studies," the boy replied. "Now you want me to get married?"

Mohamed sent him out to fetch some more tea. "I am sure by the time he finishes university ISIS will be gone," he told Munzer and me. "Or . . . they will be a superpower, in which case we will all be ISIS, and we can take care of him."

In the early days of the war, I'd known a Syrian in southern Turkey who was the kind of person who could make the best out of life as a refugee. Shadi was well educated, worldly, and happily married and found steady work quickly.

I hadn't thought about Shadi for a long time. But Munzer had heard from one of his sources that Shadi was working with ISIS. I told him that was impossible: either his information was bad or he had the wrong guy. But Munzer insisted. "I'm sure," he said. "One hundred percent."

After we left Mohamed's, I rang Shadi and said it would be good to catch up. We arranged to meet around 8 p.m. at a café where he and I had sometimes sat together for coffee. Munzer was alarmed, but I couldn't take seriously the idea that Shadi was with ISIS. And so we argued as we traveled the familiar roads.

Most of the café's tables were full. We found one in the corner, and I sat facing the door.

I remembered Shadi possessing a bright and friendly demeanor, but that was not how he arrived. He looked older and thicker and seemed to have a shadow cast over his expression. He took a seat beside me. Munzer leaned back in his chair.

Shadi wasn't sure why I wanted to meet, and I didn't want to say. We talked awkwardly, exchanging pleasantries. I asked about his wife. "Actually," he said, "we split up."

The coffee came, and I began to prod, asking my question a dozen ways without ever coming out and saying it. He winced and tried to move the conversation to something else. I knew it was all just a hall of mirrors; I was putting my old friend through an inquisition for no good reason instead of giving him my sympathy. I should have been buying him a drink, lightening the mood. And yet I wondered—what if the worst was true?

That sense of uncertainty, in which you could find yourself suspicious of anyone, had become, to me, the abiding feeling of the war. Every time I fell into it, I thought it was ISIS's greatest victory.

As Shadi and I continued our uncomfortable conversation, I looked up and noticed a man at a table near the door. He was alone, staring at us. He had long hair and a ratty beard and wore a winter beanie and a peacoat over jogging pants. His hands rested on the table, and one of them held a set of prayer beads, almost like a prop, which he fingered methodically. I looked back at him, and he didn't avert his gaze. I started to get nervous. So did Shadi. We continued talking, and the man got up and sat at another table, continuing to finger his beads and stare at us. I paid the bill, and we walked outside. I looked back into the restaurant and saw that the man had switched tables a third time. He was sitting in the seat that Shadi had just vacated, keeping us in his sight line.

I said good-bye to Shadi, and he asked where we were staying. This time I tried to change the subject. He asked me twice more. I wondered if he was trying to hurt us. I wondered if I was being rude. I told him the name of our hotel, even as I could feel Munzer silently screaming.

It was late that night when I caught the bug myself. I'd been staring out the window of my hotel room, watching the street. There was a man lingering near the hotel's entrance. I called Munzer over, and we looked down together, becoming increasingly unnerved. The man was probably just drunk—there was a bar next door—and waiting for his ride, but once the idea is in your head, everyone seems threatening. We packed our bags and slipped away into the night.

CHAPTER 31

DRIFTING

Mosul, Iraq. Hay al-Noor neighborhood. February 2017.

AHMED THE BULLET HAD DIED IN HIS HUMVEE IN MID-DECEMBER. He was standing in the turret on a street in Mosul, keeping guard as his comrades cleared houses. A car bomb emerged suddenly, bearing down on the men. "You guys run," Ahmed said on the radio. All he could do was open fire one last time, his bullets bouncing off the vehicle's armor as it sped closer.

The explosion was powerful. When Ahmed's distraught friends searched for pieces of his body, they could find no trace of him.

From there, as Major Salam and his men pushed deeper into Mosul, the deaths mounted. A beloved sergeant was killed by another car bomb. A sniper killed a newly minted ICTF member and the eleven-year veteran who rushed out to save him. And so it continued.

Iraqi forces announced control of the eastern half of the city on January 18. Two weeks later, I flew back to Erbil and met Jaff at our usual hotel.

Abdul-Wahab, the manic ICTF veteran and driver, arrived early the next morning to take us to Mosul. He sped his pickup, swerving through traffic, screaming and chattering into his ever-ringing phone. At the last

Kurdish checkpoint, a long line of trucks carrying supplies like flour and fuel waited in the morning fog. Abdul-Wahab drove along the shoulder to pass them. He barked something at the checkpoint guard and hit the gas, and then we were on the Iraqi side. The familiar destruction marked the approach to Mosul. Then there were the soldiers in their black uniforms, warming themselves around a fire, and the black Humvees parked at a makeshift base.

With victory declared in the eastern half of the city, the men of the ICTF had been given some reprieve. Most had traveled home to see their families as the coalition readied for the final battle in Mosul, across the Tigris, in the city's west. Some had remained, and a general arranged for a Humvee to take us on a tour through the liberated parts of the city.

The Humvee rumbled past markets that were returning to life alongside bombed-out buildings and cratered roads, the city caught between war and recovery. We got stuck in a traffic jam of yellow taxis, teeming flatbeds, and old Opel sedans. The sky had turned blue, and the air was a clean, hard cold. The crowds were thick on both sides of the street. Market stalls were piled with color: beets, turnips, oranges, green apples, and bunches of bananas. I watched the shoppers through my reinforced window, which was dented with a bullet mark. Mosul's governor-in-exile had ordered the roads to remain closed, but before we left, the general who'd arranged our Humvee, who was in charge of all the special forces in Mosul, had told us he'd decided to disobey the directive: "Fuck it. Bring the bulldozers and open them. People need to feel that ISIS is no longer in charge." Local militiamen organized traffic. The Humvee rolled past a park set in a busy roundabout filled with residents, and shops around it were open.

"Most of the hard fighting was here," said our Humvee's driver, whose name was Malek, as we rolled down another street marked by mashed buildings and twisted metal. We crossed a tributary of the Tigris on a pontoon bridge. Beside it, the old bridge lay broken in the water. In a residential neighborhood, some houses sat untouched, pristine behind ornate gates and palm trees. Others were collapsed, and yet, as elsewhere in the city, life was simply taking hold around the wreckage, like flora around a rotted tree.

ISIS was still entrenched on the other side of the Tigris. At the river's narrowest point, it was only five hundred feet wide. ISIS had been flying jerry-rigged consumer drones across the water, tormenting soldiers and residents by dropping grenades. The Humvee rolled down a four-lane highway. To the west I could see the fortresslike profile of the Nineveh International Hotel, the five-star counterpart to the Babylon in Baghdad, where, Malek said, ISIS had housed some of its fighters and held Yazidi slaves. I asked if we could visit, but he refused, saying that Shia militia had made the hotel their base.

Though the militia and the ICTF were technically on the same side, they regarded one another warily. The militia had not been allowed to fight in the city; the coalition's planners knew these undisciplined forces would provoke sectarian tensions. And yet, as neighborhoods were secured, they were quietly carving out territory, at times blending with units of the Iraqi federal police that they had infiltrated. We left the highway and rolled around a crater where a car bomb had detonated. Finally, we arrived at the towering gates of Mosul University.

Inside the gates, entire buildings were crushed. As we walked around the deserted campus, I noticed the trees: olive, fig, and orange, some with fruit on their branches. I could imagine how peaceful the place must have been behind its walls and hedges, cut off from the bustle of the city. There were benches beneath the trees. In the quiet, I heard a bird chirping.

A man came toward us down a footpath. He was like a mirage, shuffling amiably in a baggy suit, with grey hair and a pair of tinted eyeglasses. He greeted us warmly. He was a member of the university's management department, he said, and had been coming by to check on things. Malek seemed to be wondering how he'd gotten around the soldiers who manned the gates. "It hurts," the man said, looking at the ruined grounds. "It was one of the most beautiful places in Iraq. The gardens were beautiful. The buildings, the students. When ISIS came, everything changed. Students stopped coming. I stopped coming. They canceled everything. They only allowed the medicine department. There were little factories inside the building. They were using it to make stuff. Most of the buildings were attacked by airstrikes, because ISIS used them to make bombs."

He gestured to a charred building. Through the frame, I could see bookshelves toppled on the floor. "This is the library," he said. "One of the biggest libraries in the world. It had 850,000 books, and many were very unique and old books. ISIS burned everything."

A spent mortar lay beneath a sign that read, "Mosul University Department Physics, Chemistry and Science." Inside, in a room with rows of lab tables, a curtain slumped from a severed rod, and paint peeled from the walls. Four red pails hung from a rack beside a gas tank. On a broken shelf were dust-caked bottles and test tubes. ISIS had used the building to make chemical weapons, Malek said. Shortly after the ICTF captured the campus, he recalled, a team of Americans had arrived and, wearing gloves and gas masks, carried items away.

ISIS fighters from several surrounding neighborhoods had gathered at the university to make a final stand. As we wandered the grounds, Jaff overheard Malek describe what he'd seen to another soldier. "It was six days of fighting," Malek said. "There were a lot of dead. We buried a lot of ISIS fighters in mass graves around here. We didn't want journalists to see."

We left the university, passing civilians with shovels clearing rubble from the streets. A man sat on a stool, painting his front door. We got stuck in traffic again. "You know what's funny?" Malek said. "The cars are not afraid of us. They don't give a fuck. Which is a good thing."

I wanted to check on one of the Kurdish commandos who'd been injured during our embed with Captain Saeed and the CTU four months earlier. In the moments after the mortar blast, after I ducked for cover in a Humvee, Jaff had snapped a photo of the man, twenty-two-year-old Shirwan Shikho. It showed him slumped in the arms of his comrades, his eyes rolled back in his head. Both legs were wounded; one, with half its foot missing, dangled unnaturally. Somehow, Shirwan had survived. After our visit to Mosul University, Jaff and I returned to Erbil, rented a Land Cruiser, and drove deep into the Kurdish mountains to meet him.

We headed north and east, away from Mosul, toward the borders with Turkey and Iran. The snow was thick around the road as it cut through the peaks of the Shaxi Karox range. We stopped at a house in a town called Soran, where we found Shirwan propped up on some cushions on the living room floor, a blanket covering his legs.

With him was his wife, Nazeera, and their two-year-old daughter, Shivar. His iPhone lay by his thigh. His face had regained its vigor in the time since his injury, but his muscles were weak, and his arms were thin. Hidden beneath the blanket, both legs had been amputated below the knee. They were wrapped in white bandages.

In America, the war against ISIS was pitched to the public as a war without sacrifice, but local forces were paying for it. By now the Kurds' role in the battle was complete, giving them time to assess the damage—a preview of the more drastic accounting the Iraqis would one day face.

We were one hundred miles from the battlefield and four months on from Shirwan's injury. On his phone, he showed me a photo of himself taken before the Humvees rolled out from behind the berm at Tel Skof that day. In it, he stood proudly, posing in his combat gear as the sun rose. He was strapping and lean, with a smile on his face. With the battle for Mosul still in its early days, he felt he was just where he was supposed to be. He came from a long line of soldiers, and he was advancing on ISIS's most important stronghold as the gunner with a Humvee in the lead convoy, backed by U.S. warplanes. After all the atrocities that ISIS militants had committed, he felt he had no choice but to stop them, and as he stepped into his turret, he believed he was fighting both to free Kurdish land from ISIS and to end the group's international campaign of violence.

Sitting with his wife and daughter, Shirwan tried not to dwell on what he'd lost. "It happened. It's over. If I feel bad about it, it's not going to change anything," he said. "You have to be realistic."

Other family members joined us in the room, and they filled in details about the hard days Shirwan had faced. Some he didn't remember, and others he didn't want to discuss. More than forty of his kin had rushed to the hospital when he arrived. They found him pale and rigid from blood loss, close to death. At times he thought he was still among his fellow soldiers, shouting, "Mortars! Get down!" His left leg was amputated there. The regional government then flew him to Jordan in hopes of saving the right. But after forty-five days, undergoing one surgery after the next, he lost his second leg. Then he returned to his family in the mountains.

As Shivar galloped around him, she was careful not to touch his legs, knowing how badly they still hurt him. Jagged scars and stitches marked the fleshy stumps, which bled daily as his body passed the pieces of shrapnel that had lodged inside it. Nazeera said Shivar had been changed by the injury and was still adjusting to the loss of the robust and active dad she knew. "Before she used to ask her father to do a lot of things with her, to play with her," she said. "Now she doesn't, because she knows he can't."

Shirwan turned frequently to his phone as the hours passed, surfing the web, messaging friends, and scrolling through the memories packed into his cache of photos. One picture showed him striding through a field with a smiling Shivar tucked beneath his arm. A video showed him dancing at a wedding, a month before his injury. "That was my favorite thing, to dance. I used to know all the moves," he said. He glided with an easy confidence in the video, dressed smartly in a trim blue suit, a slim green tie, and a white shirt that was gradually becoming untucked.

Another video showed him lying on a hospital bed as doctors worked frantically on his freshly wounded legs. They were prodding the serrated flesh, but as they operated, Shirwan looked at the camera as if there was nothing wrong. He was belting out the lyrics to an old Kurdish war song. "I didn't want to scream or show pain," he said. "So instead of that I tried to get it out by singing."

Soran was Nazeera's hometown, but Shirwan hailed from a village even deeper in the mountains. A relative carried him to an SUV's passenger seat for the winding drive home. The road climbed past snowy panoramas, and then a dirt path climbed higher, to the steps of the family home, where Shirwan's father, Qassim, took him in his arms and walked him through the door.

In the receiving room, where we sat, a wood-burning furnace blazed. Relatives filtered in to join Shirwan, sitting against the walls. The family carried scars and memories from decades of Kurdish wars—a history that stretched from the Kurdish-Iraqi wars of the 1960s and 1970s to internal conflicts and battles with the Saddam Hussein regime. Qassim's brother died fighting in 1992, and his father two years after that. Qassim himself was a veteran. Sipping tea on one side of the room was Shirwan's older brother, on leave from a front line. The previous year, three cousins were killed fighting ISIS on the same day. On the other side of the room was an uncle who wore a prosthetic on his left leg, which he had lost to a land mine long ago. "I hike. I drive. I even ride a bicycle," the uncle said.

The house was full of life, with children running from room to room and noisy preparations for dinner. Together the family seemed to be gently pressing Shirwan in an invisible embrace. They shared stories of soldiers, even a famous singer, who had lost limbs and carried on with good lives. They brought his wheelchair when it was needed, served and cleared his food, and kept a constant watch on him from the corners of their eyes.

Later, in a quieter moment on his own, Shirwan opened a small window onto his pain. "It's a big deal. I lost my legs. It's very, very sad," he said. "I'm not going to be the same person."

He talked briefly about some of the things he would miss: hikes in the mountains, soccer games.

Then he said, "Thinking about it is not going to change the reality. It happened. It's over. I have to handle it and accept it."

On the battlefield in the hours before he was injured, Shirwan had the feeling that "everybody was watching," he recalled. "ISIS, they don't exist only here. They exist in France, in Turkey, in America. If you see someone chopping off a person's head, your conscience doesn't allow you to accept it. You must do something about it. If you're a good person, you don't let it happen."

Now no one was watching but his family and neighbors—like the ones who'd driven by with sympathetic waves on the road from Soran or the checkpoint officer who'd smiled and nodded gratefully. Their attention and care kept him going, he said. He fought a war that was both global and local, but he would rely in its aftermath on the people around him and his place in their history. "We won't forget. Every time I look at myself, I know where I got injured. And some people, they gave everything," he said. "In my case, I sacrificed my legs for the people of Kurdistan. Who knows, maybe I saved someone's life."

After dinner, more bodies piled together on a sitting room floor—uncles, cousins, childhood friends. They talked, laughed, smoked, and drank tea, passing the pitch-black evening hours. Shivar burst in from the porch with a freezing gust of mountain air. A young man played the *tanbur*, an instrument like an acoustic guitar with an elongated neck and a rounded base. He tapped the base methodically as he strummed, giving his mournful music a rhythm like a heartbeat. Someone erupted into song—silencing the room with a baritone that bounced off the walls. The singer, a muscular soldier who was one of Shirwan's best friends, employed his full body as he soared through an old folk song, his torso convulsing on the high notes. It was a simple song about a woman who left a man, but it was also about suffering. Shirwan watched quietly from a corner, his blanket on his lap. Then he took over. The sound coming from his recovering body was weaker but blended with the music from the *tanbur*. Shivar tilted her forehead joyously toward the ceiling and began to twirl and dance.

The next morning was clear and bright. Sitting in the passenger seat of his father Qassim's SUV, Shirwan looked out the window as the vehicle made its way up the side of a mountain near his home, sliding along snow-covered dirt roads. At the peak, Qassim parked, carried Shirwan to his wheelchair, rolled him through the snow for a few last yards, and handed him an assault rifle. Shirwan handled the glistening weapon expertly. He took a round of target practice, shooting at rocks and into trees. He was still a good shot, and he hoped to return to his place at a machine gun in a Humvee's turret one day. Gunner was an ideal role, he said, for a soldier with prosthetic legs.

For now, though, this was just a dream to keep him going. All he had in front of him was the mountain and his family on this day. He took photos constantly, adding to the ever-growing cache on his phone. As a final test, Qassim propped a cigarette on a branch in the snow about one hundred yards away. One shot cracked, and then another, each a narrow miss. The third made the cigarette disappear. "Shooooo," Shirwan said. "That's finished."

Then he held up his phone, smiled, and took a selfie.

Jaff had caught wind of a diversion, something strange even by the standards of the war. An Iraqi street-racing outfit called Riot Gear had arranged with Iraqi special forces to stage an event in a liberated neighborhood of the city. The idea, as in one of the *Fast & Furious* films, was to race a sports car down streets where civilian traffic had not yet returned, the driver picking up speed as he approached each turn and then pulling the handbrake to send the car gliding around it, a maneuver known as drifting. The event's organizer told us it was meant to demonstrate that the city was returning to normal and that Iraq was about more than just war.

The special forces unit that had agreed to the host event, Alpha Company, had been left behind in eastern Mosul to keep the peace. Abdul-Wahab dropped us at their base, and we watched the street racers load a BMW E36 Ti compact, painted black and red, onto a flatbed. Then Jaff and I stepped into a Humvee and rolled with a convoy deeper into the city, passing a billboard that thanked the special forces for driving ISIS from the area.

The soldier in the passenger's seat was a grizzled man with a bushy moustache and big sunglasses. He played music videos on his phone while the driver lit a cigarette rolled with hash. Everyone seemed to be looking forward to the chance to blow off steam. But just in case, the two soldiers loaded their assault rifles.

I asked if they were ready for the battle in the west. Back in Erbil, Jaff and I had met with a Kurdish intelligence officer who warned that it would be much deadlier than what we'd witnessed in the east. The streets were narrower, the buildings were taller and set closer together, and the civilian population was more concentrated. Iraqi forces might be forced more often to abandon their armored vehicles and fight on foot. U.S. airstrikes would bring more collateral damage, especially if America kept its promise to use them more aggressively. On top of all this, the intelligence officer warned, ISIS had conserved fighters and weapons for a last stand in western Mosul.

The driver said he hoped the battle would start soon—"because the more time we wait, the more preparations they're going to make, and the harder it will be. Let's just get it done."

The moustachioed passenger disagreed. "We need to rest."

He said casualties in the unit weren't being replaced. Instead, soldiers were going without leave. Of the 350 soldiers the battalion had at the start of the war, he said, only 150 or so remained. Most of those had been injured and returned to battle. "I was wounded three times—my stomach, my head, and my leg," he said. He pointed to the driver. "This guy was wounded twice."

We arrived in a neighborhood in downtown Mosul, and the driver rolled the BMW from the flatbed. Residents stepped out from their houses and gathered on the sidewalk as he revved the engine. The tires spun, and the car sped off down the street.

Jaff and I took some time to wander. On one corner sat a burned-out car. The back seat was covered in a sea of hair, black and brown and grey, from men who'd shaved their beards.

A boy on a hoverboard approached us down a deserted street. "Uncle," he said to Jaff, "take a picture of me."

There was a metallic shriek and then the rumble of a bomb blast. ISIS drones had appeared overhead, dropping grenades. The streets emptied again. We ran to the sidewalk and crouched beneath a trellis covered in vines.

There were more explosions. Then it was quiet. The drift team wanted to give it another try. We followed the slowly rolling sports car until the Green Mosque, a Mosul landmark, sat before us across a wide avenue. I heard the buzz of another drone behind my head and began to run, but Jaff stopped me—this one belonged to the Riot Gear crew, who were filming a video for their website. The car sped by, its tires spinning, spitting smoke, its exhaust pipe screaming.

CHAPTER 32

BLEEDING

Mosul, Iraq. Tel al-Rayan neighborhood. February 2017.

IT WAS THE SECOND DAY OF THE ICTF'S ASSAULT INTO WESTERN Mosul when the ISIS car bomb came like a spaceship at Jaff and me, leaving us bracing in our Humvee, stuck atop a dirt barricade, as Red jammed the accelerator in vain. The day began with an attack hours earlier on the ICTF forward base, in the outer neighborhood of Tel al-Rayan, as we were all eating breakfast in the Humvee. With me and Jaff was Red, the hefty driver who looked Irish, along with Mohamed, the owl-eyed spotter, and the gunner, Mustafa al-Zerjawi. I was scraping the last of a pack of cream cheese onto a piece of bread when a clamor erupted on the radio. The soldiers outside began to panic. "A car bomb, coming at us," Jaff said. "Get out of the Humvee." I grabbed my helmet and ran with the group into a house.

Tel al-Rayan was rural in the way that some Iraqi neighborhoods can be even when on the edge of a city. As we strapped on our helmets, chickens and geese waddled around. Red had taken the radio with him, and it blared with the sound of shouts and gunfire. I could also hear gunfire in the air; the soldiers seemed to be firing in all directions from the base. Mohamed opened his mouth so that the blast wouldn't burst his eardrums. I knelt on the floor, covering my head. The car bomb exploded before it reached the battalion, but it had gotten close. The house shook, and debris pelted the roof.

The radio sounded again: a second car bomb was approaching. Again Mohamed opened his mouth, and there was a similar explosion, a similar shower of debris. We stepped outside. Bits of hay were floating in the air. Two geese looked up at me inquisitively. The soldiers were shooting again, this time into the air. "Drones!" someone said. We hurried back into the house. Mohamed crouched under a door frame, watching the sky.

I wondered if the battalion was ready for what was coming in western Mosul. In addition to all their battlefield losses, the men were also fighting without their leader. Major Salam had been assigned to a two-year officers' training course with the U.S. military at Fort Hood in Texas. His superiors wanted him ready to lead the next war, whatever it might be. It would mean a promotion and a likely end to his time as a field commander. I knew he had debated the decision until the last minute; at the start of the battle in October, he'd been hoping it would finish before the new assignment began. I'd heard that in the last days of the battle in the east, he'd become unusually meditative, walking the war-torn blocks, trailed by his dog, a German shepherd he'd had sent from his home in Baghdad. In the end, after eastern Mosul was secured, he'd boarded the plane to Texas.

Some of the men grumbled that Major Salam had abandoned them. In his place was a well-liked and competent officer, Major Ali, who was a longtime ICTF veteran at the age of thirty-three. Muscular and athletic, with a crew cut and intense brown eyes, he spoke with the soft and scratchy voice of a movie gangster and had a reserved but quietly confident manner. After the first day of battle, he'd remarked that ISIS fighters had seemed unusually determined. Normally, when they knew a neighborhood was lost, they'd slip away. This time they stayed, and the soldiers had heard them yelling "Allahu akbar" as they cut them down. "We saw nine dead bodies. And how many more were killed by airstrikes, we don't know," Major Ali had said. "They are fighting face-to-face. They don't have an option. They're trapped."

He'd added that the next morning would tell him for sure what kind of fight western Mosul would be—and judging by the early assault of car and drone bombs, it seemed he had his answer. Mohamed, still watching the sky, signaled for us to return to the Humvee, and then Red drove us to a street where the attacking convoy was mustering. Word came on the radio that ISIS fighters were on the move around us. Two more car bombs were prowling.

I sat in the back as usual, behind Red. Jaff was in the passenger's seat. Mohamed sat behind him, on the other side of the gunner Mustafa's dangling legs from me. His bulletproof window was partly lowered, and when one of the car bombs exploded, with a metallic screech, he winced as debris pelted his side of the Humvee. He shut the window. I saw someone stepping down from the vehicle in front of us, much taller than any of the soldiers, his blue flak jacket too small for him. It was Ayman Oghanna, the British Iraqi photographer. I ran out to greet him, and he gave me a dour look. "I made all of this effort to come to the worst place in the world," he said.

He told me that Colonel Arkan had been wounded. A drone had crept up on him as he called in airstrikes, and when he dove for cover, shrapnel from a grenade hit his foot. There was a commotion around us—the second car bomb was approaching. We said good-bye and jumped back into our vehicles. Out my window, I saw a soldier in a black ninja mask sprint past. Another grabbed a bazooka and ran toward the threat. Bullets began to whiz by. "Probably snipers," Red said. Small puffs of dirt kicked up in front of my window. Mortars rained down around us, and the drones whirred like cicadas. ISIS was using the video feeds on its drones to help coordinate the mortar attacks, which were surprisingly accurate. A mortar hit near the spot where Ayman and I had been standing, cutting into a pair of soldiers. One of them limped over to a Medevac vehicle, holding his side. The other was carried to it.

Red rolled the Humvee a few blocks, to a place where the road passed through a village wall. Beyond the wall, the road descended fifty yards into the next neighborhood, which was ISIS territory. Major Ali's Humvee went through the wall first, his gunner firing from the moment the vehicle crossed the threshold. There was a hard knock on my door, and I rushed to check the lock. But it was only the battalion's portly cook. He handed us five Styrofoam containers with our lunch. Then Red rolled the Humvee forward into combat.

Mustafa fired on the homes below. Bullets flew back at us.

Halfway down the hill, Red passed Major Ali. Our Humvee was now in the lead.

To my right, I could see a second column, from another ISOF unit, attacking ISIS on its flank.

As both sides exchanged fire, this unit's lead Humvee burst into a hell-red ball of flames, destroyed by an antitank rocket. Mustafa responded by unleashing a wild fusillade. Bullets sparked like fireflies along the streets and rooftops.

When Jaff and I began to feed Mustafa the belts of golden ammo—with the militant in green, who had fired the antitank rocket, still on the loose before us—I knew we'd crossed a line. Our lives seemed to depend on it as Mustafa fired without pause.

The man in green had walked out with his rocket launcher so casually, stepping from behind a building at the end of the street. As he did so, he seemed to be conversing with someone, and I imagined a huddle of militants pressed against the wall beside him, their hands on their weapons. Then the man calmly walked back into cover.

Dust-covered sedans were parked along the empty street that stretched between us. The two-story houses were tan and beige and yellow and grey. Smoke billowed from the second story of one of them, through the windows and the bullet holes in its walls. A man ran out from the front door, waving at the soldiers for help, but realized it was more dangerous to be outside.

When an airstrike hit the building that the man in green had used for cover—bringing it down in an instant, along with a second building behind it—I was relieved, though I also knew there might be civilians in them.

I watched for signs of life as we rolled onward. On the street where the man in green had been, an armored bulldozer shoved the sedans into makeshift barricades to guard against car bombs. A toddler's scooter dangled from a balcony. Laundry hung from another, pink and red and white. A small woman in a headscarf crept out from a doorway, waving a white flag, trailed by an old man. From the turret, Mustafa waved them back. The Humvee rumbled on.

There was a violent crash just above my head; a drone had hit the roof with a grenade. It knocked me into a momentary daze. I heard a sharp whistling sound and panicked, thinking it was my eardrum, though it was probably one of the Humvee's big tires deflating. "We got hit," Jaff said, sounding distant. "That's rude."

There followed what felt like a prolonged moment of quiet. We had parked at an intersection. Mohamed's window, on the Humvee's right, looked onto the next street the battalion planned to secure. A bulldozer was busy pushing up dirt berms along one side of it. The nose of our Humvee faced a berm that the bulldozer had pushed up already, and beyond this berm was a modest, two-story house. Mohamed was staring through the windshield at its rooftop. He said, "Someone peeked." Dust kicked up as Mustafa patted the roof with probing fire. Then, from the front door, an old man emerged, waving a white flag. Mustafa stopped firing. The man looked back, motioning for someone in the house to step outside, and a small boy joined him. They started walking toward the Humvee, thinking it was safe. Red jumped out from the driver's seat, waving both arms frantically above his head. "Arja! Arja!" he screamed in his duck-like voice. "Go back! Go back!"

And the two finally catch his drift and scurry back, ducking fearfully as they run.

That was the last thing I wrote in my notebook.

Then I heard the familiar call: *Sayarrah, mufakhakha*. Car bomb. This time it wasn't on the radio. It was Mohamed, screaming as he looked out his window. His eyes were opened wide. He was bouncing in his seat.

"It's next to me! On the street! Coming toward us! Just go! Drive toward the barricade! Drive toward the barricade! Get away from here!"

I saw it out his window, closing on us, as we rolled slowly forward—its makeshift armor gleaming white, the metal strip that covered the windshield hiding the madman at the steering wheel. There was no way to stop him, and with the berm right in front of us, there was nowhere to go. It was there in everyone's eyes—not the chance of death but its certainty. As the Humvee stalled on the dirt berm, Mustafa closed the hatch above him and crouched beside me. Jaff grabbed his flak jacket from the floor and, putting his head between his knees, ducked under it.

I looked through the cracked windshield at the sky and heard my mother's voice. Maybe it was my earliest memory, the first time I was conscious of being something distinct. It was just my name: *Michael.* I heard it again. *Michael, Michael.* I thought I felt the earth turn, but without me on it. My heart reached out to those I loved but was trapped in my chest. I felt loneliness and guilt that seemed to swallow me and saw my fiancée step alone down a city street. There was no way to make it better; there was nothing to do.

My body surged forward in the shock wave of the blast as shrapnel flew in a sandstorm over the Humvee. I realized that I was still thinking. Blood dripped down from Red's right ear.

We staggered out of the Humvee. The bulldozer, just a few steps behind us, beside an exterior wall, was crisped and aflame. A freak chance had made the difference. The edge of the car bomb's boxy, spaceship frame had snagged on a tooth of the bulldozer's shovel. The pilot had jammed the gas, trying to shake loose. Then the bomb had detonated. No one else had been hurt—even the bulldozer's driver had managed to dive away to safety.

———·———

Red went to the medical clinic at the battalion's rear base and came back with a bottle of ear drops and a note from the doctor. His eardrum was ruptured; he thought it was an aggravation of a prior injury, from a prior car bomb. In the house where we were staying, he stripped down to a pair of spandex shorts, buried himself under some blankets, and was snoring before the sun set.

That night, after dinner, it was time to put in the drops, which caused an intense burning sensation inside his head. He laid on his side, his belly stretched out on the concrete floor, writhing in his spandex, as Jaff kneeled over him and administered the medicine.

Red would rest at the rear base, but Mohamed and Mustafa would return to battle in the morning, in the same Humvee, which the mechanics were fixing. These soldiers were grinders, pressing ahead through an endless war.

Back at the base, as Red recovered, I saw him panic for the first time. I asked about his wife, and he replied, "Why? Did she read something?" He was worried that I'd published his photo online, because he'd been telling her that he was an administrator for the ICTF, working a desk job far from the front lines. He was the crew's most senior member, having been with the battalion since its early days, and after Mosul he hoped to turn his lies about a desk job into a reality. He dreamed of finding a post at the defense ministry in Baghdad's well-secured Green Zone, so he could commute from home. He'd lost track of how many times he and his crew had almost died. "All of us when we reach that moment that is very close to death, we all feel the same—guilty," he said. "But life is hard, and sometimes you have to make something for yourself. If I tell you I'm only doing it for my country, that's bullshit. That's one of the reasons. But I also want to build a future for myself."

Around noon the next day Mustafa and Mohamed returned to the rear base in a tow truck, which dragged the Humvee behind it, crumpled like a paper cup.

They'd been third in the attacking convoy, with Mohamed at the wheel. A car bomb came straight at them again. It chased them for blocks as Mohamed sped through the streets, its pilot ignoring other Humvees as he pursued them. "The son of a bitch, he was passing other Humvees and he wouldn't push the button," Mohamed said.

Just as Red had done the day before, Mohamed had rolled the Humvee into a barricade. This time he and Mustafa were able to jump out and take cover behind it just before the car bomb exploded.

Covered in dirt, his thinning hair standing on end, Mohamed looked at me with disbelief. "Azrael was chasing me," he said, using the Arabic name for the Angel of Death.

That was the last time Jaff and I embedded with the ICTF. Soon after, an Iraqi general ordered us to leave, saying journalists were no longer allowed in combat. I was shaken by the close call and happy to obey. I tracked the fate of the battle and of the battalion from afar for a while. In the spring, the coalition began its assault on the final ISIS stronghold in western Mosul, in the winding streets of the Old City. Major Ali was killed by a sniper. His death prompted a heartbroken Facebook post from Major Salam, who was guilt ridden about having left a war from which it seemed that death alone could release the men of the ICTF. "I left you alone," the unit's old commander wrote from Texas. "I take the blame. It's my fault. Forgive me."

CHAPTER 33

CASUALTIES

Mosul, Iraq. May 2017.

THE CAMPAIGN TO FREE MOSUL HAD BROUGHT URBAN DESTRUCTION reminiscent of World War II, and it had been defined by airstrikes, with the coalition launching more than 24,000 munitions into the city, a number that also included artillery strikes and the HIMARS missiles I'd seen at "Rocket City" at the U.S. base in Qayyarah. Yet there had been no accounting of the suffering the battle had brought to civilians. ISIS restricted communications, and independent documentation of strikes was impossible when the sites were still under their control, while the coalition had been slow to investigate civilian casualties. It had assigned two service members to sift through thousands of allegations.

Abdul-Wahab, wearing civilian clothes, snuck Jaff and me around eastern Mosul's checkpoints, complaining that Shia militiamen dressed as Iraqi federal police were appearing at ever more of them, quietly extending their reach. In a middle-class neighborhood called Falah, we stopped at a fruit store across from a mosque and asked if anyone knew civilians who'd been killed by airstrikes. We could have picked any street in Mosul and done the same. A shopkeeper guided us to a peaceful block, where birds chirped in the trees and a single home sat destroyed. It had been a two-story house with concrete walls. It was caved in the middle, and two poles of rebar stuck into the air like antennae. At the sidewalk, in front of the rubble, a metal gate was still standing, its door locked.

The shopkeeper described rushing over in the aftermath of the strike. "These guys didn't have anything to do with the situation," he said. "But there was a small ISIS base in the house behind it. They hit the house first, then later the base. They hit it with four missiles. When we got here, the old lady was thrown from the house, with both of her arms torn off."

He called the household's only survivor. "His mother, his dad, his pregnant wife, and his five-year-old son were all killed," he said as he dialed.

Mohamed Ghassan Salem arrived ten minutes later, holding a set of keys. He was a burly and soft-spoken thirty-one-year-old with pale skin and red hair. He owned an electronics store down the road and had been at work when the strike hit. "I just heard it," he said. "And the fire and the smoke were unbelievable. So I ran and . . . "

He took a big key and opened the gate.

"My mother was lying down here by this tree," he said, walking through debris strewn with twisted metal and his family's belongings. "My brother was just over here next to the door. My wife and son were in the basement, dead. There was fire—fire everywhere. I couldn't get to the basement. I tried to get down, but I couldn't. I couldn't take out my wife and son until the next day."

On the floor amid the rubble were women's and children's clothes. A blanket was buried beneath cinder blocks. The walls and the sunken roof were charred black. Beside a woman's shoe, a set of stairs led to nowhere. "One of the rockets hit here," Salem said, pointing around. "They were sleeping right here. This was the kids' room. This was my room, our bedroom. On top it was my father's bedroom."

Salem seemed hollowed out by the tragedy, exhausted. He'd petitioned to get the coalition to admit its mistake because it was the only fight he could wage on behalf of his dead family. He had failed. "I understand that ISIS is putting bases in civilian houses. But it's the coalition that made the mistake," he said. "At least someone needs to take responsibility."

A short drive away, a large lot where a home once laid was flattened and empty; a bulldozer had cleared away the rubble. The concrete wall of an adjacent home was still covered in soot, and children had pressed handprints onto it and drawn hearts with their fingers. Across the street, three large houses that residents said ISIS had used as a headquarters and arms depot remained untouched; either the intelligence or the coordinates for the strike had apparently been just off. The strike killed eight members of an extended family. Four more women from the family were wounded, and two neighbors were also killed. "Whoever was able to pulled out the bodies," a neighbor said.

I saw an old man leaning against the outer wall of the house next door, favoring his right leg. Khayradeen Abdur Razzaq, a retired laborer, was in his garden when the strike hit. It covered him with rubble and broke his leg in three places. His neighbors had been buried in his small front yard, where their bodies remained for weeks until family members came and moved them to a cemetery.

He invited us to tea, and his family joined—his wife, his sons and daughters, and their children. One of his granddaughters, a little girl dressed in yellow, stared at me, her eyes wide. She'd been wounded in the fighting, he said, and had shrapnel in her chest. One of the men sitting with us had recently escaped from western Mosul with his wife and four children. "Everything is destroyed," he said. "I left at night, through the bushes. I ran toward the Iraqi army."

I asked if ISIS still cared whether civilians fled. His answer was immediate: "It's execution. Right away." He recalled the constant fear of living in ISIS territory. Residents knew the militants were always at risk of being targeted by airstrikes. He said that one way ISIS enforced its hated regime of fines—which were levied for everything from owning a hookah to using a mobile phone—was to take a relative as collateral. "If you couldn't pay, they might take your son and hold him at one of their bases," he said. "And all the time their bases were getting hit by airstrikes. You would do anything to pay and get your son back."

Whenever we stopped in a new neighborhood, people could quickly point the way to the wrecked houses, detailing which had held ISIS militants and which had held only civilians. Standing outside one rubbled home, residents of another quiet street in eastern Mosul recounted how, even five months on from the strike that destroyed it, their former neighbor still returned. He made his pilgrimage about once a week, climbing through the crushed concrete and twisted iron, stooping to dig for mementos—a photo, a scrap of clothes. Then, he would sit and cry.

Hassan Ali Hassan, forty-five, was a Jordanian who'd lived for three decades in Mosul, where he married a local woman and raised a family. In June 2014, after ISIS captured the city, he'd tried to escape with his wife and three daughters, but the militants seized their passports and ordered them to stay. Hassan and his family were still trapped in the city on December 14, 2016. The fighting had not yet reached their neighborhood, and they shared a late breakfast before Hassan stepped out to get gas for the generator. Barely a minute had passed when a massive explosion erupted behind him. He ran back to find his home demolished and engulfed in flames, pulverized by an airstrike. Body parts littered the street.

"We found some on the other houses here," recalled a neighbor.

Jaff and I took Hassan's phone number from the man, and we called him later that evening. "Just everything was in pieces," he said. "Everyone was dead."

"Everything happened before my eyes," he kept repeating.

When Hassan, an electrician, moved to Mosul from Jordan in the 1980s, he wasn't sure if he'd stay. But he fell in love with the city—he found it beautiful, with the Tigris cutting through downtown and wooded areas and waterfalls nearby. He met his wife, Sabah, through his sister, who was studying at the city's famous university, and after they married in 1992, he thought he'd live there forever. "She was a gift from God," he said. The couple first had a son, who was studying in Jordan, and then three daughters, who were sixteen, eighteen, and twenty when they were killed, along with Sabah and her brother, a high school principal. In the days after the strike, Hassan dug through the rubble and gathered what he could of the remains. "I kept looking. Sometimes I was finding a hand, sometimes I was finding a foot," he said. "I buried some of my family in the west of Mosul. And the rest, after I found more pieces, I buried them in another part of my neighborhood."

Half of one of his daughters was still missing. Once he found the rest of her remains, he said, he hoped to leave. "I don't give any thought to the U.S. or the coalition or the Iraqi government," he said. "I lost everything. All I want now is some help in finding my daughter's body and burying her. Then I want to go back to Jordan. I don't want money. I don't want a house. I don't want anything."

In western Mosul, the destruction was on a scale far greater than in the east—it was not intermittent but constant. It was as if a dam had burst, unleashing death and violence.

In some neighborhoods, entire blocks had been ravaged by airstrikes and artillery. House after house was destroyed. The coalition had begun deploying white phosphorus, an incendiary weapon that drifts down from the sky in a burning cloud. It was clear that far more civilians were being killed in western Mosul than had died in the battle for the east. As a U.S. military officer who was there told me later, at some point the coalition had decided, simply, to "make it hurt."

One attack came in a neighborhood called al-Jadida. A U.S. airstrike aimed at ISIS snipers taking cover on a rooftop destroyed a large house where civilians had been sheltering, killing more than one hundred people. It was one of the deadliest U.S. attacks on civilians in the last quarter century and perhaps the worst in Iraq since the 2003 invasion. The building looked to me like any of the hundreds around Mosul that had been destroyed in similar strikes. There was the same broken concrete, contorted metal, and tangled wires, a pink umbrella, pink children's shoes. A neighbor had lost six members of his family in the strike. He'd been at home early in the morning when it hit. "All that I saw was like fire," he said. He and other witnesses said there had been 137 people living in the building; many were sheltering there after fleeing their homes elsewhere in the city. Of them, around 100 were confirmed dead, the witnesses told me.

The bodies of the rest were still missing. "There are still a lot of dead bodies underneath," an old man said.

"No matter what they do, the Americans, they're not going to bring them back," said the man who'd lost six family members. "Even if the strike killed one or two ISIS guys, does it make sense?"

He pulled out his phone. "Do you want to see a photo of my dead brother?"

I wanted to return to Tel al-Rayan, where the car bomb had nearly killed Jaff and me in Red's Humvee. I remembered how, before that car bomb, we'd been tormented by the man in green with the antitank rocket launcher, until an airstrike knocked down the building he'd been hiding behind and another one beside it. I wanted to walk in the destruction from that strike, one of many over the previous months that may have saved our lives, and find out if any innocent people had died because of it.

After we entered Tel al-Rayan, we noticed that we were being followed by a dusty vehicle that looked like a souped-up dune buggy. From the back flew the flag of the Hashed al-Shaabi, the umbrella force of the Shia militia. They'd taken control of the neighborhood after it was liberated. Just as before, I saw no other outward signs of life, except for a little market stall that was open. Jaff wanted to turn back, but I insisted on seeing the site of the airstrike. As Abdul-Wahab drove deeper into the neighborhood, the buggy drew closer behind us. We could see four men in plain clothes sitting inside it. The one in the passenger's seat held his gun out the window. The driver flashed his lights. Abdul-Wahab stopped the pickup. The man from the passenger's seat stepped out, wearing a black tracksuit. He circled the pickup, sizing us up, and stopped at Abdul-Wahab's window.

"What are you guys up to? What are you doing?" he said.

Abdul-Wahab's every movement was calculated—he casually grabbed his Iraqi special forces ID and thrust it at the man, almost flippantly, wanting him to believe that we were soldiers on a mission, that backup could be on the way. "We're with the special forces," he snarled. "Look at it."

The man in the tracksuit read the card. He paused. Then he handed it back. "We're your brothers from the Hashed al-Shaabi," he said flatly.

And with that, the men drove slowly off, watching us through their windows as they passed.

We sat there for a moment. I looked at Jaff in the passenger's seat. Through all our travels in Iraq, this was the only time I saw him unnerved. I asked if he thought we'd really been close to trouble. What he said next, I thought, made a fitting end to our time in Mosul, a reminder of how ordinary any death is in a war. "That guy would have killed us and thrown our bodies in a ditch," he said. "Then he would have gone back to his base, taken a shit, and had some tea."

EPILOGUE

ESCAPE

Istanbul, Turkey. September 2017.

WITH THE CALIPHATE ON THE VERGE OF COLLAPSE, ISIS MEMBERS escaped by following some of the same smuggling routes that had taken them into the war originally.

It was July 2017 when Iraqi forces declared victory in Mosul. That left Raqqa as the last major city controlled by ISIS, and it was surrounded by a force led by the Syrian-Kurdish YPG, with whom I'd tracked the rise of ISIS in late 2013. Following the coalition's model from Iraq, the YPG worked alongside U.S. special forces and was backed by U.S. airstrikes. In Washington, U.S. government officials were proclaiming that most ISIS members had died on the battlefield and the rest would be killed or captured in Raqqa and eastern Syria. In the months since I'd returned to Istanbul from Iraq, though, Munzer and I had been speaking with sources in the smuggling networks that ran between Syria and Turkey. They were telling a different story.

For almost a year, a steady stream of ISIS members and their families had been sneaking out of ISIS territory. Some of the escapees were foreign fighters, and others were Syrians and Iraqis. They slipped through the dragnet of U.S.-allied soldiers outside Raqqa and crossed the Syrian border into Turkey, where they could access the migrant routes that extended to Europe, Asia, and beyond. Some were headed home. Others were seeking status as refugees. Still others were linking up with ISIS's growing roster of global affiliates in places like Libya, Afghanistan, and the Philippines. I learned later that, despite the U.S. government's optimistic public statements, American intelligence officials were tracking this exodus with mounting concern.

One trafficker told Munzer and me that he'd retrieved ISIS members and their relatives from the usual smuggling hot spots all along the Turkish border. He was a Syrian refugee, a former electrician. "I smuggled Iraqis, Syrians, and people who did not speak Arabic," he said.

We were talking on an encrypted phone call as Munzer and I huddled at my desk in Istanbul. The former electrician messaged us a location pin indicating that he was in an obscure corner of Turkey near the border with Iraq, waiting for his next ISIS clients.

Working for a network of Turkish traffickers, he was tasked with driving his charges from the border regions deeper into Turkey, to cities like Adana and Ankara, where he handed them off to other members of his team. He said that "saving these people," especially the foreigners, made him happy. "We have to help those people who came to support us," he said.

"And frankly," he added, the work was "also a good way to make money."

Munzer and I knew two Syrian smugglers based along the border who over the years had worked for all types of clients, from rebels to refugees to ISIS. It was just business. When we reconnected with them, they explained that they were busy smuggling Saudi ISIS members from Raqqa to Turkey, along with a handful of Westerners. They could make as much as $50,000 for each client, the money wired to them via ISIS-linked contacts in Syria or overseas. They paid a portion of these funds to a battalion run by a rebel leader allied with the YPG, and his men spirited the jihadis to from ISIS territory to the border. Once an ISIS member arrived at a safe house the two smugglers kept in Turkey, they took a video of him, to prove that he was alive and well, and sent it to the person who'd hired them, who released the money. They shared one of the videos. In it, the camera scanned the face and limbs of a bearded man wearing a white tank top and white boxer shorts.

"Are you okay? Can you sit and stand?" the cameraman asked.

"Yes," the man replied, speaking Arabic with a Saudi accent.

He turned from side to side, squatted up and down, and said, "Praise be to God, I am fine."

He presented a Saudi ID card to the camera and stated his name and the date. The surname was that of an influential Saudi clan. The smugglers told us that in Raqqa, the man had been channeling money to ISIS via a relative back at home, and when we checked with a well-connected Islamist source, we learned that he was known as a funder for the group in Syria. The two smugglers didn't know what happened to the men once they left their safe house in Turkey, but they'd obtained forged Syrian passports for some of them.

Money made all the difference as to who could leave ISIS territory. We spoke one day to a former ISIS member who'd recently left Raqqa and recalled that his commander had approved of his departure, telling him and other fighters that they should wait in Turkey until they were called to return. (Instead, he said, he'd defected.) To escape from Raqqa, he said, he and another ISIS member paid a smuggler to guide them down a road guarded by YPG soldiers. "The road was open, and the smuggler told us that [the YPG soldiers] are watching us," he said. The pair were then picked up in a car and driven along a circuitous route to the border with Turkey, where they paid another smuggler to cross. Another man, who claimed he was a teacher, had come to Turkey all the way from Mosul, via Syria. He said he paid more than $30,000 for the journey with his wife and four children. They were smuggled first from Mosul, then across the Iraqi border, and then to Raqqa. From Raqqa, the family passed right through YPG territory, their smuggler bribing soldiers along the way. "My trip was very comfortable, because I paid a huge amount," the man said.

The smugglers were drawn to ISIS members, especially well-known ones, because they could charge them a premium. They also had the most money. The group had spent years extorting cash from the population and looting local resources like oil and antiquities. In parts of eastern Syria, as U.S.-backed forces closed in, ISIS had forced civilians to exchange their American dollars and Syrian pounds for a new ISIS currency. The people who remained in Raqqa tended to be those who couldn't afford to leave. "It's easy for ISIS people to escape," one smuggler told us. "Civilians, they can't. They're trying to escape and they don't know what to do. So there are many important ISIS officials who left, and many civilians are stuck there in the end."

The underground networks that had served ISIS for so long were whirring into action once more, fueled by the illicit wealth ISIS had taken such care in building. True to form, Mohamed, the former oil smuggler, had found a way to get involved and was running a side business helping ISIS members move onward from Syria. Over dinner at his home near the border, he explained that he'd hosted about a dozen Syrians whose roles with ISIS had ranged from rank-and-file soldier to internal security officer to regional administrator. Most chose to remain in Turkey, he said, but several had traveled by sea to Greece.

He said he didn't know their intentions. All told him the same thing: that they'd quit. "They told me they defected," he said. "How can you know? Everyone tells me the same story. They say, 'We like ISIS, and we know that they are fighting [for the right cause], but now because of the siege on Raqqa we just want to support our families, and we chose to defect.' I don't know if they really defected or not."

I wondered, once again, about Mohamed's place in this. He'd always kept a partial distance from ISIS—derisive of its extremes, chagrined by its senseless violence, aware that, in the end, just like the Assad regime, it had oppressed Syrians. He also still maintained his sympathies for ISIS as an underdog foil to the United States. And it helped him make a living. Governments could target ISIS members more easily than people like Mohamed, who were its occasional supporters and enablers and who could be motivated to play a role, when needed, at least as long as the war in Syria continued. Since he wasn't officially with ISIS, he didn't need to escape—he could just remain where he was.

Munzer and I said good-bye to Mohamed and made the long drive to Sanliurfa, where we met another Syrian who was smuggling ISIS members into Turkey. He told us about two who showed how surprisingly easy it could be even for well-known jihadis to escape. One was Tareq Kamleh, an Australian medical doctor who'd joined ISIS in 2015 and featured in its propaganda, making him one of its most recognizable Western faces. Traveling with him was another senior ISIS member, a cardiologist from Deir Ezzor who'd helped to oversee the group's medical facilities, and who has the adult sons living under asylum in Europe. The smuggler explained how from Raqqa the two men had been driven right to the border with Turkey, before traveling to Istanbul. After some time, Kamleh had returned to Syria, but his colleague quickly landed a job in Istanbul. He was working at a medical center not far from the Hagia Sophia.

Eventually, Munzer and I were detained by Turkish intelligence officers at a shopping mall in Sanliurfa. They took our ID cards, brought us to a small room off a stairwell, and looked through the messages on Munzer's phone. After a while, they agreed to let us go. "Leave Sanliurfa, and don't come back," one of them told me. That night, as we slept at our hotel, preparing to fly home in the morning, someone broke into Munzer's apartment in Istanbul. His downstairs neighbor heard heavy steps on the old wood floor. When Munzer returned, the only thing missing was the backup phone he'd left on his desk.

———·———

As summer turned to fall, rescue workers were still pulling bodies from the rubble in western Mosul. Much of the city was destroyed—a grim preview of the battle in Raqqa, which would see its neighborhoods laid to waste on a similar scale. And soon enough, Donald Trump would be declaring a premature victory—even as across its former territory, ISIS launched the kind of insurgent-style attacks that would have been familiar to the U.S. troops battling AQI a decade prior.

As in the past, America was looking to move on from the region before its war was really over—leaving much of Iraq and Syria in ruins and ISIS still a threat. This was an impulse that I embodied too. As Colonel Arkan had once explained, the thing about going to war far from home is that you can always walk away from it. In October 2017, I said good-bye to friends and sources who were still trapped in the conflict and prepared to return to the United States. Munzer had been planning to join me, applying for a journalism fellowship at the University of Missouri, but he was blocked from entry, like any Syrian, by Trump's travel ban. And so we said farewell over beers in Istanbul on a crisp fall night.

There was a lot about Munzer's time in prison in Syria that he hadn't told me. He opened up a little more as we drank.

After he'd been arrested for handing out flyers and helping to arrange the protests in Daraa, he'd been kept in an underground prison with dozens of men, but it was so dark that even up close, he'd never seen their faces.

Some of them had died as the weeks dragged on, and Munzer had wept in the blackness as he tripped over them.

He'd been pulled from that subterranean cell into a bright interrogation room and tortured under the glare of its lights. He was beaten with electric cables. He was hung from his feet.

Friends of his, fellow activists, had appeared in the interrogation room from time to time, pointing at him with false accusations, stories their own interrogators had invented. His heart broke for his broken friends, and when his turn came, he did the same.

He signed papers that said he was terrorist.

He was, in fact, the truest kind of journalist, one with no allies. To the Syrian regime he was a terrorist; to many Western governments he was a potential terrorist too. He was under threat from ISIS, and from the Nusra Front in Syria, and from other rebels he'd investigated. We worried that he might also be at risk from the authorities in Turkey, wondering if they'd broken into his apartment to send a message.

I knew that, beneath the facade of normalcy he presented to the world, he had to be suffering. He told me that there were still nights when he woke up feeling terrified, though he couldn't say why, and his mind refused to let him get back to sleep. And that was how I left him as I flew back across the ocean, pacing his apartment through the twilight hours.

ACKNOWLEDGMENTS

THIS BOOK IS DEDICATED TO MY WIFE, MY PARTNER THROUGH everything.

I want to thank my parents and siblings for a lifetime of love and support and for sticking with me despite what my work and travel put them through. This goes especially for my mother, who has been my role model for as long as I can remember.

Thank you to my godmother for always pushing me to follow my dream of writing for a living and to my late grandfather, whose enthusiasm for that idea always inspired me.

I have been truly fortunate for the many teachers who have made an impact on my life. Two stand out. Lori Cariello first gave me the idea of pursuing writing as a career, and I have been grateful since. Bro. Stephen Balletta, S.M., did more than anyone to make me into the writer I am today. I can't thank him enough for taking so much time and care in teaching me to write and most importantly to edit—and for the lesson that it's always worth as much time as it takes to get it right.

I have been lucky, too, to work under some incredible editors. Thank you to Scott Smith for giving me a shot and to Richard Thurmond for teaching me to write deeply and to revise. And to Margaret Downing for teaching me how to be a professional, how to be edited, how to investigate, and how journalism, when done right, can be a calling.

Thank you to Louise Roug for everything—from helping me get the hell out of New York to teaching me how to be a foreign correspondent. To Jack Livings for getting me in the door. And to Tina Brown for giving me the chance to be a correspondent, and then a second chance. Thank you to Ben Smith for letting me be part of what felt at the time like the best place in the world to be a journalist and to Paul Hamlios for being a friend, an occasional therapist, and an expert editor at once. And thank you especially to Miriam Elder: for the years of guidance and friendship, for your constant concern and courage, for never running with the crowd, and for helping me do the kind of work that made us proud.

I have made some incredible friends through journalism, and all of them have helped me immeasurably in their own ways. Thank you to Matt McKenzie for helping me get through my first job. To Roman Kessler for giving me a home and a much-needed friend in Germany and beyond. To Paul Knight and Chris Vogel for making some of the darkest times the best ones. To Ross Schneiderman, Joel Schectman, Rob Verger, and McKay Coppins for the solidarity as underlings. To Christian Cecchi and Claire Ludden for making sure I wasn't stuck in London on my own. To Yusuf Sayman for helping me make Istanbul into a real home, for being a companion through so many difficult assignments, and for bringing out the best in me through his dedication and unique vision. To Eliot Stempf, Jason Reich, and the Antares crew for keeping me safe. To Warzer Jaff for helping me stay sane and alive through some of the worst of it and most importantly for all of the advice on life. To Ayman Oghanna for being so generous in sharing his contacts with ISOF and the ICTF and for all the good times and all the very bad ones in the field and at home. To Dmytro Tkachenko and Andriy Glushko for being so welcoming in Ukraine. In Cairo, to Maged

Atef, one of the world's best investigative journalists, for everything. To Zaher Said in southern Turkey for helping me so many times over the years, and for all the laughs. To Munzer al-Awad, whom I miss as a friend and colleague every day. And to Mitchell Prothero for being a friend and mentor when I've needed it most.

Thank you to David Halpern, my agent, who had the patience and old-school decency to help me through years of uncertainty until I found the idea I was looking for in this book, and then guided me through every stage of conceiving, pitching, and producing it. To Jim Hornfischer for the much-needed push and to Andrew Miller at Knopf for the early feedback and encouragement. Thank you to Clive Priddle at PublicAffairs for believing in the book and enabling me to do it, from the early ideas sessions through the last edits. Thank you to the friends and neighbors who helped me through the writing process and the transition to life in America that came with it—especially the people at CFSS, the original noon crew, and Marcos Hernandez, who was a comrade-in-arms through some of the most difficult stages. Thank you to Bryan Di Salvatore for swooping in with incredible edits and for being such a pleasure to deal with at a time when the work was feeling pretty rough. Thank you to Mitch Prothero for going above and beyond in helping with the fact check. And thank you to Matthew McAllester for being so generous with his time and wisdom in giving me the feedback I needed to make this the book I wanted to write.

NOTES

PROLOGUE

Because I understood Abdul-Wahab's story about Will as a ghost story—like many war stories are—I don't mean for it to be taken as fact or to cast aspersions onto a particular soldier or unit.

I don't know for certain which aircraft were circling overhead as the ICTF convoy made its approach to Tel al-Rayan or to which command centers the drones were beaming their video. I've based this description on my general understanding.

The fact that both ISIS and the coalition were using an American specialist to deal with drone frequencies was relayed to me after the battle by the ISOF colonel Arkan, who appears later in this book.

I'd like to thank Dr. Joseph Amar of the University of Notre Dame, a scholar who has produced fascinating work on the Biblical history of the region, for reviewing my interpretation of the passage from the Book of Jeremiah that's cited in this chapter.

In passing ammunition to the Humvee's gunner during a frantic moment in the battle in Tel al-Rayan, I crossed a journalistic line for the first and only time in years of war reporting. I was painfully aware at the time of the additional risk I'd caused our escorts to incur by displacing one or two well-trained soldiers from the convoy's lead Humvee, and all of our lives seemed to be at stake. Even so, I regret this.

CHAPTER 1: THE MARTYR

Wael Ghonim was not the only person behind the We Are All Khaled Said page. He collaborated with the Egyptian activist AbdelRahman Mansour and others, including Nadine Wahab, an Egyptian-American activist. Nadine was based in Washington, DC during the protests but in their aftermath moved to Cairo, where she lives today, still committed to the causes of human rights and social justice.

CHAPTER 2: LEO

Leo wasn't the only Syrian who hoped that Assad would use his momentous speech in March 2011 to bring unity and reform. I detailed those hopes in a 2014 article for *BuzzFeed*, "The Speech That Changed Syria."

Parts of my description of Damascus and the early protests there are drawn from a 2011 article I published in *Newsweek*, "Syria: The Republic of Fear," to which Katie Paul, a journalist then working in Damascus, contributed. I believe certain descriptions of Damascus—of the mall, bazaar, and mosque, for example—are based on her accounts.

The Impossible Revolution, a book by the Syrian writer Yassin al-Haj Saleh from which I took the passage cited in this chapter, is a must-read for anyone interested in understanding the tragedy of the civil war.

CHAPTER 3: BORDER

I know that Tom Holland, the writer and popular historian cited in this chapter, is controversial for his treatment of and views about Islam, including in the book from which I've taken the passage on Antakya. But his writing about that ancient city and its place in history is insightful and worth citing.

My reporting on the early efforts of the CIA program can be found in more detail in a 2013 article in *Newsweek*, "Did The CIA Betray Syria's Rebels?"

CHAPTER 4: REVENGE

For numbers on arrests and casualties from the massacre at Rabaa and related crackdowns, I refer to an in-depth report from Human Rights Watch, "All According to Plan," which was published in August of 2014.

The number of protesters who were at Rabaa that day, as well as the number of protesters who turned out to support the military coup, have always been disputed, and so I have turned, regretfully, to generalities.

Shawkan was finally released from prison in March of 2019, after more than five years of unjust confinement.

CHAPTER 5: SIGNS

With Yusuf and me as we were smuggled into Syria was Jamie Dettmer, a journalist with *Voice of America* and *The Daily Beast*, and his traveling companion, an Egyptian doctor. Our two parties split up after visiting Qamishli. After that, Jamie experienced a harrowing ordeal in which he was nearly detained by Syrian security forces—a sign of how uncertain the truce between the YPG and the Assad government was at the time. He recounts this in detail in an article for *The Daily Beast*, "How I Escaped Assad's Army in Syria."

The idea that ISIS and/or Nusra members went into battle with keys around their necks and spoons in their pockets, which was recounted to me several times by awestruck Kurdish civilians, seems unlikely. This may have been an exaggeration based on some combination of hearsay and YPG propaganda, and it suggested to me that the fighters were taking on mythical qualities in the minds of many locals.

ISIS and Jabhat al-Nusra were in the process of splitting in late 2013 as part of a larger rift between al-Qaeda and AQI. The signs I found on the floor of the warehouse near the border had the names of both groups written on them, as detailed in a 2013 article for *BuzzFeed*, "Inside Syria: Al-Qaeda Was Here."

CHAPTER 6: ABU AYMAN

For a summation of Abu Ayman al-Iraqi's biography, I have relied in part on the analysis of the journalist Hassan Hassan, and on my own reporting. Daniele Raineri of *Il Foglio* has also tracked Abu Ayman extensively.

A 2014 *Vice* documentary, "Syria: Wolves in the Valley," by the journalist Aris Roussinos, focuses on the rebel commander Mohamed Zaatar and his men.

CHAPTER 7: FEAR

I spoke with the sergeant who'd been posted to the Ghazlani base outside Mosul by phone, from Baghdad, in July of 2014, along with several soldiers who relayed similar accounts of the Iraqi military's collapse. The sergeant requested anonymity during the interview, and I wasn't able to reconnect with him afterward to ask his permission to use his name.

Because the Iraqi captain cited at the end of the chapter had abandoned his military post to go into hiding, he cannot be named here.

CHAPTER 8: EAGLE

There is more information on Okab later in the book. Because he lives abroad as a refugee—and because he might face retaliation from ISIS for speaking so critically of it—he can't be identified beyond the details I received his approval to relay in 2016, for a story in *BuzzFeed*.

CHAPTER 9: ARRIVALS

Abdulrahman is a pseudonym. He still lives between Syria and Turkey and cannot be identified due to the same security risks—from local police, as well as from ISIS—that led me to grant him anonymity in the fall of 2014, when I first interviewed him for a story in *BuzzFeed*.

CHAPTER 10: FRONTIER

Mohamed is a pseudonym. I'd hoped to be able to identify sources such as him in this book, or at least to provide more personal details about them, but as

I set about writing it, I realized this was naive. In the summer of 2019, as this book approaches publication, the war in Syria continues. ISIS, while weakened, remains a threat to locals when it wants to be, with underground networks continuing to target its perceived enemies across Iraq and Syria. Some 3.5 million Syrian refugees remain in Turkey, where they face as uncertain a future as ever. Those Syrians who have returned home to areas under government control have been harassed, extorted, arrested, and tortured by Assad's security forces, as detailed in a June 2019 report by Louisa Loveluck in the *Washington Post* and elsewhere. In short, many of the same risks that caused Syrian sources to request anonymity when I first interviewed them for articles in *Newsweek* or *BuzzFeed* remain. I regret that I can't share more about these people and their personal stories.

Abu Salah is a pseudonym. He now lives in Europe with his family, and I don't want his wartime work along the border to tarnish his new life in any way.

CHAPTER 11: BEHEADING

Malik is a pseudonym.

CHAPTER 12: GATEWAY

In researching Aksaray's history as a point of transit for refugees and migrants, I was struck by a passage from the self-published autobiography of an Iranian exile, *Nemesis*, by Amir K. Alai. In it, he describes his own arrival in Turkey in the 1980s. At the airport, Alai writes, "I looked at myself and around me thinking where can I go, what can I do? The answer was one choice only; in fact, I had no other selection but to take a taxi to an unknown hotel. This is what happens for everyone arriving at an airport. However, there was a difference here; I had no plan, no future to think of, and no person to go to. It was neither a tourist nor a business trip. It was just being dropped off into an ocean of wilderness." From the airport a taxi driver took the author "directly to a hotel in Aksaray, as soon as he found out I was an Iranian.[. . .] After a day of walking around I realized why: thousands of Iranians were living there, mostly distressed and in poverty. Refugees, or rather I should say fugitives, who ran away from the Islamic Republic, of all walks of political sectors." Alai describes Aksaray as "run-down buildings with narrow dark stairways, back alleys, abandoned building lots. It was home to Roma, Kurds and poor Turks living on the margins of society."

I've tried to give a small sense of Istanbul's unique character through my description of its old-style shopping districts. Hugh Pope's 2016 essay "A Farewell to Istanbul" is well worth a read for its discussion of pop-up restaurants, and much more.

I mention in this chapter that ISIS wanted to convince Muslims everywhere—especially those living in the West—that they were in conflict with the West, whether they wanted to be or not. Murtaza Hussain of *The Intercept* has covered this subject well, including in a 2015 article titled "Islamic State's Goal: 'Eliminating the Grayzone' of Coexistence Between Muslims and the West."

CHAPTER 13: DINNER

Khalil is a pseudonym. I'm no longer in touch with him and have kept to the agreement on anonymity that I made in 2015, when I met him while reporting an article for *BuzzFeed*. The steps I took to confirm his identity and his story are detailed in part in this chapter and in the article "ISIS Operative: This Is How We Smuggle Jihadis to Europe." This included verifying his role with ISIS and his personal history with a rival Syrian rebel commander, who sent me a photo of Khalil so I could be sure we were speaking about the same person, in addition to interviews with the Syrian intermediary and the smuggler mentioned in this chapter. Through another Syrian contact with well-established ties to ISIS, I also independently contacted Khalil's superior, who confirmed his story. Before publishing the 2015 article, I had a colleague in Washington, DC, relay its details to the chairman of the Senate Intelligence Committee, who said he'd been briefed on operations similar to the one Khalil described, which at the time had not been publicized.

Nabil is a pseudonym.

CHAPTER 14: BODIES AND BOMBS

The fact that peshmerga EOD technicians were dying in the field because they couldn't obtain cheap plastic or ceramic wire cutters was a damning indictment of both Kurdish leadership and the U.S. government, whose failure to provide this basic equipment to its allies six months into the war effort showed a surprising lack of concern and urgency. This spoke to wider problems with the way America carried out the war effort, especially early on.

CHAPTER 15: PASSPORTS

Samir is a pseudonym. He was one of several human traffickers Munzer and I knew over the years who smuggled refugees and migrants to Europe relatively openly—a testament to the fact that the Turkish government was seldom if ever seriously concerned with cracking down on these efforts and at times seemed even to welcome them.

CHAPTER 16: ARTIFACTS

Talib is a pseudonym.

The idea that conflict antiquities from Syria and Iraq have often made their way to buyers in Europe and America has been contested by some in the antiquities industry. Reporting from myself and others suggests that they are wrong. I laid out the case in more detail than is presented here in a 2015 article for *BuzzFeed*, "This Is How Syrian Antiquities Are Being Smuggled And Sold."

CHAPTER 17: BREAKING POINT

The full details of our investigation into civilian casualties from U.S. airstrikes in Syria can be found in a 2015 story for BuzzFeed, "The U.S.–Led Fight Against ISIS Has Killed Far More Civilians Than It Admits."

The difficulty of adequately vetting the rising number of refugees and migrants who were arriving in Europe in 2015 was reported in news accounts. I also saw this firsthand during a visit to the German city of Passau, on the border with Austria, that fall. My account of this appears in an article in *BuzzFeed*, "Paris Attacks Stoke Fears Of Refugees, And That's What ISIS Wants."

CHAPTER 18: DEATH COMES TO YOU

It's difficult if not impossible to say how many Yazidis remained in ISIS captivity in November of 2015. The 3,000 figure I use in this chapter was an estimate by Matthew Barber of the NGO Yazda and was cited in press reports at the time.

CHAPTER 19: DEFECTORS

As mentioned in the notes for Chapter 8, Okab cannot be identified for two reasons—because he lives abroad as a refugee, and because he might face retaliation from ISIS for sharing his story—that also apply to the other sources who have been granted anonymity here. The story of Okab and the other defectors appeared in a 2016 article for *BuzzFeed*, "How to Lose Your Mind to ISIS and Then Fight to Get It Back."

CHAPTER 20: FOREIGNERS

Ahmed is a pseudonym. The parents of his cousin—the Canadian ISIS member described at the end of this chapter—have not gone public with their story. When I reported on him for a 2016 article in *BuzzFeed*, I agreed to keep Ahmed anonymous and not to use his cousin's name for that reason.

CHAPTER 21: COUNTERTERROR

Ayman Oghanna, the British Iraqi photographer who appears throughout this book, provided the introduction to the ICTF for Jaff and me. He saw ISOF's importance in the war against ISIS earlier than most, if not all, Western journalists. He first contacted them in 2014 and began pushing for an embed, which they were not accustomed to granting. After our reporting trip for the IED story in February of 2015, he traveled with them to Ramadi, where they were engaged in a desperate and ultimately losing battle to hold off ISIS. From there he connected with the ICTF, and he and Jaff spent grueling weeks with the battalion in early 2016 to film a harrowing report for *Vice*, "Fighting the Islamic State with Iraq's Golden Division: The Road to Fallujah."

I've included ranks with the names of various ISOF officers starting with captain.

For security reasons, only some of the ISOF soldiers who appear in the chapters in this section can be named in full. None of the names are pseudonyms.

Some of the material about the ICTF in this section originally appeared in a 2017 *BuzzFeed* article titled "The ISIS Killers."

CHAPTER 22: ARMIES IN THE NIGHT

The first line of this chapter is an homage of sorts to the first line of a 2003 article by Evan Wright in *Rolling Stone*, "The Killer Elite," which has been stuck in my head for over a decade.

For more on the role that U.S. special operations forces played in the war against ISIS, please see my 2016 report in *BuzzFeed*, "Inside The Real U.S. Ground War On ISIS." There are further details in a 2019 *BuzzFeed* article, "How Trump's Withdrawal Threatens The Secretive Hunt For ISIS In Syria."

CHAPTER 23: COMMANDOS

The story of Joshua Wheeler and the role of both the CTU and U.S. special operations forces in Iraq are covered in the 2016 *BuzzFeed* report mentioned earlier, "Inside The Real U.S. Ground War On ISIS."

CHAPTER 24: "MOVE SLOW, NO BLEEDING"

If you type my name and "Iraqi forces" into a video search on Google, you can view a short clip of a scene described in this chapter, in which a soldier in a baseball cap steps out from his Humvee to fire his assault rifle.

CHAPTER 25: BASE CAMP

Ayman informed me when I fact-checked this chapter with him that he and Jewan had been traveling with a pair of hand grenades not with the intent of ever hurling them at ISIS, but because they'd made a pact to kill themselves if they faced imminent capture by ISIS. They preferred this to the idea of being beheaded on camera for propaganda purposes.

CHAPTER 26: KEY WEST

Jaff and I did end up traveling with the Fifteenth Division for a day. While it was not a combat embed, we found them just as unsteady as the Iraqi journalist had warned. We also spoke with other Iraqi journalists who'd embedded with the Fifteenth and had similar impressions.

CHAPTER 27: "PUT DOWN YOUR WHITE FLAG"

The information in this chapter about the nationalities of ISIS's suicide bombers and how it chose to publicize these attacks is taken from a 2016 article I published with my colleague Mitchell Prothero in *BuzzFeed*, "ISIS Suicide Bombers in Mosul Are Terrifyingly Effective." The reporting for this information is his, and he agreed to let me use it here.

CHAPTER 28: ELECTION DAY

The American soldier with whom I discussed the election results is still employed by the U.S. government and can't be identified.

CHAPTER 29: COMRADES

At around the time I interviewed Colonel Arkan, observers such as David M. Witty, a retired Green Beret who trained ISOF during the Iraq War, were becoming increasingly alarmed by the scale of their casualties. Witty tracked ISOF's fate exhaustively during the Mosul offensive, and told me at the time that the casualties were skyrocketing. "What Iraq is missing is infantry to do this dirty work. ISOF are being used in that role now, and it's got to be bleeding them dry," he told me. "When a very elite unit like that takes those kinds of losses—you know some of those guys have been training with the U.S. since 2003—they can't really be replaced. And they're the ones that need to secure the peace."

Abuses by Iraqi security forces in Mosul were a serious problem with long-term implications. Perhaps the most shocking report of this came from the veteran journalist Ali Arkady, who recorded video of Iraqi soldiers torturing captives and obtained another video in which a man in handcuffs was executed. The soldiers in question were from the Interior Ministry's Emergency Response Division, one of the worst forces in this regard, aside perhaps from the militias that fought under the banner of the Popular Mobilization Front. The problem, however, was widespread. A June 2017 article by Susannah George of the *Associated Press*, "Iraqi Officer Seeks Vengeance In Mosul, Where Killings Mount," featured admissions from sources in three different branches of the Iraqi security services that revenge killings had taken place. ISOF faced fewer allegations than other forces. Some are detailed in two 2017 reports from Human Rights Watch, "Iraq: New Abuse, Execution Reports of Men Fleeing Mosul" and "Iraq: Execution Site Near Mosul's Old City." I didn't see such abuses from the ICTF, and their commanders denied that they'd taken part in them, but it's worth noting that the ICTF was ISOF's most professional unit.

CHAPTER 30: SUSPICION

I apologize to my old friend. I still have a hard time believing he could have had anything to do with ISIS. The point of this anecdote is to highlight the sense paranoia that ISIS was working to instill around the world, which affected me as well. Shadi is a pseudonym.

CHAPTER 31: DRIFTING

Ayman Oghanna wrote a moving tribute to Ahmed the Bullet after his death in an article for the *BBC*, "Mosul Battle: Remembering Iraqi Special Forces Soldier 'Spongebob.'"

News reports have established that ISIS did in fact develop chemical weapons at Mosul University and elsewhere. Joby Warrick details this in a 2019 report for the *Washington Post*, "Exclusive: Iraqi Scientist Says He Helped ISIS Make Chemical Weapons."

CHAPTER 32: BLEEDING

The anecdote about Major Salam walking through war-torn neighborhoods of eastern Mosul with his German shepherd was relayed to me by Ayman Oghanna, who was there at the time. Ayman described him as "the lone man of the apocalypse," or something to that effect.

CHAPTER 33: CASUALTIES

Allegations that the coalition was deploying white phosphorus in Mosul were detailed in a 2017 Human Rights Watch report, "Iraq/Syria: Danger From US White Phosphorus," and elsewhere.

The U.S. military officer cited in this chapter remains employed by the U.S. government and can't be named.

The full results of my investigation into civilian casualties from U.S. strikes in Mosul were published in a 2017 article for *BuzzFeed*, "These Are the Victims of the U.S.–Led Campaign Against ISIS." That report led the coalition to admit responsibility for the deaths of thirty-six civilians in Mosul. When I later followed up on these admissions, I learned that neither the U.S. military nor the coalition had made any effort to contact the families of the victims or to offer condolence payments, as was common practice during the Iraq War. I detailed this problem in a follow-up report, "BuzzFeed News Investigation Leads To U.S. Admission It Caused Civilian Deaths In Mosul."

EPILOGUE: ESCAPE

The issue of ISIS escapes from Iraq and Syria is covered in depth in a 2017 report that Munzer and I published in *BuzzFeed*, "The Escape."

INDEX

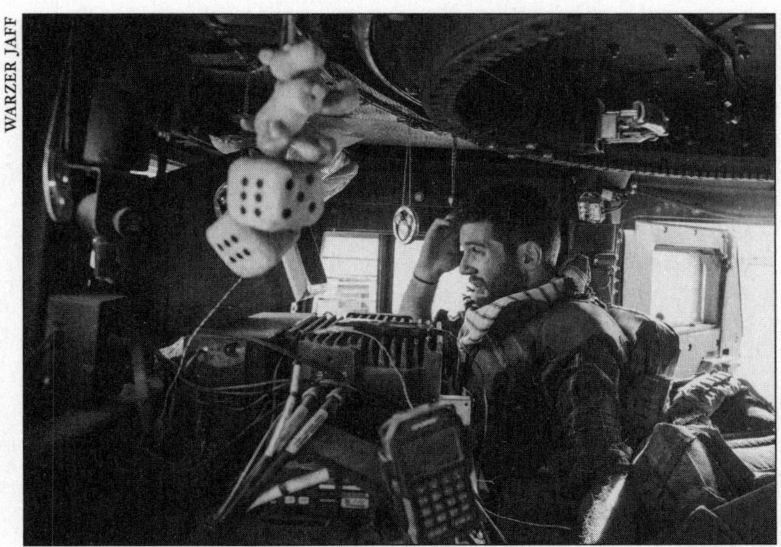
WARZER JAFF

Mike Giglio is staff writer at *The Atlantic* based in Washington, DC. He has reported extensively on the conflicts in Iraq, Syria, and Ukraine, and he spent five years based in Istanbul as a foreign correspondent for *Newsweek* and *BuzzFeed*. His work has twice been a finalist for the Livingston Award and has won the Arthur F. Burns Prize. He is a graduate of Davidson College and native of New York.

PublicAffairs is a publishing house founded in 1997. It is a tribute to the standards, values, and flair of three persons who have served as mentors to countless reporters, writers, editors, and book people of all kinds, including me.

I. F. STONE, proprietor of *I. F. Stone's Weekly*, combined a commitment to the First Amendment with entrepreneurial zeal and reporting skill and became one of the great independent journalists in American history. At the age of eighty, Izzy published *The Trial of Socrates*, which was a national bestseller. He wrote the book after he taught himself ancient Greek.

BENJAMIN C. BRADLEE was for nearly thirty years the charismatic editorial leader of *The Washington Post*. It was Ben who gave the *Post* the range and courage to pursue such historic issues as Watergate. He supported his reporters with a tenacity that made them fearless and it is no accident that so many became authors of influential, best-selling books.

ROBERT L. BERNSTEIN, the chief executive of Random House for more than a quarter century, guided one of the nation's premier publishing houses. Bob was personally responsible for many books of political dissent and argument that challenged tyranny around the globe. He is also the founder and longtime chair of Human Rights Watch, one of the most respected human rights organizations in the world.

• • •

For fifty years, the banner of Public Affairs Press was carried by its owner Morris B. Schnapper, who published Gandhi, Nasser, Toynbee, Truman, and about 1,500 other authors. In 1983, Schnapper was described by *The Washington Post* as "a redoubtable gadfly." His legacy will endure in the books to come.

Peter Osnos, *Founder*